DEWEY DECIMAL CLASSIFICATION

A PRACTICAL GUIDE

LOIS MAI CHAN

JOHN P. COMAROMI

JOAN S. MITCHELL

MOHINDER P. SATIJA

DEWEY DECIMAL CLASSIFICATION

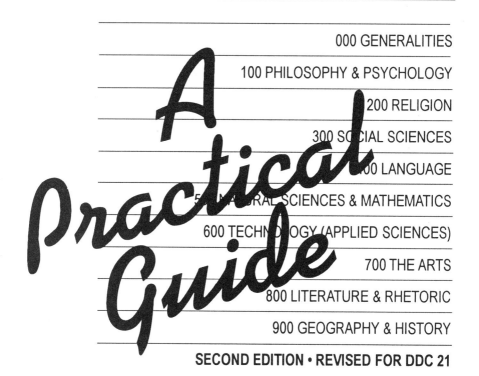

000 GENERALITIES

100 PHILOSOPHY & PSYCHOLOGY

200 RELIGION

300 SOCIAL SCIENCES

400 LANGUAGE

500 NATURAL SCIENCES & MATHEMATICS

600 TECHNOLOGY (APPLIED SCIENCES)

700 THE ARTS

800 LITERATURE & RHETORIC

900 GEOGRAPHY & HISTORY

SECOND EDITION • REVISED FOR DDC 21

Forest Press

A Division of OCLC Online Computer Library Center, Inc.
Albany, New York 1996

Library of Congress Cataloging-in-Publication Data

Chan, Lois Mai
    Dewey decimal classification : a practical guide / Lois Mai Chan ...
[et al.]. -- 2nd ed., rev. for DDC 21.
        p.   cm.
    Includes bibliographical references and index.
    ISBN 0-910608-55-5 (alk. paper)
    1. Classification, Dewey decimal.
Z696.D7C48   1996
025.4'31--dc20   96-16307
                                                          CIP

The paper used in this publication meets the requirements of
ANSI/NISO Z39.48-1992 (Permanence of Paper).

CONTENTS

CHAPTER 3
STRUCTURE AND ORGANIZATION OF THE SCHEDULES:
NOTES AND INSTRUCTIONS

CHAPTER 4
SUBJECT ANALYSIS AND CLASSIFICATION OF A DOCUMENT

CHAPTER 5
USING THE MANUAL

CHAPTER 6
USING THE RELATIVE INDEX

CHAPTER 7
SYNTHESIS OF CLASS NUMBERS OR
PRACTICAL NUMBER BUILDING

CHAPTER 8
TABLE 1: STANDARD SUBDIVISIONS

CHAPTER 11
TABLE 4: SUBDIVISIONS OF INDIVIDUAL LANGUAGES
AND TABLE 6: LANGUAGES

CHAPTER 12
TABLE 5: RACIAL, ETHNIC, NATIONAL GROUPS
AND TABLE 7: GROUPS OF PERSONS

CHAPTER 13
NUMBER BUILDING FOR COMPLEX SUBJECTS

PREFACE

This book introduces the reader to the methods of classifying and arranging library collections according to the Dewey Decimal Classification (DDC). It begins with a brief history of the DDC, followed by discussions on the notation (its numbers), its uses, the concepts of practical classification, the methods of analyzing the subject content of documents to be classed, and the proper procedures for assigning class numbers. The guide's aim is to explain the proper methods of applying the DDC schedules; of locating and assigning the appropriate class numbers; and of synthesizing a class number if need be. Because notational synthesis is at the heart of applying Dewey, a great deal of emphasis is placed on building numbers with notation from the schedules and the auxiliary tables.

We hope both beginning classifiers and experienced DDC users will find this book useful. It contains an overview of the Classification for readers who are new to the DDC. It also contains many detailed explanations and instructions that experienced users will find helpful. The theoretical basis and historical overview are provided to help in the understanding of current practice.

This second edition of this book is designed to accompany Edition 21 of the Dewey Decimal Classification. The first three chapters cover the basic tenets of the DDC. Chapter 4 discusses subject analysis in general and assigning class numbers from the DDC in particular. Chapter 5 describes the Manual. Chapter 6 explains the structure of the Relative Index and its application. Beginning with Chapter 7, the process of number building is discussed in detail with step-by-step explanations and multiple examples. Chapter 7 explains and illustrates number building with notation from the schedules only. Chapters 8-12 cover the auxiliary tables. For readers interested in further discussion and examples, Chapter 13 contains examples and explanations of building complex numbers, many of them requiring the use of notation from various sources within the schedules and from two or more tables. Each of the chapters dealing with the practical application of Dewey includes exercises designed to reinforce the examples and explanations through practice. The answers are given in an appendix.

The examples and exercises are based on Edition 21. Examples are drawn from all over the world because that is the domain of the DDC; its users and students are found everywhere. Though we provide excerpts from the text to expedite the learning of DDC matters, the reader must have access to the DDC schedules, tables, Manual, and Relative Index in order to benefit fully from the explanation and illustrations.

For the convenience of users, the glossary in this book includes the terms and definitions found in the glossary in volume 1 of the DDC, Edition 21. The glossary also contains additional terms used in this book.

The authors wish to acknowledge the following persons for their contributions to this book: Julianne Beall, Winton E. Matthews, Jr., and Gregory R. New, assistant editors of the Dewey Decimal Classification, for reading the manuscript and making many invaluable suggestions on the text and exercises; Peter J. Paulson, executive director, OCLC Forest Press, for his encouragement and support; Judith Kramer-Greene for editing and supervising the production of the book; Theodora Hodges for proofreading the manuscript and preparing the index; Nancy Lewis for bibliographical assistance and proofreading; and Stella Cottam for proofreading.

Library classification is an indispensable key to the temple of knowledge. We hope that the present guide to the Dewey Decimal Classification will enable readers to enter this temple with ease and efficiency.

Lois Mai Chan
Joan S. Mitchell
Mohinder Partap Satija

CHAPTER 1
INTRODUCTION TO THE
DEWEY DECIMAL CLASSIFICATION

Objectives:

The objectives of this chapter are to introduce the reader to: the life of Melvil Dewey, who devised the Dewey Decimal Classification (DDC); the history of the DDC and its various editions; and the DDC notation.

Outline:

1.0   INTRODUCTION

Classification, defined as a logical system for the arrangement of knowledge, has played a vital role in the course of the history of library and information services and management. In a modern library, books and other sorts of materials are arranged by subject to expedite the retrieval of items by and for patrons. Classification is also used for arranging entries in a classified catalog, or in a bibliography. The classified approach in Online Public Access Catalogs (OPACs) has been found to be a fruitful method in meeting information needs.[1] In the electronic environment, classification is being used increasingly as a means of organizing and accessing information.[2] A home-made system can be devised for these purposes, but constructing such a system would be a difficult and time-consuming process. The other course is to adopt an already existing system. There are several universally known general classification schemes available.

---

[1]Karen Markey and Anh N. Demeyer, *Dewey Decimal Classification Online Project: Evaluation of a Library Schedule and Index Integrated into the Subject Searching Capabilities of an Online Catalog: Final Report to the Council on Library Resources* (Dublin, OH: OCLC, 1986). Report No. OCLC/OPR/PR-86/1.

[2]Diane Vizine-Goetz, "Online Classification: Implications for Classifying and Document[-like Object] Retrieval." In *Knowledge Organization and Change: Proceedings of the 4th International ISKO Conference, Washington, D.C., 1996.* Edited by Rebecca Green. (Frankfurt/Main: INDEKS Verlag, forthcoming).

Among them are the Dewey Decimal Classification, the Library of Congress Classification, the Universal Decimal Classification, and S. R. Ranganathan's Colon Classification. The Dewey Decimal Classification (DDC), a system of American origin, is the most used, studied, and discussed classification the world over.

1.1   TERMINOLOGY

The Decimal Classification was originally designed in 1873 for arranging the books and the catalog of the library of Amherst College (Amherst, Massachusetts). It was published in 1876 for wider use in other libraries. The word "Dewey" in its current name is that of Melvil Dewey (1851–1931), who devised the Classification. The second word, "Decimal," refers to the base-ten notation that is used to denote and relate subjects. It employs Indo-Arabic numerals treated like decimal fractions. Hence the name of the classification is the Dewey Decimal Classification.

1.2   LIFE AND MIND OF MELVIL DEWEY

Dewey's full name was originally Melville Louis Kossuth Dewey, and he was born on December 10, 1851 (the tenth day of the tenth month, according to the early Roman republican calendar), an apt birthday for the creator of a decimal classification. His family was poor, and resided in a small town in upper New York State. Later (in accordance with his quest for economy in every sphere of life), he cut short his given name to Melvil, dropped his middle names and, for a brief period of time, even spelled his family name as Dui. He invented his system when he was twenty-one and was working as a student-assistant in the library of Amherst College.

In those days the classification of books involved reclassification each time the collection grew beyond the shelf space available to it, because classification schemes were generally tied to shelf locations. Librarians always had to seek to accommodate new books at their proper places on the shelves. The methods of classification used then are known now as "fixed-location" systems. In such systems books were placed in a fixed physical space in the library, not in an intellectual space in a classification system. Every time the library grew beyond its shelving capacity, there was the expense of having to reclassify the collection. Fixed location could not work from building to building because the number of ranges and shelves were different, and fixed location was based upon these physical characteristics. Dewey asked himself: Why not classify a book once and for all? Why not give a book a notation that is true from shelf to shelf, from range to range, and from building to building? With these questions in mind he set out to seek a solution. He studied writers on library economy (which in those days meant the administration and management of the services of libraries), and visited many libraries.[3] In retrospect, Dewey recounted his thoughts in an essay published in 1920, using his characteristic phonetic spelling:

> In visiting over 50 libraries, I was astounded to find the lack of efficiency, and waste of time and money in constant recataloging and reclassifying made necessary by the almost universally used fixt system where a book was numberd according to the particular room, tier, and shelf where it chanced to stand on that day, insted of by class, division and section to which it belonged yesterday, today and forever. Then there was the extravagant duplication of work in examining a new book for classification and cataloging by each of a 1000 libraries insted of doing this once for all at some central point.[4]

Day and night Dewey thought about the problem. Then, as the story goes, one morning in May 1873, when he was sitting in the Amherst Chapel attending to religious obligations, an idea flashed across his mind that put the problem to rest:

> After months of study, one Sunday during a long sermon by Pres. Stearns, while I lookt stedfastly at him without hearing a word, my mind absorbed in the vital problem, the solution flasht over me so that I jumpt in my seat and came very near shouting "Eureka"! It was to get absolute simplicity by using the simplest known symbols, the arabic numerals as decimals, with the ordinary significance of nought, to number a classification of all human knowledge in print; . . .[5]

Thus, Dewey decided to use decimal fractions to denote the subjects of books, rejecting ordinal integers that represented positions in space, e.g., 1, 2, 3, 4, . . . representing the first, second, third, and fourth books acquired by a library in a particular category. Dewey's invention of relative location made it possible for growth without having to renumber books because he numbered books according to their intellectual content, not according to their physical location—the latter changes, the former never does.

Dewey thus divided the world of knowledge into ten main classes, each class into ten divisions, and each division into ten sections, and on and on until a point was reached where further branching would produce subjects of such

---

[3]"Preface," *A Classification and Subject Index for Cataloguing and Arranging the Books and Pamphlets of a Library* (Amherst, MA, 1876), p. 3.

[4]Melvil Dewey, "Decimal Classification Beginnings," *Library Journal,* 45:151 (Feb. 15, 1920).

[5]Dewey, "Decimal Classification Beginnings," p. 152.

specificity that no works were likely to be written upon them. The universe of knowledge is mapped in a hierarchy from the broadest subjects to the narrowest. For notation, or the numbering system used in a classification, Dewey employed Arabic numerals 0 to 9 on each level of the hierarchy. For example, 3 represents social sciences, 34 represents law, 341 international law, 3416 international law of war, and so forth. Each additional digit renders greater detail for the content of the book and places it next to other books on the same or related topics. Note each number behaves like a decimal fraction that provides linear order for the subjects of the entire library—that is, the numbers above are actually .3, .34, .341, .3416. It was a simple and a revolutionary idea.

On May 8, 1873, Dewey submitted the plan to the library committee of Amherst College and obtained approval to apply his idea in organizing both the library collection and the classified subject catalog. His work created a revolution in library science and set in motion a new era of librarianship. Melvil Dewey is deservedly called the father of modern librarianship.

Dewey focused his energy and intellect on transforming librarianship from a vocation to a modern profession. He helped establish the American Library Association (ALA) in 1876; he was secretary of ALA from 1876 to 1890 and president during the 1890/1891 and 1892/1893 terms. He co-founded and edited *Library Journal*. He was a promoter of library standardization and formed a company to market library supplies, which eventually became the Library Bureau. He was a pioneer in library education. In 1883 Dewey became the librarian of Columbia College (now Columbia University) in New York City. While there he founded the first ever library school on January 1, 1887. Two years later, because of policy disagreements with Columbia's trustees about the school, Dewey was forced to leave his position at Columbia.[6] In December 1889, he became the director of the New York State Library at Albany, retiring from that position in 1906. His range of knowledge and work was wide and varied. He took keen interest in co-education, metrics, and simplified spelling. He was a reformer and a crusader who inspired others to join in his work. He is primarily known, however, for the classification system that bears his name.

Dewey died from a stroke on December 26, 1931. Six decades after his death he remains unsurpassed in librarianship for his ingenuity and versatility, for his vision, and for bringing grand library projects to successful conclusion and fruition.

1.3   HISTORY OF THE DDC

The Dewey system, published anonymously in 1876 in Amherst, Mass., was entitled *A Classification and Subject Index for Cataloguing and Arranging the Books and Pamphlets of a Library*. It was a pamphlet of 44 pages, and, as its name implies, was designed primarily as a practical scheme for arranging library books.

---

[6]John P. Comaromi, *The Eighteen Editions of the Dewey Decimal Classification* (Albany, N.Y.: Forest Press, 1976), p. 3.

The Dewey Decimal Classification, the system that began with that pamphlet, still serves this function in tens of thousands of libraries throughout the world more than a century after its first publication.

The second edition of the Classification (thoroughly revised and enormously expanded) was published in 1885. In many respects, the second edition may be considered one of the most important editions because it established the form and policy of the scheme for the next 65 years.

Another major event in the history of the DDC occurred in the late 1890s. The newly founded (September 1895) International Institute of Bibliography, now called the International Federation for Information and Documentation, requested and received permission from Dewey to translate and adapt the DDC for the purpose of preparing a universal bibliography. The European effort eventually resulted in a considerably modified classification now called the Universal Decimal Classification. It was first published in 1905 in French, but since then has appeared in several dozen languages and in various levels of development: full, medium, and abridged. It is widely used in Europe, Africa, and South America.

Till his death in 1931, Dewey helped his editors (Walter S. Biscoe, Evelyn May Seymour, and Dorkas Fellows) by overseeing their efforts in expanding and developing the Classification. The 13th edition (1932), published the year after Dewey's death, was designated the Memorial Edition. For the first time it bore Dewey's name in the title. The enlarged and somewhat unwieldy size of the 14th edition (1942) was criticized by many librarians who asserted that most of its growth had been disproportionate and imbalanced.[7] To check this lopsided growth, the 15th edition, known as the "Standard Edition," displayed all fields of knowledge evenly but in skeletal detail. Only libraries of 200,000 volumes or fewer would be served by the Standard Edition, which was reduced to one-tenth the intellectual (numerical) size of its predecessor, Edition 14. Edition 15 was an almost complete failure and, ironically, was not accepted by the profession that had called for it and that had participated in its planning.

The very survival of the system was now at stake. The 16th edition (1958) was produced with support from the Library of Congress under the able editorial direction of Benjamin A. Custer. Custer gave the Classification a new lease on life by modernizing it and establishing a diplomatic balance between tradition and change. Edition 17 (1965) was revolutionary in many respects, including its emphasis on subject relationships and on classification by discipline, a new area table, and especially its new index. The index represented a drastic reduction from that of Edition 16; there were far fewer entries and many more cross references. The index, severely criticized for these changes,[8] was eventually replaced at no cost by a new one based on the Edition 16 pattern.

---

[7]Comaromi, *Eighteen Editions*, pp. 359–60.

[8]Frances Hinton [Review of the Dewey Decimal Classification], *Library Resources & Technical Services*, 10:393–402 (Summer, 1966).

With Edition 18 (1971), the DDC made a giant step towards a faceted approach. Five new auxiliary tables were added, providing much greater possibilities for number building. It was the first edition to be produced in three volumes (1—Introduction, Tables; 2—Schedules; 3—Relative Index). Edition 19 (1979) was the last edition published under the direction of Custer. Edition 20 (1989), in four volumes, was supervised by John P. Comaromi, who was editor from 1980 to 1991. Edition 20 was the first to be produced by an online editorial support system, a result of which was a database that could be used to produce future editions and a variety of products. Edition 21 was begun under the editorial direction of John P. Comaromi. After his death in 1991, Joan S. Mitchell assumed the position of editor in 1993 and completed the edition.

The scheme is published by Forest Press, which is located in Albany, New York. In 1988, Forest Press became a division of OCLC Online Computer Library Center, Inc.

1.3.1 DEVELOPMENT OF THE DDC

Revising Dewey is a lengthy, systematic, and democratic process that pays heed to user needs and new developments in classification and knowledge. The Dewey editorial office is located in the Decimal Classification Division of the Library of Congress in Washington, DC. The Division applies over 110,000 numbers annually to works cataloged by the Library of Congress. The Dewey editorial office has been located at the Library of Congress since 1923, and the application of DDC numbers to bibliographic records distributed by the Library of Congress has continued unbroken since 1930. Having the editorial office within the Decimal Classification Division means that the editors are very close to the application of numbers by classification specialists. By classifying titles and working closely with the specialists, the editors can detect trends in the published literature and incorporate them into the Classification.

The Classification is revised and developed by the editor and three assistant editors. The process of developing a schedule includes researching the subject area, discussing problems and potential changes with the classification specialists, looking at the published literature for literary warrant, conferring with subject experts, and considering the impact of proposed changes on users and on the rest of the Classification. The editors depend on the Library of Congress online catalog and the OCLC Online Union Catalog for guidance on literary warrant and use of the Classification. Terminology for indexing is gleaned from current literature, *Library of Congress Subject Headings*, *Sears List of Subject Headings*, thesauri, and reference sources. The resulting draft schedule is reviewed by the editors and then sent to the Decimal Classification Editorial Policy Committee (EPC) for review and recommended action.

The development and review process is more elaborate for a major revision. EPC evaluates the initial draft for outside review. Various review committees and individual experts then study the draft and submit a formal report to EPC. Review committees' comments are considered carefully, and may result in a revised draft for EPC's review.

1.3.2   DECIMAL CLASSIFICATION EDITORIAL POLICY COMMITTE (EPC)

The Decimal Classification Editorial Policy Committee (EPC) is a ten-member international board whose main function is to advise the editors and OCLC Forest Press on matters relating to changes, innovations, and the general development of the Classification. It is a joint committee of OCLC Forest Press and the American Library Association (ALA), and includes official representatives of OCLC Forest Press, ALA, the Library of Congress, and the (British) Library Association. EPC represents the interests of DDC users; its members hail from public, special, and academic libraries, and library schools.

1.3.3   EDITIONS OF THE DDC

The Dewey Decimal Classification is published in two editions, full and abridged. The current full edition, Edition 21, was published in 1996. An abridged edition usually appears about a year after the publication of the full edition. The latest Abridged Dewey (Edition 12) was published in 1990. Abridged Edition 13 is planned for publication in 1997. Though it is intended for small libraries that are unlikely to grow significantly, the abridged edition can easily accommodate collections of up to 20,000 volumes.

The Dewey Decimal Classification is kept up-to-date between editions through additions and corrections published in *Dewey Decimal Classification: Additions, Notes and Decisions (DC&)*. *DC&* carries news relating to the Classification, feature articles and letters from users and interested persons, and lists of additions and corrections to the full and abridged editions of the DDC.

Beginning in 1993, the twentieth edition of the Dewey Decimal Classification became available in a DOS version called Electronic Dewey. The entire schedules, tables, Relative Index, and Manual of DDC 20 are stored on a CD-ROM. Electronic Dewey also includes up to five frequently used Library of Congress subject headings linked to each DDC number and a sample bibliographic record for the most frequently occurring subject heading. Electronic Dewey can be searched by words or phrases, numbers, index terms, and Boolean combinations. An update was issued in March 1994, which included the changes announced in *DC&* 5:5 and a new feature, segmentation information to show the logical breaks in Dewey numbers.

Dewey for Windows, a Microsoft Windows®-based version of Electronic Dewey, was released at the same time as publication of Edition 21. Dewey for

Windows is based on the Edition 21 database and includes the same features as the DOS version along with several enhancements. Users may take advantage of the Windows environment to display multiple records from anywhere in the Classification simultaneously. Data may be moved between windows by "dragging and dropping" with the click of a mouse. Dewey for Windows is LAN-compatible, i.e., the database may be loaded on a single CD-ROM drive and shared by multiple users across a local area network. Users can annotate records in the Dewey for Windows database to reflect local classification decisions. Annotations can be carried over from one update to the next. In addition to statistically mapped Library of Congress subject headings, Dewey for Windows includes selected LC subject headings mapped to DDC numbers in the major revised schedules in Edition 21.

1.3.4 USE OF THE DDC

The DDC is the most widely used library classification system in the world. It is used in more than 135 countries. In the United States, the DDC is used by 95% of all public and school libraries, 25% of all college and university libraries, and 20% of special libraries.[9]

The popularity of the DDC outside North America is also considerable. The scheme has been translated into over 30 languages. Translations of Edition 20 are available in Italian, Spanish, and Turkish. Abridged Edition 12 has been translated or is in the process of being translated into Arabic, French, Greek, Italian, Hebrew, and Persian. There is also a French intermediate edition that is based on Abridged Edition 12 plus selected expansions from Edition 20. Work is underway on a Russian translation of Edition 21. Currently, slightly more than half of the sales of the DDC are to international users. The DDC is a general classification scheme that aims to classify books and other material on all subjects in all languages in every kind of library; it is the *lingua franca* of librarians.

1.4 NOTATION (NUMBERING SYSTEM)

The Dewey Decimal Classification is basically a number-building machine that provides both intellectual order and physical location in one step. The engine of the DDC is the notation. Notation may be defined as a systematic series of shorthand symbols used to denote classes and their subdivisions, and to reveal relationships among subjects. It mechanizes the arrangement of books in a library or of records in an electronic database. Brevity is implied in notation, but contrary to popular belief it is not the prime concern of notation.

---

[9]Melvil Dewey, *Dewey Decimal Classification and Relative Index*, Ed. 21, edited by Joan S. Mitchell, Julianne Beall, Winton E. Matthews, Jr., and Gregory R. New (Albany, NY: OCLC Forest Press, 1996), v. 1, p. xxxi.

Its primary role is to make the system work by revealing the classification conceptually and visibly.

As mentioned earlier, to denote subjects Dewey decided to use the pure and simple notation of Arabic numerals treated like decimal fractions. The decimal notation from which the scheme derives part of its name is its characteristic feature and remains the most revolutionary contribution of Melvil Dewey to the development of library classification. Before one learns to use the Classification, it is important to understand the nature of its notation.

The notation of the DDC is pure; that is, it uses an unmixed (a single) set of symbols—here 0–9. Dewey's immediate purpose in using decimal notation was to reveal the coordination and subordination of subjects; his second purpose was to employ a notation capable of expansion without disturbing other topics already classed.

Though notation cannot reveal the importance or value of a subject, it can display the subject's relative status and location among other subjects in the universe of knowledge. Notation can also show the relative breadth or depth of a subject and its relation to the subjects to its left and right on the shelf. The DDC uses a hierarchical notation. This means that coordination and subordination of subjects are depicted through notation. For example, of three subjects denoted by 8, 81, and 9 respectively, we say that 81 is subordinate to 8, and 8 and 9 are coordinate. This is possible only if the notation is made up of decimal fractions. Note that 9 is not subordinate to 81; it merely comes later in the ordinal series of decimal fractions. On the other hand, .82 is coordinate with .81 and .83–.89.

1.5   BASIC PLAN OF THE CLASSIFICATION

The DDC is a universal scheme that treats knowledge as a whole, dividing it into ten mutually exclusive main classes that are denoted by Arabic numerals used as decimal fractions as follows:

0   Generalities
1   Philosophy, paranormal phenomena, psychology
2   Religion
3   Social sciences
4   Language
5   Natural sciences and mathematics
6   Technology (Applied sciences)
7   The arts   Fine and decorative arts
8   Literature (Belles-lettres) and rhetoric
9   Geography, history, and auxiliary disciplines

A digit stands for a main class; that is, 5 stands for the sciences. Strictly and mathematically speaking, the numbers denoting the main classes are decimal numbers and should have been written as .0 Generalities, .4 Language, .5 Natural sciences and mathematics, and so on. The .5 is extended, like a decimal fraction, to indicate the subdivisions of the sciences; that is .59 stands for zoology, .599 stands for mammals, .5996 stands for ungulates, .59963 stands for even-toed ungulates, .599633 stands for pigs, and .5996332 stands for wild boars. The decimal fractions reveal the intellectual hierarchy of the subject. But for brevity, simplicity of notation, and ease of reading, the decimal point is placed after the third digit in the full DDC number; hence, 599.6, 599.63, etc.

1.5.1   CONVENTION OF A MINIMUM OF THREE DIGITS

To simplify the ordinal value of the decimal fractions as Dewey uses them, and for ease of arrangement, there is a convention that no number in the DDC shall have fewer than three digits. If any number has fewer than three significant digits, additional zeros are added to the right or to the left of the significant digits to make up a three-digit number, for example, 001, 010, 100. The ten main classes are now denoted as:

000   Generalities
100   Philosophy, paranormal phenomena, psychology
200   Religion
300   Social sciences
400   Language
500   Natural sciences and mathematics
600   Technology (Applied sciences)
700   The arts   Fine and decorative arts
800   Literature (Belles-lettres) and rhetoric
900   Geography, history, and auxiliary disciplines

This is called the *first summary* of the DDC schedules. For the beginner it is the first practical step in learning the system.

1.6   SUMMARY

The Dewey Decimal Classification was conceived in 1873 and published in 1876 by Melvil Dewey (1851–1931), considered to be the father of modern librarianship. The continually revised Classification is now in its twenty-first edition, and is published in print and electronic form. The DDC uses decimal fractions to denote the ten main classes from 0 Generalities to 9 Geography, history, and auxiliary disciplines. Decimal fractions can be expanded infinitely to accommodate new subjects, are universally understood, and reveal the intellectual hierarchy of the subjects they represent.

CHAPTER 2

STRUCTURE AND ORGANIZATION OF THE TEXT OF THE DEWEY DECIMAL CLASSIFICATION, EDITION 21

Objectives:

The objectives of this chapter are to explain: the physical organization of the four-volume text of the DDC; the makeup of a schedule page and the typographical devices used therein; how to interpret the schedules; and the concept and uses of centered entries.

Outline:

2.0   OVERALL STRUCTURE OF THE PHYSICAL VOLUMES

The current edition of the DDC is the twenty-first in the series that began in 1876. Its bibliographic details follow:

> Dewey, Melvil. *Dewey Decimal Classification and Relative Index* / devised by Melvil Dewey. Ed. 21 / edited by Joan S. Mitchell, Julianne Beall, Winton E. Matthews, Jr., and Gregory R. New. 4 volumes. Albany, NY: Forest Press, a Division of OCLC Online Computer Library Center, Inc., 1996. ISBN 0-910608-50-4

From Editions 1 through 15 revised (1876–1952), the DDC was published in one volume. The 16th edition (1958) and the 17th (1965) were issued in two volumes, which eased the handling of the growing system. The second volume was devoted primarily to the index (called the Relative Index). The 18th (1971) and the 19th (1979) editions were issued in three volumes. The 20th (1989) and the 21st editions (1996) are each contained in four volumes.

The parts of the DDC and their location in the four-volume set are:

Volume 1: Prefatory material, New Features, Introduction, Glossary, Index to Introduction and Glossary, Tables 1–7, Relocations and Reductions, Comparative and Equivalence Tables, Reused Numbers

Volume 2: Schedules: 000–599

Volume 3: Schedules: 600–999

Volume 4: Relative Index, Manual, Library of Congress Decimal Classification Division Policies and Practices

In this chapter, we will describe volumes 1 and 4, and briefly volumes 2 and 3. A fuller description of volumes 2 and 3 will continue in chapter 3.

2.1   VOLUME 1: INTRODUCTION, TABLES, OTHER MATTERS

Volume 1 contains the publisher's foreword regarding recent developments in the DDC and a preface by the chair of the Decimal Classification Editorial Policy Committee (EPC). As its name suggests, EPC is the powerful policy-making body of the system. The preface describes the committee's work as well as features and policies of Edition 21; it is followed by the acknowledgments. The next section, "New Features in Edition 21," describes the major changes in the edition and includes lists of selected revised numbers in the tables and schedules. It is followed by "The Introduction to the Dewey Decimal Classification," which explains the nature and structure of the Classification, and provides instruction on how the DDC is to be applied. The introduction also provides guidance in determining the subject of a book (subject analysis), so that the appropriate class number can be located. In doing so, it provides rules to further synthesize (extend) a number either from the schedules or from any of the auxiliary tables. To understand these instructions fully is to have complete mastery over the system. Though written in a clear, simple style, the ideas presented in the introduction can be difficult to grasp; the text is divided therefore into small sections to facilitate comprehension. Time spent studying the introduction will be repaid many times over in mastering the application of Dewey. The gist of the instructions in the introduction is explained with ample illustrations in the course of the remaining chapters in this book.

The introduction is followed by the glossary, which has provided useful assistance since its first appearance in Edition 18. It explains the various technical terms used in the application of Dewey. Familiarity with these terms is helpful in understanding the theory of classification as well as the practice of the DDC.

2.1.1 AUXILIARY TABLES

The bulk of volume 1 is devoted to the seven auxiliary tables:

Table 1   Standard Subdivisions
Table 2   Geographic Areas, Historical Periods, Persons
Table 3   Subdivisions for the Arts, for Individual Literatures, for Specific
           Literary Forms
    T3-A   Subdivisions for Works by or about Individual Authors
    T3-B   Subdivisions for Works by or about More than One Author
    T3-C   Notation to Be Added Where Instructed in Table 3-B, 700.4,
           791.4, 808–809
Table 4   Subdivisions of Individual Languages and Language Families
Table 5   Racial, Ethnic, National Groups
Table 6   Languages
Table 7   Groups of Persons

Use of these tables will be explained one by one in other chapters of this book. The tables provide the means of representing complex subjects in minute (close) classification. They are never used alone, but are required at times to specify aspects of a subject not expressed in the main numbers in the schedules. Chapters 8-12 discuss these tables in detail with examples of their application.

2.1.2 LISTS OF CHANGES

The next segment of volume 1, "Relocations and Reductions," is meant for classifiers intent on tracking changes from Edition 20 to Edition 21. This list is followed by "Comparative and Equivalence Tables" for the major revisions in Edition 21. These tables help classifiers who are familiar with the location of a topic in the old schedule in the previous edition see its placement in the revision in the new edition. The last table, "Reused Numbers," is a short list of numbers (other than those in major revisions) whose meanings have changed completely from those in the previous edition.

2.2 VOLUMES 2–3: SCHEDULES

The schedules consist of a long table of all DDC numbers with captions indicating their topical significance and notes explaining their use. In Edition 20, the schedules were split into two volumes for the first time: volume 2, 000–599; volume 3, 600–999. This was done because the schedules as a whole could not be bound in one volume that could be easily manipulated. This arrangement is continued in Edition 21.

The schedules form the core of the Classification. To use them correctly and efficiently, it is necessary to know their typographical devices, and to understand the various constraints regarding the headings and the instructions accompanying them.

2.2.1 SUMMARIES

Volume 2 begins with the three summaries of the Dewey Decimal Classification. The summaries are important in understanding the overall structure of the DDC. These three outlines of the scheme are given in order of increasing specificity and detail. The *first summary*, also called the ten main classes, is the broadest; it is the first outline of the universe of knowledge as reflected in recorded literature. Some find it worthwhile to memorize the first summary, because knowing the overall structure improves efficiency in the use of the scheme. The first summary is found in section 1.5 of chapter 1 in this book.

The *second summary*, the hundred *divisions*, includes the ten main classes, each further divided into ten branches that are called divisions. The second summary appears on the opposite page.

The *third summary* divides each of the hundred divisions into ten parts. Together, the divisions and their parts form one thousand entries called *sections*. The sections enumerate the scope and content of the hundred divisions.

There is no need to memorize the sections. However, with constant and daily use, many people find they have committed the most frequently used sections to memory.

The summaries give the numbers and their captions. Together, the three summaries provide, in varying detail, an overview of the intellectual and notational structure of classes in the DDC. However, they do not always reveal the substance of what the numbers represent. To understand the breadth of each number and caption, one must consult the schedules.

2.2.2 STRUCTURE OF A SCHEDULE PAGE

Basically, each page of the schedules consists of a sequence of entries. An entry in the schedules is "a self-contained unit consisting of a number or span of numbers, a heading, and often one or more notes" (see glossary, p. 220). For example, p. 1189 of volume 2, which appears on page 16, has entries ranging from 599.54 to 599.63.

SAMPLE SUMMARY PAGE

Second Summary*
The Hundred Divisions

000	**Generalities**		**500**	**Natural sciences & mathematics**
010	Bibliography		510	Mathematics
020	Library & information sciences		520	Astronomy & allied sciences
030	General encyclopedic works		530	Physics
040			540	Chemistry & allied sciences
050	General serial publications		550	Earth sciences
060	General organizations & museology		560	Paleontology Paleozoology
070	News media, journalism, publishing		570	Life sciences Biology
080	General collections		580	Plants
090	Manuscripts & rare books		590	Animals
100	**Philosophy & psychology**		**600**	**Technology (Applied sciences)**
110	Metaphysics		610	Medical sciences Medicine
120	Epistemology, causation, humankind		620	Engineering & allied operations
130	Paranormal phenomena		630	Agriculture & related technologies
140	Specific philosophical schools		640	Home economics & family living
150	Psychology		650	Management & auxiliary services
160	Logic		660	Chemical engineering
170	Ethics (Moral philosophy)		670	Manufacturing
180	Ancient, medieval, Oriental philosophy		680	Manufacture for specific uses
190	Modern western philosophy		690	Buildings
200	**Religion**		**700**	**The arts Fine and decorative arts**
210	Philosophy & theory of religion		710	Civic & landscape art
220	Bible		720	Architecture
230	Christianity Christian theology		730	Plastic arts Sculpture
240	Christian moral & devotional theology		740	Drawing & decorative arts
250	Christian orders & local church		750	Painting & paintings
260	Social & ecclesiastical theology		760	Graphic arts Printmaking & prints
270	History of Christianity & Christian church		770	Photography & photographs
280	Christian denominations & sects		780	Music
290	Comparative religion & other religions		790	Recreational & performing arts
300	**Social sciences**		**800**	**Literature & rhetoric**
310	Collections of general statistics		810	American literature in English
320	Political science		820	English & Old English literatures
330	Economics		830	Literatures of Germanic languages
340	Law		840	Literatures of Romance languages
350	Public administration & military science		850	Italian, Romanian, Rhaeto-Romanic
360	Social problems & services; association		860	Spanish & Portuguese literatures
370	Education		870	Italic literatures Latin
380	Commerce, communications, transportation		880	Hellenic literatures Classical Greek
390	Customs, etiquette, folklore		890	Literatures of other languages
400	**Language**		**900**	**Geography & history**
410	Linguistics		910	Geography & travel
420	English & Old English		920	Biography, genealogy, insignia
430	Germanic languages German		930	History of ancient world to ca. 499
440	Romance languages French		940	General history of Europe
450	Italian, Romanian, Rhaeto-Romanic		950	General history of Asia Far East
460	Spanish & Portuguese languages		960	General history of Africa
470	Italic languages Latin		970	General history of North America
480	Hellenic languages Classical Greek		980	General history of South America
490	Other languages		990	General history of other areas

*Consult schedules for complete and exact headings

SAMPLE SCHEDULE PAGE

599	*Animals*	599

.54   *Other Odontoceti (toothed whales)

> Other than dolphins and porpoises
>
> Class comprehensive works on Odontoceti in 599.5
>
> > *For false killer, pilot whales, see 599.53; for killer whale, see 599.536*

.542   *Delphinapterus (Beluga, White whale)

> Class here Monodontidae
>
> > *For Monodon, see 599.543*

.543   *Monodon (Narwhal)

.545   *Ziphiidae (Beaked whales)

.547   *Physeteridae

> Including dwarf and pygmy sperm whales
>
> Class here Physeter (sperm whale)

.55   *Sirenia (Sea cows)

> Class here manatees

.559   *Dugongidae

> Class here dugong
>
> Class Steller's sea cow in 599.559168

.6   ***Ungulates**

> Class here hoofed mammals, comprehensive works on big game animals
>
> Class Sirenia in 599.55; class big game hunting in 799.26
>
> > *For a specific kind of nonungulate big game animal, see the kind, e.g., bears 599.78*

SUMMARY

599.63	**Artiodactyla (Even-toes ungulates)**	
.64	**Bovidae**	
.65	**Cervidae (Deer)**	
.66	**Perissodactyla (Odd-toed ungulates)**	
.67	**Proboscidea (Elephants)**	
.68	**Hyracoidea (Hyraxes)**	

.63   *Artiodactyla (Even-toed ungulates)

> Including Tragulidae (chevrotains, mouse deer)
>
> Class here Ruminantia (ruminants)
>
> Class comprehensive works on Artiodactyla and Perissodactyla in 599.6
>
> > *For Bovidae, see 599.64; for Cervidae, see 599.65*

*Add as instructed under 592–599

There are over 23,000 entries printed in the schedules. The total number of available schedule numbers is far greater than that figure, since numbers may be extended by various number-building procedures, which will be discussed in later chapters. In addition there are over 8000 entries in the seven auxiliary tables in volume 1 that may be added to most schedule numbers, thus producing an almost countless set of class numbers.

Each page consists of two columns:

(1) Number column: the column of class numbers printed vertically on the left-hand side of the schedule page

(2) Heading and notes column: the column to the right of the number column. The heading is a word or phrase, i.e., a verbal term, giving the meaning of the number on the left.

The columns and their corresponding headings are printed in varying type sizes depending upon their positions in the hierarchy. Type size decreases as we go down the hierarchy. For example, note the type sizes of the following numbers and their headings in volume 2:

Number	Heading	Type size
303	**Social processes**	12 point bold
303.3	**Coordination and control**	10 point bold
303.32	Socialization	10 point light

When a number is expanded beyond the decimal point, the three digits for the section are only given once, at the top of each number column.

2.2.3 HIERARCHY

Hierarchy means the sequence of subjects in their successive subordination. Hierarchy in the DDC is expressed through both structure and notation. Structural hierarchy means that each topic, other than those represented by the main classes, is subordinate to and part of the broader topics above it. Logically, whatever is true of a general topic is true of all of its subordinate topics, a principle referred to as "hierarchical force."

In the printed schedules, whole-part and genus-species relationships, or increasing specificity of subjects, are shown by means of a shift of indention of the verbal heading to the right, and by the addition of a meaningful digit to the number in the left column. For example:

300	Social sciences
330	Economics
332	Financial economics
332.4	Money
332.41	Value of money
332.414	Factors affecting fluctuations in value

In the example shown, each heading, except Social sciences, is subordinated to the immediately superordinate heading. Note the lengthening of the digit chain in the number column and the shift in typographical indention to the right in the corresponding headings. Also, in the schedules themselves, note the type size used in printing these entries of varying specificity. These are devices to show the relations and status of subjects. Therefore, when reading any page of the schedules, it is important to watch for such typographical devices and their logical effects—much of the beauty and utility of the Classification lies in its depiction of subject relations.

2.2.4   SEQUENCE OF NUMBERS

The entire schedules have been arranged in a single numerical sequence from 000 to 999; therefore, it should not be difficult to locate a desired class number. For the convenience of users and for rapid location, the section numbers, i.e., three-digit figures, are always printed on the top outer corner of each page.

2.3   VOLUME 4: RELATIVE INDEX AND MANUAL

Volume 4 is devoted to the Relative Index and the Manual.

2.3.1   RELATIVE INDEX

An index is always an important part of a classification. In the DDC it is called the Relative Index. It is more powerful than a simple alphabetical index, and is considered one of Melvil Dewey's most important and enduring contributions to library classification.

The Relative Index not only arranges subject terms alphabetically, but also links the terms to the context (discipline) in which they appear in the schedules. It is called "relative" because it relates subjects to disciplines. In the schedules, subjects are distributed among disciplines; in the Relative Index, however, subjects are arranged alphabetically, accompanied by terms identifying the disciplines in which they are treated. Under each subject, names of disciplines and terms implying disciplines (e.g., "area planning" implying "Civic art" in the following example), are subarranged alphabetically:

Airports	387.736
architecture	725.39
area planning	711.78
engineering	629.136
institutional housekeeping	647.963 9
international law	341.756 77
law	343.097 7
military engineering	623.66
public administration	354.79
transportation services	387.736
see also Aircraft	

As a topic, airports may appear elsewhere in the schedules other than under the numbers listed in the Relative Index. There may be a song about airports, or a movie, or a poem, or a short story, or a bibliography, or a social service number for protecting people at airports. But the Relative Index cannot list them all. In such cases, the classifier must first determine the context in which the topic of airports is treated in the work and then examine the schedules for the most appropriate number. For example, for a short story with airports as a theme, the correct number would be found in the class for literature.

Since the Relative Index is a key to the schedules, a full chapter (chapter 6) will be devoted to a discussion of its importance, status, frequent use, and complexity.

2.3.2 MANUAL

The Manual follows the Relative Index in volume 4. The Manual first appeared as part of the DDC four-volume set in Edition 20; a Manual on the use of Edition 19 was published separately in 1982.[1] The Manual gives advice on classifying in difficult areas, provides in-depth information on revised schedules, and explains the policies and practices of the Decimal Classification Division at the Library of Congress. It is arranged by Dewey numbers for quick reference. References from the schedules and tables refer the classifier to the Manual for additional information about a specific number, range of numbers, or choice among numbers. The Manual is explained in greater detail in chapter 5.

---

[1]John P. Comaromi and Margaret J. Warren, *Manual on the Use of the Dewey Decimal Classification: Edition 19* (Albany, NY: Forest Press, 1982).

2.4   READING THE SCHEDULES

Based on the principle of hierarchy, the corresponding heading for every number does not describe the full range of the meaning of the subject; what is given is enough to describe the specific contents of that particular number within the context of the superordinate numbers. For example:

342.052   Duties, functions, powers

If this entry is taken in isolation, we would not understand whose duties, functions, and powers were being discussed. But if we read it in conjunction with (or in the context of) its immediately superordinate heading (i.e., the heading found at 342.05), then its meaning becomes clear—it is the duties, functions, and powers of the legislative branch of government. This meaning can be perused further in the context of its superordinate number twice removed. In this case we would have the constitutional law (342) of the powers, functions, and duties of the legislative branch of government.

The brief heading is used as a straightforward and convenient method of avoiding unnecessary repetition and clutter on the schedule page. It is also useful in chain indexing, a type of index that lists each heading, or the important part of it, in its hierarchical chain. For example:

Constitutional law—Legislature—Duties, functions, powers

In Edition 21, the practice of using headings consisting solely of adjectival or prepositional phrases was discontinued. However, many headings can only be understood in the context of their hierarchy. The advantage of economy in printed words on the page, however, can be a disadvantage in an online version of Dewey, because the user often sees a heading in isolation without its superordinate entries. The electronic version overcomes this difficulty by offering a display function for the hierarchy of any number.

2.5   TRANSCRIPTION OF A CLASS NUMBER: DOT AND SPACES

In a DDC class number:

(1)   the digits are treated as decimal fractions;

(2)   there are at least three digits, e.g., 5 is written as 500, 53 as 530; and

(3)   a dot is put between the third and the fourth digits, e.g., 324.3, 362.14, 386.24, when a class number extends beyond three digits.

2.5.1   DOT

All digits in a DDC class number are treated decimally. The dot is not a decimal point in the mathematical sense. It is a psychological pause to break the monotony of numerical digits and to ease the transcription and copying of the class number. Also, educational psychologists believe that 324.12 is more easily remembered than 32412. The dot assists the eye and the memory.

2.5.2 SPACES

In the print version, if a class number extends beyond six digits, the remaining digits are printed in groups of three, with a space between each group. For example:

341.758 2   [International law of] Copyright
621.388 002 88   [Television] Maintenance and repair

This space has exactly the same purpose as that of the dot, namely to ease the transcription, copying, and remembering of the class numbers. The spaces have no meaning beyond this, and should not be confused with the segmentation of numbers provided in Library of Congress cataloging to show the logical breaks in numbers.

2.6   NUMBERS IN SQUARE BRACKETS

There are many class numbers at various levels in the schedules and tables that are enclosed in square brackets. For example:

[309]   [Unassigned]
204[.5]   Christian mythology

Any number enclosed in square brackets is not valid, and is empty of any content at the moment. Such a number is not to be used. There are three kinds of bracketed numbers:

(1)   Numbers never assigned any content in the scheme: Such numbers have always been vacant. For example:
       [009] [Never assigned]
       The number of such entries is decreasing, as gaps are used to accommodate new topics or fields of study. Some libraries also assign special meanings to such numbers for local use.

(2)   Currently unassigned numbers: Some bracketed numbers, which were once valid, remained vacant since some previous edition. Such numbers carry the heading [Unassigned] and a note stating when the number was last used. For example:
       [007] [Unassigned]
              Most recently used in Edition 16
       [426] [Unassigned]
              Most recently used in Edition 18

The number of such temporarily vacant numbers has increased from edition to edition; they result from revision of the DDC.

(3)   Vacated numbers: These bracketed numbers have been vacated for the current edition; that is, their contents have been shifted to other numbers. As a matter of policy, such numbers are not immediately reused in order to minimize confusion and inconvenience to users. The shifting of a topic or a heading from a number to another number is called a *relocation*. There is always a note that tells where the contents of the number have gone. Numbers can be vacated, but the meaning or topic represented by the vacated number normally remains somewhere in the scheme. Examples:

> [207]   Education, research, related topics of Christianity
> Relocated to 230.007
>
> 641[.1]   Applied nutrition
> Relocated to 613.2

2.6.1   DISCONTINUED NUMBERS

Discontinued numbers are also enclosed in square brackets. A *discontinued number* is a number from the previous edition that is no longer used because the concept represented by the number has been moved to a more general number in the same hierarchy, or has been dropped entirely. For example:

> 526[.92]   Land (Boundary) surveying
> Number discontinued; class in 526.9

2.7   NUMBERS IN PARENTHESES

In classification, subjects may be treated in more than one way. To provide flexibility to libraries that wish to arrange certain subjects in ways different from those adopted officially, optional numbers are provided for certain subjects.

The DDC lists standard notation for English-language users. At certain places in the schedules, options are provided for users whose needs are not met by the standard notation. Options are a means of accommodating cultural differences, and provide a mechanism for emphasizing topics of local importance. For example, in order to give prominence to the religion, literature, or language of a particular country, libraries may insert letters in the notation or use briefer notation (e.g., as indicated under 292–299 Religions other than Christianity).

In the schedules, optional numbers are enclosed in parentheses. These numbers may be used by individual libraries if preferred. They are not part of the standard notation. Examples:

(330.159)   Socialist and related schools
                 (Optional number; prefer 335)

(819)   American literatures in English not requiring local emphasis
                 (Optional number and subdivisions; prefer 810–818 for all
                 American literatures in English. Other options are described
                 under 810–890)

2.8   CENTERED ENTRIES

In the schedules there are often headings denoted not by one number but by a span of numbers identified by the symbol > in the number column. For example:

>   250–280 Christian church

>   381–382 Internal and international commerce (Trade)

These are called centered headings or centered entries. The entry is called "centered" because the span of numbers is printed in the center of the page rather than in the number column on the left side of the page. A centered entry is used to indicate and relate structurally a span of numbers that together form a single concept for which there is no specific hierarchical notation available.

Normally, a broad subject that has subdivisions should be represented by a single number. In the case of centered entries, however, such a subject is covered by a span of coordinate numbers. This device shortens the notation for each of the subdivisions by one digit, but results in the loss of hierarchy in the notation.

Centered entries occur at all levels of hierarchy, and hundreds of them can be found in the DDC schedules and tables.

Not all spans of numbers, however, are centered entries: some spans are given to save space. For example:

809.1–.7 Literature in specific forms

In such cases the span is given in the number column.

2.9   SUMMARY

Edition 21 of the DDC is in four volumes. Volume 1 contains prefatory and introductory materials, the seven auxiliary tables, and lists of changes from Edition 20 to Edition 21; volumes 2 and 3 contain the schedules, which form the core of the system with entries arranged in one sequence of decimal fraction numbers from 000 to 999; volume 4 contains the Relative Index and the Manual. Every entry in the schedules is to be read in the context of its superordinate headings. Class numbers given in square brackets are not to be used, and those in parentheses are optional. A centered entry uses a span of numbers to represent a single concept without hierarchy in the notation.

CHAPTER 3

STRUCTURE AND ORGANIZATION OF THE SCHEDULES:
NOTES AND INSTRUCTIONS

Objectives:

This chapter is a continuation of the previous chapter, which describes the makeup and entries of a schedule page. The specific objective in this chapter is to explain the various types of notes and instructions found in DDC entries, with special emphasis on number-building notes.

Outline:

3.0   Introduction
3.1   Notes That Describe What Is Found in a Class
3.2   Notes on What Is Found in Other Classes
3.3   Notes Explaining Changes or Irregularities in the Schedules and Tables
3.4   See-Manual Notes
3.5   Number-building Notes
3.6   Importance of Notes
3.7   Summary

3.0   INTRODUCTION

In the previous chapter we studied the makeup of a schedule page and its entries. Apart from the class number and its corresponding heading, an entry often contains notes. By definition, notes are a part of entries. There are various types of notes, each with a different function. Notes help to explain and interpret the meaning, scope, and limitation of the subject covered in the entry. Some notes refer to a more appropriate number, and others to a comparable or related number. Because the Manual is now part of the scheme, notes referring to pertinent entries in the Manual are provided under individual numbers in the schedules and tables. Of greatest importance are the notes that extend (synthesize) a number; these are called number-building notes.

Notes used in the DDC are described in the following paragraphs.

3.1   NOTES THAT DESCRIBE WHAT IS FOUND IN A CLASS

In many cases, the caption accompanying a class number is not sufficient for identifying what is included in the number. Notes are provided to clarify the meaning of the caption, to delineate the scope of the number, or to indicate topics included in the number which are not clearly stated in the caption. With the exception of "including notes," notes that describe what is in a class have hierarchical force (see 2.2.3).

3.1.1 DEFINITION AND SCOPE NOTES

More often than not there is no consensus among scholars on the boundaries of a subject or discipline. Scope, connotations, and boundaries of a class likewise differ from scheme to scheme and from time to time within the same scheme. Invariably, all classification schemes define the boundaries of a class by listing all its subtopics. In other words, they follow the principle that any class is the sum total of all its enumerated subdivisions and their unlisted family members. However, in addition to enumeration, some notes and devices are employed to make class numbers more explicit and specific.

3.1.1.1 DEFINITION OF A CLASS

In Dewey, the definitions of some classes and their subdivisions are given in notes under the appropriate number. A *definition note*, if there is one, normally appears immediately below a heading. For example:

321.03 Empires
    Systems in which a group of nations are governed by a
    single sovereign power

334   Cooperatives
    Voluntary organizations or enterprises owned by and
    operated for the benefit of those using the services

Definition notes are given when: (a) the heading is broader or more limited in meaning than is commonly accepted; (b) the heading has multiple or ambiguous meanings in *Webster's Third New International Dictionary of the English Language* and other general unabridged dictionaries; or (c) the term is new to the language.

3.1.1.2 NOTES STATING AND ILLUSTRATING THE SCOPE OF A CLASS

Scope notes limit the heading to the characteristics listed in the note. For example:

579.16 Miscellaneous nontaxonomic kinds of organisms
    Not provided for elsewhere

658.042 Partnerships
    General and limited

The first example instructs the classifier to use 579.16 for nontaxonomic organisms for which provision has not been made elsewhere in the same schedule. In the second example, only general and limited partnerships are allowed at number 658.042. Those, of course, may be all that there are, in which case the scope note need not have been given. But if there were other kinds of partnerships, they would not be classed at this number.

Some scope notes expand rather than contract the contents of a number. For example:

021.8   [Library] Relationships with government
          Regardless of governmental level

782.1   Dramatic vocal forms   Operas
          Regardless of type of voice or vocal group

3.1.2   FORMER-HEADING NOTES

When the wording of a heading has been revised from one edition to the next to the extent that the new heading bears little or no resemblance to the former heading, a *former-heading note* is given to assist in the identification of the former heading. In such cases, there is usually no change in the meaning of the number. For example:

005.12   Software systems analysis and design
          Former heading: Program design

3.1.3   VARIANT-NAME AND FORMER-NAME NOTES

Variant-name notes, containing synonyms or near-synonyms of the caption, also help indicate what is found in a class. For example:

305.235   Young people twelve to twenty
          Variant names: adolescents, teenagers, young adults, youth

Earlier names of geographic areas in the same number are given in *former-name notes*. The following example is from Table 2:

—466   País Vasco autonomous community
          Former names: Basque Provinces, Vascongadas

3.1.4   CLASS-HERE NOTES

Class-here notes list major topics that are included in a class even though they may be broader or narrower than the heading, overlap it, or define another way of looking at essentially the same material.[1] For example:

576.5   Genetics
          Class here heredity. . .

The note means that heredity, though not strictly speaking genetics, is to be classed with genetics at 576.5. Two more examples:

---

[1]Topics in class-here notes are said to *approximate the whole* of a class. That means that class numbers for such topics may be extended by means of the auxiliary tables, which will be discussed in later chapters.

006.31   Neural nets (Neural networks)
            Class here connectionist learning, neural computers

372.357   Nature study
            Class here environmental studies

Class-here notes are also used to indicate that interdisciplinary and comprehensive works[2] on the topic in question are also classed in the number under which the note appears. For example:

305.231   Child development
            Class here interdisciplinary works on children

368.82   Burglary, robbery, theft insurance
            Class here comprehensive works on crime insurance

3.1.5   NOTES IDENTIFYING TOPICS IN STANDING ROOM

Including notes identify topics that have "standing room" in the number where the note is found. Including notes list topics that are considered part of the class, but are less extensive in scope than the concept represented by the class. Standing-room numbers provide a location for topics with relatively few works written about them, but whose literature may grow in the future, at which time they may be assigned their own number. These notes are introduced by the term "Including."[3] For example:

372.358   [Elementary education in] Science and technology
            Including metric system

The note conveys the sense that, logically speaking, metric system may not seem to be a part of the entry. At the same time, the subject metric system is not fully developed in elementary education, because the literature on the topic is not substantial enough to justify its having its own class number. Therefore, for the time being, the subject of elementary education in the metric system is classed at 372.358. Let us take another example:

340.55   Medieval European law
            Including feudal law, medieval Roman law

Whether or not one considers feudal law or medieval Roman law to be medieval European law, they are to be classed at this number. We say "at" to convey the message that no additional notation can be added to 340.55 for works on feudal

---

[2]In Dewey, the term *interdisciplinary work* refers to a work treating a subject from the perspective of more than one discipline, and the term *comprehensive work* refers to a work treating a subject from various points of view within a single discipline.

[3]Standard subdivisions cannot be added to topics in standing room, nor are other number-building techniques allowed.

law and medieval Roman law; such works are assigned 340.55 and no more. Works on medieval European law in general, however, may have additional notation appended to them.

In Edition 21, including notes have replaced the following types of notes found in earlier editions: contains notes (for major components of the number that do not have their own subdivisions), example notes (examples of an abstract category), and common-name notes (common English names for scientific taxonomic terms).

Entries in the taxonomic schedules may have two including notes. The first including note contains the scientific taxonomic names above the level of family; the second contains the common and genus names. For example:

584.38   Iridales

Including Burmanniaceae

Including blackberry lily, crocuses, freesias, gladiolus (sword lilies), saffron, tigerflowers

Including notes are also used to indicate where interdisciplinary or comprehensive works on a topic are classed. Unlike their mention in class-here notes, interdisciplinary or comprehensive works in including notes are considered to be in standing room. For example:

583.48   Betulales

Including alders, filberts (hazelnuts), hornbeams; comprehensive works on ironwoods

If the literature were to grow on ironwoods in the future, then a number would be developed for comprehensive works on these trees.

3.2   NOTES ON WHAT IS FOUND IN OTHER CLASSES

Several types of notes alert users to topics outside of the scope of the number in question. These include *class-elsewhere notes, see references,* and *see-also references.* Each of these notes has hierarchical force.

3.2.1   CLASS-ELSEWHERE NOTES

Class-elsewhere notes are in direct contrast to class-here notes and including notes: they lead to topics not located at the number in which the note is located. Class-elsewhere notes give the location of interrelated topics or distinguish among numbers in the same notational hierarchy. They are used to show preference order among topics, to lead to broader or narrower topics in the same notational hierarchy, to override the first-of-two rule, or to lead to the comprehensive or disciplinary number for the topic. A class-elsewhere note takes the form of "class ... in ..." There are several kinds of "class ... in ..." notes. The simplest is straightforward:

025.341 6   Rarities
             Class rare manuscripts in 025.3412; class archival materials
             in 025.3414

In this example, the class-elsewhere note instructs the classifier to prefer the number for manuscripts (025.3412) over the number for rarities (025.3416) when classifying a work about cataloging rare manuscripts.

Another kind of "class ... in ..." note scatters the topic to several numbers. In this circumstance, all that can be given is an instance of the scattering. Here are two examples:

353.463   Public investigations and inquiries
           Class legislative oversight hearings on administrative
           matters with the subject in public administration, e.g., on
           administration of social welfare 353.5

613.711   Fitness training for sports
           Class a specific kind of fitness training with the kind, e.g. weight
           lifting 613.713. . .

3.2.1.1 "CLASS COMPREHENSIVE WORKS IN..." TYPE

A special type of "class ... in ... " note, the *comprehensive-works note*, is used for topics that fall in several classes in the same discipline. For example:

551.3   Surface and exogenous processes and their agents
         Class comprehensive works on landforms in 551.41;
         class comprehensive works on sedimentology in 552

Comprehensive-works notes are also used for topics listed under a centered entry (explained in 2.8). Centered entries are signaled by an arrow > at the left margin. The comprehensive-works note assigns a single class number for a work that covers all the topics in the centered-entry span. For example:

>   307.1–307.3   Specific aspects of communities
                    Class comprehensive works in 307

That is to say, if you had a work on communities that encompassed planning and development (307.1), movement of people (307.2), and the structure of communities (307.3), then it would be classed in 307.

Every centered entry contains a note that tells users where to class comprehensive works on the topics in the span. This note is needed because no book is ever assigned a span of numbers. For example:

> 172–179 Applied ethics
>> Class comprehensive works in 170

> 250–280 Christian church
>> Class comprehensive works in 260

In other words, a comprehensive work on the Christian church is classed in 260, with Christian social and ecclesiastical theology.

3.2.1.2 "CLASS INTERDISCIPLINARY WORKS IN..." TYPE

A similar note with broader coverage than the comprehensive-works note is the *interdisciplinary-works note*. Such notes are used when topics fall in two or more disciplines. Marriage, for instance, may fall in ethics, religion, sociology, law, customs, music, and literature, to name only the most obvious. A work that treats marriage in more than one discipline is classed in 306.81 (the sociology number):

306.81 Marriage
        Class here interdisciplinary works on marriage

An important consideration in using such an interdisciplinary number is that the work must contain significant material on the discipline in which the interdisciplinary number is found (in this example, sociology).

Interdisciplinary-works notes can be class-here notes as well as class-elsewhere notes (see discussion in 3.1.4). The same is true for comprehensive-works notes. For each "class ... in ... " note, there is usually a reciprocal class-here note (or including note) in the entry to which the class-elsewhere note refers.

3.2.1.3 SEE REFERENCES

See references lead from a stated or implied comprehensive number for a concept to the component (subordinate) parts of the concept. See references take the form "*For ..., see ...*" and appear in italics. For example:

004.16 Digital microcomputers
        Class here laptop, notebook, palmtop, pen, personal, pocket
        computers; personal digital assistants, workstations,
        comprehensive works on minicomputers and microcomputers
        For minicomputers, see 004.14

004.16 is the *stated* comprehensive number for minicomputers and microcomputers, and the see reference leads to the component part, minicomputers, in another number. An example of the use of a see reference with an *implied comprehensive* number follows:

> 001.42   Research methods
> > Class here scientific method
> > *For historical, descriptive, experimental methods, see 001.43*

See references may also lead from the interdisciplinary number for a concept to treatment of the concept in other disciplines. For example:

> 181.45   Yoga
> > Class here interdisciplinary works on the practice of yoga and yoga as a philosophical school
> > *For yoga as a religious and spiritual discipline, see 291.436; for Hindu yoga as a religious and spiritual discipline, see 294.5436; for physical yoga (hatha yoga), see 613.7046*

See references are also used to lead from comprehensive or interdisciplinary works in including notes to component parts in other numbers. For example:

> 613.9435 Mechanical methods of birth control
> > Including intrauterine devices, comprehensive works on condoms
> > *For use of condoms for disease prevention, see 613.95*

Another type of see reference, a *scatter see reference,* is used to lead to component parts of the topic scattered throughout all or part of the Classification. The note includes an example of one of the scattered parts. For instance:

> 579.82   Minor divisions of algae
> > Class here . . . comprehensive works on flagellates . . .
> > *For a specific kind of flagellate, see the kind, e.g., Zoomastigophorea 579.42 . . .*

3.2.2 SEE-ALSO REFERENCES

See-also references point to topics that are tangentially related to the topic where the note is given. See-also references appear in italics and follow see references in the same entry. For example:

> 306.872   Husband-wife relationship
> > *See also 613.96 for sexual techniques*
> 780.266   Sound recordings of music
> > *See also 781.49 for recording of music*

3.3 NOTES EXPLAINING CHANGES OR IRREGULARITIES IN THE SCHEDULES AND TABLES

Four types of notes explain changes from earlier editions or irregularities in the schedules or tables resulting from special provisions. These include revision notes, discontinued notes, relocation notes, and do-not-use notes.

3.3.1 REVISION NOTES

Revision notes alert users to major changes that have occurred in a schedule since the previous edition. They are used to introduce *complete* or *extensive* revision of a division or section in a particular edition of the DDC. In Edition 21, complete revision notes are given under the headings for Table 2 —47 Eastern Europe   Russia, 350 Public administration and military science, and 570 Life sciences   Biology. For example:

350   Public administration and military science
             Except for military science (355–359), this schedule is new
             and has been prepared with little or no reference to previous
             editions. Most numbers have been reused with new meanings

             A comparative table giving both old and new numbers for a
             substantial list of topics and equivalence tables showing the
             numbers in the old and new schedules appear in volume 1 in
             this edition

Extensive revision notes are given under the headings for 370 Education, 560 Paleontology   Paleozoology, 580 Plants, and 590 Animals. For example:

370   Education
             This schedule is extensively revised, 370.1, 370.7, 375–377,
             and 378.14–378.19 in particular departing from earlier editions

             A comparative table . . .

3.3.2 DISCONTINUED NOTES

Discontinued notes identify numbers in which all or part of the contents have been moved to a broader number in the same hierarchy, or have been dropped entirely. Discontinued notes take several forms:

502[.822] Simple microscopes
             Number discontinued; class in 502.82

637.14   Processing specific forms of cow's milk
          Use of this number for comprehensive works on processing
          cow's milk discontinued; class in 637.1

533.295   Vortex motion
          Provision for cavitation discontinued because without
          meaning in context

In the first example, the note shows that the complete contents of the number have been moved to a broader number in the same hierarchy. In this case, the number was discontinued because the topic does not have a sufficient literature. Any literature on the topic will henceforth be found at the listed superordinate number. In the second example, comprehensive works on the processing of cow's milk were moved to the broader number for milk processing, 637.1, because the processing of cow's milk represents the bulk of milk processing. In the third example, the topic of cavitation has been dropped entirely because it has no meaning in the context of vortex motion in pneumatics.

3.3.3 RELOCATION NOTES

Relocation notes indicate that all or part of the contents of a number in the previous edition have been moved to a different number in the current edition. A note is usually given at the new location that indicates where the topic used to be located (see 3.3.3.1). For example:

799[.242] [Hunting of] Upland game birds
          Relocated to 799.246

649.68   Home preschool education
          Home schools and schooling relocated to 371.042;
          techniques of study for parents relocated to 371.30281

Sometimes topics are relocated because of dual provision, that is, the inadvertent provision of more than one place for the same aspect of a subject in the DDC. For example:

641.566   Cooking for Christian church limitations and observances
          Cooking for Christmas relocated to 641.568

Cooking for Christmas was implicitly also located at 641.568 Cooking for special occasions; the relocation eliminates the dual provision for this topic.

Certain topics are relocated throughout part or all of the Classification. These are called scatter relocations. For example:

346.033   Torts against the person
          Malpractice pertaining to a specific profession relocated to
          the profession in 342–347, e.g., malpractice of notaries
          347.016, malpractice of lawyers 347.05041

Thus, malpractice pertaining to a specific profession has been relocated to the profession ("scattered") throughout 342–347.

3.3.3.1 FORMERLY NOTES

Formerly notes are always associated with relocations. The note is part of the caption or part of a class-here note and given in the form of *[formerly ...]* or , in the case of a dual provision, *[formerly also ...]*. The notes are printed in italics and followed by the former number. For example, the formerly notes corresponding to the relocation notes in 799.242, 649.68, and 641.566 are as follows:

799.246   [Hunting of] Upland game birds *[formerly 799.242]*

371.042   Home schools *[formerly 649.68]*
             Class here home schooling *[formerly 649.68]*

371.302 81   Techniques of study
             Class here techniques for parents *[formerly 649.68]* . . .

641.568   Cooking for special occasions
             Including Christmas *[formerly also 641.566]* . . .

Formerly notes cannot be provided for relocations scattered throughout part or all of the Classification ("scatter relocations").

Formerly notes trace the changing structure and the revision process of the DDC. They are mostly of historical interest, but they are also a guide to users of both the new and previous editions.

3.3.4   DO-NOT-USE NOTES

Do-not-use notes instruct the classifier not to use all or part of the regular standard subdivision notation or an *add table* provision under a particular class number in favor of special provisions or the standard subdivision notation (see discussion in chapter 8) at a broader number. For example:

640[.288]   Maintenance and repair [in home economics]
             Do not use; class in 643.7

The note conveys the information that the standard subdivision number 640.288 for maintenance and repair of the home by the homemaker is not to be used; material on the topic is to be classed in 643.7, the number for renovation, improvement, remodeling.

3.4   SEE-MANUAL NOTES

Since the Manual was incorporated into the Classification beginning with Edition 20, many numbers in the schedules and tables now carry references to specific passages in the Manual. The references appear in the form of a note beginning with the phrase *"See Manual at ..."* *See-Manual notes* appear in italics, and follow see-also references. For example:

302.230 8 History and description [of media] with respect to persons
See Manual at 302.2308

280 Denominations and sects of Christian church
See Manual at 230–280: Biography; also at 280: Biography; also at 291 Denominations and sects

A see-Manual reference may lead to a full note on the topic, a portion of a note on a topic, the discussion of several numbers, or other situations. A detailed discussion of the Manual is provided in chapter 5.

3.5 NUMBER-BUILDING NOTES

The DDC began as an enumerative scheme that listed ready-made numbers for all the subjects it could classify. Over the years, in order to cope with the constantly swelling tide of literature and under the influence of faceted classification schemes such as the Universal Decimal Classification and Ranganathan's Colon Classification, Dewey has shed its rigid enumerative pattern and gradually made provisions for *number building*, also referred to as *notational synthesis*. Number building is the process of making a given number appropriately more specific by adding notation from the tables or other parts of the schedules.

To a certain extent, the system is still enumerative, in the sense that it does not allow all possible combinations; also, numbers for many complex subjects are still enumerated in the schedules. Nevertheless, over the years, it has incorporated many elements of a faceted classification scheme. Each new edition of the DDC has included more facilities for number building. Several of the major revisions in recent editions feature notational synthesis as a basic feature of the schedule, e.g., 780 Music, 351–354 Public administration, 570 Life sciences Biology. The Editorial Policy Committee has endorsed the general trend towards more notational synthesis in the schedules.[4]

A facet is a characteristic belonging to a class of works. For instance, in the DDC, literature has four facets: (1) Language, e.g., Russian; (2) Literary form, e.g., fiction; (3) Period, e.g., Victorian; and (4) Theme and feature, e.g., realism. In number building, these facets are combined ("synthesized") to reflect the content of the work being classified.

In Edition 21, almost every number in the schedules can be further extended by notation either from one or more of the auxiliary tables or from the schedules themselves. The two methods discussed below explain most of the notational synthesis in the scheme.

---

[4]Minutes of Decimal Classification Editorial Policy Committee, Meeting 103, November 3–5, 1993, EPC Exhibit 104-3, p. 11.

3.5.1   WITHOUT INSTRUCTIONS

Any number from Table 1 Standard Subdivisions can be added[5] to any number in the schedules for a topic that equals or approximates the whole of the class without specific instructions to do so. Occasionally there are instructions that this cannot be done. Standard subdivisions are not to be added for topics in standing room, or when their significance would be redundant. For example, a number meaning history from Table 1 should not be added to a class number that already implies history. In Edition 21, to assist the user in determining whether standard subdivisions may be added in specific situations, *standard-subdivisions-are-added notes* are provided under multiterm headings to indicate whether standard subdivisions may be added to one or all of the terms in the heading.[6] For example:

636.73   Working and herding dogs
Standard subdivisions are added for working and herding dogs together, for working dogs alone

3.5.2   ONLY ON INSTRUCTIONS

Adding a number from Tables 2–7 or from the schedules to any other number in the schedules can be done only when so instructed in the schedules or tables. The instruction for this kind of synthesis or number building is given in a note that usually takes the form of "Add to base number . . . the number following . . ." Proper understanding and implementation of such number-building notes, or *add notes*, are central to the synthesis of class numbers in the DDC.

Add notes can be further divided broadly into two categories, as follows:

3.5.2.1 INDIVIDUAL ADD INSTRUCTIONS

An individual add note that appears under a specific entry is intended solely for that entry. For example:

333.314–.319   Land reform in specific continents, countries, localities of modern world
Add to base number 333.31 notation 4–9 from Table 2, e.g., land reform in Latin America 333.318

Each add note includes one or more examples, as shown above.

---

[5]In number building in the DDC, "to add" means "to append" or "to attach to," rather than "to add mathematically."

[6]For further discussion of adding standard subdivisions, see chapter 8.

3.5.2.2 COLLECTIVE INSTRUCTIONS

In the print version of the DDC, sometimes an add instruction applies to a series of numbers occurring on a single page or a number of pages of the schedules. In such a case all the numbers to be synthesized are marked with an asterisk (*) or some other symbol, and at the foot of each page containing such entries is a footnote giving the location of the appropriate add instruction. The footnote applies to all the numbers marked by the symbol. This is done to avoid repetition of add notes in each entry. An example of such a collective add note can be seen on p. 892 of volume 2 where 495.1, 495.6, 495.7, and 495.8 have been marked with asterisks:

495.1 *Chinese
  .6 *Japanese
  .7 *Korean
  .8 *Burmese

At the bottom of the page, a footnote provides the add instruction:

*Add to base number as instructed under 420–490

The note means that all of the asterisked numbers can be further extended, if desired, according to the instructions given under the centered entry at 420–490:

>   420–490 Specific languages
>   Except for modifications shown under specific entries, add to base number for each language identified by * notation 01–8 from Table 4, e.g., grammar of Japanese 495.65. The base number is the number given for the language unless the schedule specifies a different number

Add notes are the backbone of the number-building equipment of the DDC. Moreover, they are a major factor in the correct use of Dewey. For this reason the majority of the following chapters in this book will be devoted to number building and the various kinds of add notes.

3.6   IMPORTANCE OF NOTES

Many entries have more than one note. In such cases no one note inhibits another. DDC schedules abound with numerous definition, scope, including, class-here, and class-elsewhere notes; and see references. These notes help immensely in the correct classifying of a document. They also help achieve uniformity in the interpretation of entries and therefore promote consistency in the application of the DDC in all libraries in all countries. The notes in the schedules and tables are essential, therefore, in helping explain the positions, boundaries, and scope of various subjects.

3.7   SUMMARY

An entry in the DDC, especially one that is frequently used, may contain various notes that help interpret the scope and jurisdiction of the class number. Definition and scope notes formally define, illustrate, or explain the scope of the entry and its various topics. Variant-name, class-here, and including notes list the topics classed in a given class number. Class-elsewhere notes and references direct users to a better or more specific class number for a related topic. Revision, discontinued, relocation, and do-not-use notes alert users to changes or special applications. Such notes are of great importance and are possibly the only way to avoid the problem of the lack of consensus on the boundaries of different subjects. Central to the process of synthesis of numbers or number building are the various add notes that have increased the capacity of the DDC to classify more and more subjects in ever greater detail.

CHAPTER 4
SUBJECT ANALYSIS AND CLASSIFICATION OF A DOCUMENT

Objectives:

The objectives of this chapter are to explain: the technique of determining the specific subject of a document; how to separate the subject proper from the author's viewpoint, the form of presentation, and the physical medium or form; and how to assign to a document the appropriate class number by following the hierarchical highway mapped in the schedules.

Outline:

4.0   INTRODUCTION

The work of practical library classification, in its essence, is to find the appropriate place for a document in the overall scheme of the classification system, and to assign the appropriate notation from the classification schedules to the document. Therefore, the work of classification requires knowledge of both the contents of the document and the structure and mechanism of the classification system. The work of a classifier is analogous to that of a matchmaker. For a happy pairing, one must know the hearts and minds of both parties.

The layout of the DDC system, especially of the schedules, has already been explained in the first three chapters. This chapter sets forth the process of subject analysis of documents.

The work of subject analysis is of paramount importance in bibliography and library science. Though many people approach a library collection by way of an author or title, the basis for their particular interest is most frequently a subject. This is true even in recreational reading. The smallest error at the subject analysis stage of classification can defeat the purpose of classification, because misclassed works are lost to readers. Those who browse a collection will not find them, and those who use the subject catalog as a starting point often pass over records with class numbers that do not reflect their topic. Thus, care and circumspection must be constant companions in subject analysis.

4.1   ANALYZING THE SUBJECT CONTENT OF A DOCUMENT

Determining the subject of a document is the first step in classification. The classifier often begins with the title and other preliminary material in the document, such as the author's preface, table of contents, and the bibliography, if any. Accompanying material such as the case of a sound recording may also be of help. As a last resort, the classifier may consult subject experts.

In analyzing the subject of a document, the classifier first determines the subject proper. Other aspects to be considered are the author's viewpoint, the form of presentation, and the physical medium in which it appears.

Some documents treat two or more topics and/or one or more aspects of a topic. In subject analysis, these individual topics and aspects must be identified.

4.1.1   FROM THE TITLE

The title of a work and its subtitle (if it has one) must be read carefully. A subtitle immediately follows the title proper; it is also called the secondary or explanatory title. A subtitle normally elucidates or clarifies the theme of the book. For example, in *Winston Churchill: A Life* the subtitle explains that the work is a biography. In a majority of cases the title and the subtitle of a work, taken together, sufficiently reveal the subject of the work. The subtitle is often the more revealing of the two. Authors seek to seize attention by the title proper; they intend to inform with the subtitle. Here are a few examples in support of this assertion:

(1)   Returning to Eden: animal rights and human responsibilities
(2)   The image of eternity: roots of time in the physical world
(3)   Winning: the psychology of competition
(4)   A story of Christian activism: the history of the National Baptist Convention, U.S.A., Inc.
(5)   Beyond the Milky Way: hallucinatory imagery of the Tukano Indians
(6)   Small finds: ancient Javanese gold
(7)   Secret city: photographs from the USSR
(8)   The monster with a thousand faces: guises of the vampire in myth and literature
(9)   Matthias: a novel
(10) The Arctic Grail: the quest for the North West Passage and the North Pole, 1818–1909

4.1.1.1 FANCIFUL OR CATCHY TITLES

If the title of the work is a fanciful one or one that has been deliberately made ambiguous, it will probably not reveal the subject of the work. Note the following titles:

(1) The eagle and the dragon
(2) Silicon idol
(3) Tiger's milk
(4) Asian drama
(5) Third wave
(6) Asking for trouble

The actual subjects of these works, as gathered from their subtitles or elsewhere, are:

(1) Foreign relations between the United States and China
(2) A work on computer chips
(3) A book on housewives and their routines
(4) Economic conditions of Third World countries
(5) A futuristic look into the coming society
(6) Memoirs of a vice-chancellor of an Indian university

To help the library user, the classifier has to look beyond titles.

4.1.1.2 INCOMPLETE TITLES

Some titles seem to be incomplete, at least from the classifier's point of view. For example, a book entitled *Shakespeare* could be a biography, a critical appraisal, or a collection of Shakespeare's works. A work entitled *Canada* does not reveal the aspect of Canada portrayed; it could be a treatise, a travel guide, or an atlas.

On the other hand, a title may seem to be complete in itself, but is incomplete from the classifier's perspective. For example, a book entitled *Reign of Henry VII* will have to be read in the context of the history of England, even though England does not figure in the title. Such incomplete titles will require the classifier to seek assistance elsewhere in the work.

4.1.1.3 REDUNDANT WORDS IN TITLES

Many titles contain adjunct, supernumerary, or self-praising words that have to be removed from consideration when classifying. For example, a book entitled *Rudiments of Economics* will get the main class number for economics (330). Rudimentary, elementary, intermediate, advanced are terms often used in book titles. They mean nothing to the classifier unless the classification makes these distinctions. Edition 19 of the DDC contained separate numbers for elementary, intermediate, and advanced algebra in 512.9042–.9044; in Edition 20, these were discontinued to 512.9 Foundations of algebra. On the other hand, Edition 21 contains separate entries for elementary, intermediate, and advanced levels of accounting at 657.042–.046.

Regarding *A Memorable and Rewarding Journey to Nepal*, whatever the author thinks of his subject, the subject still is only a journey to Nepal. The rest of the words in the title are superfluous with regard to classification, however important and true they may be to the author. Remember: we classify not by the title but by the subject of the work.

4.1.1.4 CLEAR BUT OBSCURE TITLES

Some titles may be crystal clear to those who understand the subject, but their meaning would doubtless be lost upon the classifier who knows little about the subject. Such titles are usually scientific, technical, or esoteric. For example:

(1) Introduction to compression neuropathy
(2) Fundamentals of tribology
(3) Fundamentals of acoustics
(4) An analysis of the Zend Avesta

The first two contain technical terms: the first deals with the cause of carpal tunnel syndrome, the second with friction; the third title may be either the physics or technology of sound, and the last deals with the holy scriptures of the Parsees. To a layperson or a novice classifier these terms may not be known. But then sometimes even nontechnical and nonesoteric terms may not be well known. Take the following:

(1) Nuremberg Trials
(2) War of the Roses
(3) Third Reich
(4) The Great Depression
(5) Crimean War
(6) Whistled languages

These titles are neither fanciful nor obscure. They are all apt, yet their meanings may not be altogether familiar to the classifier. For unfamiliar terms, an appropriate encyclopedia or dictionary must be consulted. For this reason, some libraries maintain a reference collection in their cataloging departments.

4.1.1.5 TERMINOLOGY

The title of a work may be clear and complete, yet it may contain a term for a concept that differs from the terminology in the schedules. For example, a work on the Japanese Diet, like a work on the U.S. Congress, will get the number for legislative bodies. In Nepal such a body is called the Rashtriya Panchyat. These concepts have terminology that differs from country to country. In such cases the terminology in the title must be interpreted by the classifier to conform to the standard terminology used in the DDC schedules.

4.1.1.6 LITERARY TITLES

In the case of literature, i.e., the imaginative writings that fall in 800 Literature, titles are virtually ignored as far as subject matter is concerned. The basis of classification for a literary work is determined by the language, form, and period in which it was written. For example, Thomas Hardy's novels, say, *A Pair of Blue Eyes* and *Far from the Madding Crowd*, will get the same class number, i.e., the number for English novels written in the Victorian period, to which Thomas Hardy belongs. The class numbers for the two novels would remain the same even if they had different titles.

4.1.1.7 NEVER BY TITLE ALONE

In many works the title alone does not reveal its subject content. Therefore, classifiers should never classify by the title alone, however clear and unambiguous it may seem. Titles may be incomplete or deceptive or may not reveal anything beyond the typographer's art. Whatever the case, the true subject of the work must always be verified from other parts of the work.

4.1.2 OTHER SOURCES OF THE SUBJECT FOUND IN THE WORK ITSELF

After the title and subtitle, the classifier should look for information that summarizes the purpose and theme of the work. In most cases this can be found on the left inside flap of the book's jacket (dust cover), on the back cover in the case of a paperback, on the container of a nonprint item, or in the abstract of a report or article. The preface or introduction should be read in order to learn about the author's intent and final thoughts. A preface or introduction written by someone other than the author often indicates the subject of the work and suggests the place of the work in the development of scholarship on the subject. The table of contents displays the structure of the work and lists major topics treated in the work; chapter titles often show aspects or subtopics and so help clarify content. The bibliography, the subject index, and the series to which the work belongs, if any, may also provide useful clues in determining the subject of the work.

4.1.3 OUTSIDE HELP

If such sources are inadequate and some doubts remain that subject content has been satisfactorily identified, reviews of the work may be helpful. As a last resort, subject experts may be consulted.

4.1.4 DETERMINING THE DISCIPLINE FOR A WORK

Any given subject may be treated from the standpoint of one or more disciplines. Because classification with the DDC is first by discipline and then by subject, the classifier must also determine the discipline, or field of study, of the work being classified. For example, the subject iron is scattered in the DDC among several disciplines, including metallurgy, building materials, mining, and inorganic chemistry. Thus, in order to place a work about iron properly, the classifier must determine the discipline into which the work in hand falls.

4.1.5 ANALYSIS OF WORKS WITH COMPLEX SUBJECTS

Often a particular work treats two or more subjects or two or more facets, or aspects, of a subject. DDC notation, however, does not always provide a single class number for these multitopical or multifaceted works. To complicate matters further, because class numbers are tied to shelf location in American libraries, each item is usually assigned only one class number even though two or more numbers may apply. Therefore, when it is necessary to choose among competing class numbers, it is extremely important to analyze and understand the composition of the subjects being treated in the work in hand. Complex subjects are discussed further below and in chapter 13.

4.1.5.1 MULTITOPICAL WORKS

A work may treat two or more subjects either separately or in relation to one another. The two or more subjects may belong to the same discipline or may be from different disciplines. For example, a history of France and Germany may treat the two countries separately or focus on the relationship between them, and the book entitled *Crime and the American Press* treats two subjects in relation to each other.

4.1.5.2 MULTIFACETED WORKS

A work may treat a subject with two or more facets. For example, a book about crimes in nineteenth-century France contains the main subject crimes with two facets: time and space (or place).

4.1.5.3 INTERDISCIPLINARY WORKS

A work may treat a subject from the point of view of more than one discipline. Such works are called *interdisciplinary works*. For example, a work about the social and psychological development of the child, in which the subject child is treated from the points of view of both sociology and psychology, is an interdisciplinary work.

4.1.6 ANALYSIS OF THE "NONSUBJECT" ASPECTS OF A WORK

In library classification the process of subject analysis of a work does not end with the determination of subject and discipline. The classifier has to know several other things about the work. These "nonsubject" aspects include the author's viewpoint, the form of presentation, and the physical medium of the document.

4.1.6.1 AUTHOR'S VIEWPOINT

Any core subject can be presented from various viewpoints. For example:

Theory of economics
History of economics
Research in economics

The subject of all three works is clearly economics. However, the fact that a work is theoretical or historical or a summary of the latest advances in research means that its base class number can be extended by notation that indicates these viewpoints. This will be addressed further when we take up Table 1 Standard Subdivisions in chapter 8.

4.1.6.2 FORM OF PRESENTATION

A document can be presented in many forms: it can be a bibliography, a periodical, a dictionary, or the proceedings of a conference on a specific subject. For example:

A bibliography of economics
A dictionary of economics
Proceedings of an international conference on economics held in 1996

Other forms include: statistical tables, handbooks, compilations of abbreviations, illustrations, directories, exhibits, and so on. The following examples illustrate subjects that include the author's viewpoint and/or the form of presentation:

(1) A pictorial history of England
(2) Formulas in electrical engineering
(3) Research in cataloging
(4) A handbook of data processing in banking
(5) A commission report on the relations of the U.S. President and the U.S. Congress

Separating the elements, we have:

	Subject	Form	Viewpoint
(1)	England	pictures	history
(2)	Electrical engineering	formulas	
(3)	Cataloging		research
(4)	Banking	handbook	data processing
(5)	Relations of President/Congress	report	

The notation for most of these forms and viewpoints is found in Table 1, which will be discussed in chapter 8.

4.1.6.3 PHYSICAL MEDIUM OR FORM

With the advances in information technology and publishing, we have seen documents arrive in various physical forms. A document can be a printed book, a microfiche, or a microfilm. It can be in the form of a videorecording, an audiotape, a computer disk, a compact disc (CD-ROM), or a computer file. It is possible to indicate in the DDC number some of these physical forms (again by way of standard subdivisions in Table 1). However, more often than not, information about the physical form of a document is not revealed in the class number, but is carried elsewhere in the cataloging record.

4.2   ASSIGNING CLASS NUMBERS FROM THE SCHEDULES

As noted above, subject analysis of a document is not dependent on the classification system being used: the subject must first be determined whether one is using the Library of Congress scheme, the Colon Classification, or the DDC. In practice, however, when classifying with the DDC, it is necessary to do subject analysis within the context of the disciplinary structure Dewey provides. For this reason a knowledge of the structure and intellectual basis of the DDC is a prerequisite. We begin with the underlying structure of the Classification and the order of the main classes and divisions. The DDC is divided into four parts:

(1) 000 Generalia

(2) 100/700 The realm of reason (in which the mind attempts to understand itself and the spiritual and physical world outside itself); here are found the sciences and the arts

(3) 800 The realm of the imagination (in which the mind produces literary inventions regarding the world that may or may not be based upon experience): literature

(4) 900 The realm of memory (in which the mind records events and conditions regarding human life upon earth over time): geography, biography, history

The 800s take precedence over the other realms. That is, a novel about the corruption of Wall Street finance (like *The Bonfire of the Vanities* by Tom Wolfe) is classed in American literature in the 800s, not in financial economics or in crime (both in the 300s). Shakespeare's *King Henry V* goes in English drama, not in English history. But works other than those of the imagination in whatever form are classed with the appropriate subjects. A dialogue by Plato, no matter how elegantly written, is classed in philosophy in the 100s; a poem on the circulation of the blood (in human physiology) is classed in medicine in the 600s; a counting book in rhyme in arithmetic in the 500s; and so on. One must take care in the first sorting of the nature of a work.

The realm of reason (science) is structured as follows: philosophy (which is the most general field and the field that provides system and logic for all other fields); theology (the science of the absolute); the social sciences, which include:

(1) Sociology and Anthropology—the raw materials for the study of the social sciences
(2) Statistics—raw materials in numerical form
(3) Political science
    (i) Political science—the study of the distribution and uses of power within a society
    (ii) Law—politically agreed upon constraints on individuals and groups within a particular society
    (iii) Government—maintenance of order through the law
    (iv) Social problems and service—no matter how well power is distributed, laws written, and societies governed, problems occur. They are treated here
(4) Economics—the allotment of scarce goods and services; communication, transportation, and trade regarding goods (these topics are not found together, however)
(5) Education—the introduction of individuals to the order and intellectual products of society
(6) Costume, customs, folklore—more raw material for understanding the social sciences
(7) Language—a society's best record of itself, and a connecting point between what is spiritual and what is physical

Following the social sciences are the natural sciences, which describe the laws of nature and move from inorganic phenomena on a large scale (astronomy) to organic life on an advanced scale (zoology—human beings). The natural sciences are preceded by mathematics, and are followed by the useful arts (or technology) and the fine arts.

The second realm organizes works of the imagination. These works are made up. They are none the less true for being fabricated. A young woman reading

Amy Tan's *The Joy Luck Club* was asked by an acquaintance what she was reading. When she told him, the acquaintance remarked that he did not read fiction, he only read the truth. The reader responded, "But this is the truth." Each realm deals with the truth in a different way. In the realm of the imagination, poetry, drama, fiction, essays, speeches, and letters are the vehicles for revealing the truth.

The third and last realm is the realm of history. Geography and travel, civil history, and biography and correspondence are found here, as are two auxiliary historical sciences: genealogy and heraldry.

The foregoing discussion has tried to show that there are three realms at work in the operation of classifying an item using Dewey. One usually grasps the subject fairly quickly, but grasp of the proper realm and discipline is not so readily accomplished. A classifier can acquire the knowledge of where to begin looking for a topic in the DDC by studying the ten main classes, the hundred divisions, and the one thousand sections. The more the classifier knows about them, the more efficient he or she will become.

4.2.1   SEARCHING FOR THE RIGHT CLASS NUMBER

After discussing subject analysis of the document, we shift to the schedules for an examination of assigning proper class numbers. The schedules consist of a long list of numbers for all subjects and their subdivisions arranged in logical order. There are two ways to enter the schedules. One is through the Relative Index found in volume 4 of the DDC. It is a quick method, but it does not help in understanding the structure of Dewey. The other method is to trace the class number by following the hierarchical ladder down each meaningful rung until we find the one which fits our topic best. This is the best and most effective approach to learning the DDC structure.

4.2.1.1 CLASSIFICATION BY DISCIPLINE

It should be kept in mind that the DDC is a classification divided first by discipline. Disciplines may be found in main classes, divisions, or sections. The main classes are the broadest areas of study. These classes have two zeros to the right, e.g., 200 Religion. Divisions are the next level down; they have one zero to the right, e.g., 220 Bible. Next come the sections, e.g., 221 Old Testament. Further subdivisions are occasionally referred to as subsections (four digits) or sub-subsections (five digits). To classify properly from the DDC schedules, therefore, we proceed from the broad to the narrow, from the general to the specific, from the main class to the division to the section, and so on. Some examples follow.

4.2.1.2 EXAMPLE 1

Let us say that the title of a book undergoing classification is *Married Women in the Labor Force*. To begin to classify the book we must understand that it is a subject falling in main class 300 Social sciences, and more narrowly in division 330 Economics. Our own general knowledge or the Relative Index will help us make these choices. At this point we may either scan the sections of 330 in the third summary or go directly to 330 in the schedules, where we find the sections and subsections of 330 Economics, including 331 Labor economics. Under 331 we find 331.4 Women workers, which is the right place to be, even though it is somewhat broader than our topic (that is, not all women who work are married). For that reason, our search does not end here. Scanning the subdivisions of 331.4, we find 331.43 Married women, the appropriate number for our book. Here our search ends, and we assign the number to the catalog record. We arrived at the proper number by narrowing the area of search at each stage where the ten roads diverged to different destinations. Visually, the entire path can be shown by the following structured diagram (Figure 4-1).

UNIVERSE OF KNOWLEDGE

Generalia	Philosophy	Religion	Social sciences	Linguistics	Science —>
000	100	200	300	400	500

	Sociology	Statistics	Political science	Economics	Law —>
	301–307	310	320	330	340

Labor economics		Financial economics		Land economics	Cooperatives —>
331		332		333	334

Labor force	Wages	Workers of specific age groups	Women workers	Special —> categories of workers
331.1	331.2	331.3	331.4	331.5

Specific aspects	Married women		Working mothers —>
331.41–331.42	331.43		331.44

Figure 4-1

4.2.1.3 EXAMPLE 2

We have the title *Lower House of Parliament*. We should know immediately that the work belongs in political science, and, after a little experience with the DDC, we should know that 320 is Political science. The third summary leads us to the proper section: 328 The legislative process (the work of parliaments). Under 328 in the schedules we learn that 328.3 Specific topics of legislative bodies is an available class, and it happens to have its own summary, which tells us that 328.32 is the number for lower houses of legislatures—a perfect match. We therefore end our search. Its linear course is charted below:

300	Social sciences
320	Political science
328	The legislative process
328.3	Specific topics of legislative bodies
328.32	Lower houses

To repeat, the first two rungs of the ladder may be reached from memory, and perhaps the third from experience. Then we shift to the schedules and move from general to specific, narrowing our area of search at every rung of the hierarchical ladder, often with the assistance of a summary.

4.2.1.4 EXAMPLE 3

Our last title is *Anatomy of the Large Intestine*, a work about the human large intestine. Our knowledge of the structure of the disciplines may not help us in this case. All creatures on the planet, except human beings, have their anatomy and physiology classed in 571 Physiology and related subjects, and properly so. Human beings are a special case. When the DDC was first devised, human anatomy and physiology were placed with the useful arts (medicine, specifically) to be with the technology that would be needed most often by students of these subjects. At that time, a century ago, it was physicians more than any other class of scholars who studied anatomy and physiology. That is why human anatomy is found in medicine instead of in division 570 Life sciences   Biology. As medicine is a reasonable location, it has not been moved to biology. Equally reasonable is the location of the anatomy, physiology, and pathology (illnesses) of farm animals in veterinary medicine in the technology number for farming. Needless to say, in classifying one has to know that human anatomy is located in technology, not in biology where all other anatomies (save for farm animals) are found. Thus, by way of the Relative Index or through the summaries, we have found our way to 611 Human anatomy, cytology (cell biology), histology (tissue biology). The summary there reveals that 611.3 is the number for digestive tract organs. At 611.3 we see that the intestine has been given the number 611.34, and the large intestine 611.347. Here we end our search with another perfect match of title and class. In the real world things do not always work out so nicely, of course. The route we followed is traced below:

600	Technology	
610	Medical sciences	Medicine
611	Human anatomy	
611.3	Digestive tract organs	
611.34	Intestine	
611.347	Large intestine	

4.2.2 DENOTING NONSUBJECT ASPECTS

If the subject of a work has been presented from a specific viewpoint (e.g., theoretical or historical) or in a recognized form (e.g., a periodical or dictionary), at the first opportunity we should separate the viewpoint and form from the subject proper. Both viewpoint and form are nonsubject characteristics of the document. First we should find the number for the subject, and then we can add to it the number for the viewpoint or form that we have taken from Table 1 Standard Subdivisions in volume 1. For example, if our title is *A Dictionary of Photocopying Technology*, we should recognize that "dictionary" is simply the form of presentation of the subject. First we should determine the class number for the subject proper (photocopying) in the usual way. In this case, the class number is 686.4. To this number we can add the number for a dictionary taken from Table 1 of volume 1. Then we join the two numbers, with the standard subdivision coming last, to arrive at 686.403. (For a detailed discussion of Table 1, see chapter 8.)

Often a subject is studied in the context of a geographic area; the area number to be attached to the subject number is usually taken from Table 2, where area numbers are listed. (For a detailed discussion of Table 2, see chapter 9.)

In the majority of cases the number arrived at through the structural ladder is a broad one. At that number there may be instructions in the form of add notes (discussed in chapter 3) that allow us to extend the number by another number taken either from the schedules or any of the auxiliary tables. There are seven auxiliary tables, all found in volume 1.

Name of Auxiliary Table

Table 1	Standard Subdivisions
Table 2	Geographic Areas, Historical Periods, Persons
Table 3	Subdivisions for the Arts, for Individual Literatures, for Specific Literary Forms

	T3-A	Subdivisions for Works by or about Individual Authors
	T3-B	Subdivisions for Works by or about More than One Author
	T3-C	Notation to Be Added Where Instructed in Table 3-B, 700.4, 791.4, 808–809
Table 4		Subdivisions of Individual Languages and Language Families
Table 5		Racial, Ethnic, National Groups
Table 6		Languages
Table 7		Groups of Persons

These tables will be discussed at length in chapters 8–12.

4.3   COMPLEX SUBJECTS

What is written above is, in fact, a simplistic view of practical classification. The reality is that subject analysis is not so simple—even for the experienced classifier. A document may pose unique and unimagined problems. Sometimes a work embodies a composite subject or it may be an agglomeration of seemingly unrelated subjects. Moreover, even though subject analysis has been done correctly, too often there is not a class number that fits the topic nicely; the final class that we find ourselves at is often three sizes too large or three sizes too small. In such cases we have to put the topic in the class that is too large. Interdisciplinary notes help overcome the problem of multidisciplinary subjects.

4.3.1   NUMBER BUILDING

When encountering a document with complex subject(s), the first thing to do is to look in the schedules for a ready-made number. Failing that, one must determine whether a number can be built or synthesized, either by following add instructions or by extending the schedule number for the main subject with notation from the auxiliary tables. In number building, *citation order*, i.e., the order or sequence of facets appearing in a class number, is an important consideration. For the sake of consistency, facets applicable to a particular class should be arranged in the same order in built numbers resulting from the extension of that class by means of numbers added from the schedules or from the tables. Citation order is discussed in detail in later chapters (note, in particular, 7.2.1).

Because number building is an essential procedure in the application of the DDC, it is discussed in depth in the following chapters.

4.3.2   CHOOSING APPROPRIATE NUMBERS

In spite of in-depth enumeration and the provision of synthesis of multitopical subjects, there are still cases where it is not possible to provide a coextensive (covering all facets of the subject) number for the content of a particular work. Many works treat different subjects separately or in relation to one another. Others treat a subject from different perspectives or cover one or more facets of a subject. The DDC does not always provide ready-made numbers or allow synthesis. For example, take the title *Treatment of Heart Disease According to Homeopathy*. In Dewey there is a separate number for homeopathy (615.532) and another for diseases of the heart (616.12), but it is not possible to combine the two. We may specify treatment, but will have to choose one base number and ignore the other aspect. Take another example, *Classification in Public Libraries*. Separate DDC numbers exist for library classification (025.42) and for public libraries (027.4), but there is no provision for combining them. One reason for such problems is that Dewey is still a partially enumerative classification rather than a totally faceted system aimed at complete subject analysis of documents, particularly documents on minute or very specialized topics.

In the case where a co-extensive number is not found in the schedules or cannot be built, the classifier must choose one subject or one facet/aspect and ignore the other(s). The question then is which to ignore and which to consider. The guidelines for classifying such works appear in sections 5.7–5.9 of the introduction to Edition 21[1] and are discussed below.

4.3.2.1 TWO OR MORE SUBJECTS TREATED SEPARATELY

Many works treat two or more subjects. These subjects may belong in different disciplines or come from the same discipline. In general, the discipline, subject, or aspect given the fullest treatment is preferred. If treatment is equal among the subjects or aspects, general guidelines regarding the choice of the appropriate numbers given in the introduction to Edition 21 should be followed, unless specific instructions in the schedules indicate otherwise. Specific instructions appearing in the schedules or tables override those given in the introduction.

4.3.2.1.1 TWO SUBJECTS

When the work treats two subjects separately and there is no class number covering both subjects, the number for the subject given fuller treatment in the work is chosen. When treatment is equal between the subjects, the number coming first in the numerical sequence is chosen. This is called the *first-of-two rule*. For example, a work on the fine arts and literature is classed in 700 (Arts) rather than in 800 (Literature), a work on the English language and English literature is classed in 420 (English language) rather than in 820 (English literature), and a work on gems and jewelry is classed in 736.2 (Gems) rather than

---

[1]Melvil Dewey, *Dewey Decimal Classification and Relative Index*, Ed. 21, edited by Joan S. Mitchell, Julianne Beall, Winton E. Matthews, Jr., and Gregory R. New (Albany, NY: OCLC Forest Press, 1996), v. 1, p.xxxvi–xxxviii.

739.27 (Jewelry). However, this rule does not apply when the two subjects constitute the major subdivisions of a broader (i.e., more general) number. In this case, the broader number is chosen.

4.3.2.1.2 THREE OR MORE SUBJECTS

When a work deals with three or more subjects that are all subdivisions of a broader subject, the next broader number in the same hierarchy that includes them all is chosen. This is called the *rule-of-three*.

4.3.2.2 TWO OR MORE SUBJECTS TREATED IN RELATION TO ONE ANOTHER

When a work covers two or more subjects treated in relation to one another, the number expressing such a relationship, if available, is chosen. For example, a work on church and state is classed in 322.1, the number in political science for church and state; a work on religion in public schools is classed in 379.28, the number in education for the place of religion in public schools.

If there is no class number expressing the relationship, the choice depends on the nature of the relationship. A work treating two or more interrelated subjects is classed with the subject that is being acted upon. For example, a work on Shakespeare's influence on Keats is classed with the number for Keats. This is called the *rule of application*.

4.3.2.3 INTERDISCIPLINARY WORKS

If the work treats a subject from the point of view of two or more disciplines, the interdisciplinary number, if provided, is chosen. To be a candidate for application of the interdisciplinary number the work must contain significant material on the discipline in which the interdisciplinary number is found. The interdisciplinary number may be indicated in the schedules by a note and appears opposite the first unindented term in the Relative Index. For example, a work on community-school relations that focuses on the sociological and educational benefits would be classed in 306.432, the interdisciplinary number in sociology for community-school relations. However, if the work just focuses on the mechanics of setting up a community-school partnership to improve elementary education, it would be classed in 372.119, the number in elementary education for community-school relations.

If a subject is not given an interdisciplinary number, the class number in the discipline given the fullest treatment in the work is chosen. When the work involves many disciplines, numbers in 000 Generalities are also possibilities.

Any other situation follows the rules for multitopical works.

4.3.2.4 WORKS TREATING TWO OR MORE ASPECTS OF A SUBJECT

For works that treat two or more aspects of a subject, a ready-made number, if available, is used. If such a number is not available, the classifier should determine whether a number covering all the facets can be built. If not, a choice must be made between two or more numbers each covering some but not all of the aspects. The following sections discuss the guidelines for choosing numbers.

4.3.2.4.1 ORDER OF PREFERENCE

In choosing among different potential class numbers for the same work, certain aspects are preferred over others. Decision making in such situations depends upon many factors. First of all, between two or more aspects, the one emphasized by the author may be considered foremost. Preference may also depend upon the policy of the classifying agency. If this is not the case, then the general (and common sense) rule is that the most specific aspect is to be chosen. To be sure, to determine which is the most specific aspect is not always easy. To help resolve such situations certain guidance has been provided officially in the introduction to Edition 21.

In the DDC, *preference order* is officially defined as:

> The order indicating which one of two or more numbers is to be chosen when different characteristics of a subject cannot be shown in full by number building. A note (sometimes containing a table of preference) indicates which characteristic is to be selected for works covering more than one characteristic. When the notation can be synthesized to show two or more characteristics, it is a matter of citation order (see glossary, p. 223).

In the schedules and auxiliary tables, there are *tables of preference* (previously called tables of precedence) or *preference notes* where appropriate, as well as certain other general rules for choosing among numbers for two or more aspects.

4.3.2.4.2 TABLE OF PREFERENCE

A table of preference establishes the priority of one topic or aspect over the other(s) in a multitopical or multifaceted subject. Chapter 8 includes a discussion of the table of preference in Table 1 Standard Subdivisions. Such tables also appear throughout the schedules. For example, under 155.42–155.45 [Child psychology by] Specific groupings we find the following table of preference:

Exceptional children	155.45
Children by status, type, relationships	155.44
Children in specific age groups	155.42
Children by sex	155.43

This table of preference must be observed in cases of complex subjects involving two or more aspects in a given title. For example, let us take the title *Psychology of Exceptional Sibling Children*. This complex subject can be broken into the following viable components:

Psychology of sibling children	155.443
Psychology of exceptional children	155.45

Since, according to the table of preference above, 155.45 Exceptional children is to be preferred over 155.44 or its derivatives, our class number will be 155.45. Similarly, according to the same table of preference, for a work on the psychology of preschool girls, the number 155.423 Psychology of children three to five is chosen over the number 155.433 Psychology of girls.

Another example of a table of preference is found under 658.401–658.409 Specific executive management activities:

Personal aspects of executive management	658.409
Management of executive personnel	658.407
Internal organization	658.402
Managing change	658.406
Negotiation, conflict management, crisis management	658.405
Planning, policy making, control, quality management	658.401
Decision making and information management	658.403
Social responsibility of executive management	658.408
Project management	658.404

Applying the table above results in:

(1) Decision making and information management for internal organization
658.402 not 658.403
(2) Policy making for project management
658.401 not 658.404

Examples of many more such tables throughout the schedules can be cited. In addition there are preference notes with the same effect.

4.3.2.4.3 PREFERENCE NOTES
Instead of being in tabulated form, the order of preference of topics may be given as a general instruction to use either an earlier or later number in the schedule. Examples of such instructions are given below.

4.3.2.4.3.1 USING EARLIER NUMBER
In many situations, the classifier is instructed to use the earlier number. For example:

> 331.3–331.6 Labor force by personal characteristics
> Unless other instructions are given, class a subject with aspects in two or more subdivisions of 331.1–331.6 in the number coming first, e.g., young Native American native women 331.34408997 (*not* 331.408997 or 331.6997)

In application:

Immigrant women labor
331.4 Women workers; not 331.62 Immigrants and aliens or its subdivisions

Middle-aged migrant workers
331.394 Middle-aged workers; not 331.544 Migrant and casual workers

4.3.2.4.3.2 USING LAST NUMBER

Increasingly, there are instructions to use the last number in certain situations. For example, under 365 Penal and related institutions, the instruction reads:

Unless other instructions are given, class a subject with aspects in two or more subdivisions of 365 in the number coming last, e.g., maximum security prisons for women 365.43 (*not* 365.33)

Therefore for:

Maximum security military prisons
365.48   Military prison and prison camps, not 365.33 Institutions by degree of security

Prison discipline for political prisoners
365.643   Discipline, not 365.45 Institutions for political prisoners and related classes of persons

Under 395 Etiquette (Manners), a similar note appears with an instruction to use the class number coming last in 395. For example:

Etiquette for entertainments at weddings
395.3   Etiquette for social occasions; not 395.22 [Etiquette for] Engagements and weddings

Table manners for children
395.54   [Etiquette for] Table manners; not 395.122 [Etiquette for] Children

4.3.2.4.4 GENERAL GUIDELINES

When no specific instructions are provided under a particular class, there are general guidelines for determining the order of preference. These guidelines are given in sections 5.7–5.9 of the introduction in volume 1 of the DDC.[2]

4.3.2.4.4.1 BY THE NUMBER OF ZEROS IN A CLASS NUMBER

A general guideline, called the *rule of zero*, instructs the classifier to choose the number with the fewest zeros if a comparison can be made. In other words, at the same point of a hierarchy (i.e., the same main number), a subdivision without a zero is to be preferred over a subdivision with a zero; and similarly, a subdivision with one zero is to be preferred over a subdivision with two zeros. For example:

Qualification of teachers in private schools
371.12 Professional qualifications of teachers; not 371.02 Private schools

Manufacture of metal outdoor furniture
684.18 Outdoor furniture; not 684.105 Metal furniture

Architecture of wooden ceilings
721.7 Ceiling; not 721.0448 Wood

The rationale behind such a policy is that, generally, in a particular hierarchy in the DDC, subdivisions with a zero or two zeros are used for subdivisions applicable to the topic as a whole, whereas subdivisions without a zero represent specific subtopics.

4.3.2.4.4.2 PREFERRING THE CONCRETE OVER THE ABSTRACT

When no specific guidance is provided in the schedules or auxiliary tables and the rule of zero does not apply, there is the *table of last resort* :

(1) Kinds of things
(2) Parts of things
(3) Materials from which things, kinds, or parts are made
(4) Properties of things, kinds, parts, or materials
(5) Processes within things, kinds, parts, or materials
(6) Operations upon things, kinds, parts, or materials
(7) Instrumentalities for performing such operations

This table is based on the principle of preferring the kind of thing over the part; the concrete over the abstract; thing/material over the process; and process over the agent.

[2]Dewey, *Dewey Decimal Classification*, Ed. 21, v. 1, p. xxxvi–xxxviii.

The table of last resort should be used with caution. Do not apply this table if it appears to disregard the author's intention and emphasis. For example, if the author's emphasis in a work is clearly on process over thing or material, then the general order of preference should be reversed.

4.4 SOURCES OF READY-MADE NUMBERS

In addition to the inside and outside sources of knowledge about the subject of a work, there are sources for ready-made class numbers for specific titles. These include:

(1) Cataloging copy prepared by central or cooperative cataloging agencies or libraries such as the British Library and the Library of Congress (the home of the Decimal Classification Division, where the Dewey editorial office is also located)

(2) Cataloging copy prepared by libraries sharing cataloging information found in union catalogs maintained by bibliographic utilities such as OCLC Online Computer Library Center and RLIN (Research Library Information Network)

(3) Cataloging-in-Publication (CIP) data given on the verso of the title pages of books whose publishers are enrolled in the CIP program at the Library of Congress or at the British Library

(4) National bibliographies, such as Australian National Bibliography, British National Bibliography, and Indian National Bibliography

Some of these sources, including many of the national bibliographies, appear in print form. Others appear in electronic form. For instance, MARC bibliographic records prepared by the Library of Congress form a part of the OCLC Online Union Catalog (OLUC) database. They are also available through LOCIS (Library of Congress Information System) via Internet. In addition, they are available on CD-ROM.

4.5 SUMMARY

The work of practical classification involves two operations: determining the subject of a work and determining the disciplinary context in the DDC for the topic. The first operation involves the careful subject analysis of the document being classified. The subject of the work is what the author focuses upon, what he/she describes. This can be learned from the title and subtitle, with assistance from the book jacket or container, preface, table of contents, bibliography, and subject index. The title alone is never a sufficient indication of what a work is about, however simple and clear it may appear to be. It is also important to differentiate the author's viewpoint, the form of presentation, and the physical medium or form of the document from the subject proper.

The second operation, once the subject is properly analyzed, is to find the appropriate number to represent the subject. This process of classification begins by determining the main class, the division, and the section for the subject. This could be called "disciplinary analysis." When this has been done, we scan the subsections through levels of increasing specificity until we arrive at the appropriate number. We proceed from general to specific and at every juncture we go on narrowing our search. The various summaries assist us by enabling a rapid transit down the hierarchical chain.

A number may also be further extended by another number either from the schedules or from any of the auxiliary tables. But it must be remembered that Dewey is still not an exhaustive classification, and the class number whether found ready-made or extended by any device may still not cover all the aspects of the subject. In cases where a single number does not cover all topics or aspects a choice must be made among two or more available numbers. The choices in these cases are made according to the order of preference given in tables of preference, preference notes, or instructions in the introduction to the DDC.

In order to facilitate classification by the DDC and to render the operation more cost-effective, classifiers may consult various sources for ready-made numbers assigned by cataloging agencies or other libraries. Cataloging information, including class numbers, is available in electronic form as well as in print form, such as those given on the verso of the title pages of books.

4.6   EXERCISES

Exercise 1:

Identify the class numbers for the following subjects:

(1)   Aves: a zoological study

(2)   Heart diseases

(3)   Surgery for diseases of the gums

(4)   20th-century sculpture

(5)   Reign of Elizabeth I (of England)

Exercise 2:

Classify the following subjects by using the appropriate table of preference:

(1)   Preparing luncheon for schools
(2)   Deportation for political offenses
(3)   Decorative lighting for weddings
(4)   Miniature portraits of women (paintings)
(5)   Compensation of working mothers

Exercise 3:

Identify the class numbers for the following subjects:

(1)   Educational service in adult women prisons
(2)   Veteran immigrant labor
(3)   Production (economic) efficiency in agriculture
(4)   Maladjusted young people

Exercise 4:

Identify the class numbers for the following subjects:

(1)   Evaluation of curricula in elementary schools
(2)   Color printing by photo mechanical techniques
(3)   Metallic chairs
(4)   Atomic weight of curium (chemical element)
(5)   Breeding of Oriental horses
(6)   Diseases of arrowroot

CHAPTER 5
USING THE MANUAL

Objectives:

The objectives of this chapter are to explain: the origins and use of the Manual; the types of notes it includes; its organization; and how the Manual relates to other parts of the Classification.

Outline:

5.0   INTRODUCTION

The Manual for the Dewey Decimal Classification gives advice on classifying in difficult areas, provides in-depth information on the major revised schedules, and explains the policies and practices of the Decimal Classification Division at the Library of Congress.

The Manual was first published as part of the Classification in volume 4 of Edition 20. Its direct predecessor was *Manual on the Use of the Dewey Decimal Classification: Edition 19*,[1] which was published separately three years after the publication of Edition 19. The Edition 19 Manual was intended as a pragmatic guide to the Classification for practicing classifiers and students. In "New Features in Edition 20," the relationship between the Edition 20 integrated Manual and the Edition 19 Manual is described:

> The Manual represents the core of a much larger body of notes first introduced in the separately published 1982 *Manual on the Use of the Dewey Decimal Classification: Edition 19*. . . .The briefer notes of

---

[1]Comaromi, John P., and Margaret J. Warren, *Manual on the Use of the Dewey Decimal Classification: Edition 19* (Albany, NY: Forest Press, 1982).

the 1982 Manual, and those that need to be used frequently, have been incorporated in the Schedules and Tables.[2]

In Edition 21, the Manual has been expanded. The Edition 20 practice of incorporating brief and/or frequently used information directly in the schedules and tables has continued. At the same time, many new notes have been added to the Manual, and references to the Manual have been incorporated in the Relative Index.

5.1   SCOPE OF THE MANUAL

The Manual is not an exhaustive guide to the Classification. It is a selective guide that includes assistance on choosing among numbers, detailed instructions on the use of complicated schedules (e.g., Table 3, 004–006, 780, 800), and lengthy introductions to major revisions. Information is placed in the Manual when it cannot be succinctly represented within the framework of notes in the schedules and tables, or when its inclusion in the schedules would be distracting or annoying.

The Manual contains three kinds of notes:[3]

(1)   Notes on problems common to more than one number

(2)   Notes on problems involving only one number (or a single number and its subdivisions)

(3)   Notes on differentiating numbers (the notes linked by "vs.," e.g., 500 vs. 600)

The Manual also includes an appendix on the policies and practices of the Library of Congress Decimal Classification Division (see section 5.7).

5.2   NOTES ON PROBLEMS COMMON TO MORE THAN ONE NUMBER

The Manual contains explanations of problems common to more than one number. The issues addressed may occur in a span of numbers, or a group of related numbers. For example:

281.1–.4

Early church

The early church is considered to be undivided by denominations until the schism of 1054. Therefore, the history of the Church prior to 1054 is classed in 270.1–.3, not here. . .

---

[2]Melvil Dewey, *Dewey Decimal Classification and Relative Index*, Ed. 20, edited by John P. Comaromi, Julianne Beall, Winton E. Matthews, Jr., and Gregory R. New (Albany, NY: OCLC Forest Press, 1989), v. 1, p. xix.

[3]For an explanation of the sequence and format of Manual notes, see section 5.5.

The treatment of the early church is explained succinctly in the Manual note at 281.1–.4. For a classifier who occasionally uses these numbers, it provides a welcome clarification of the terminology. For the classifier who uses the 200 Religion schedule on a regular basis, reading this note once will be sufficient.

Similarly:

> T1—081 and T1—082, T1—08351, T1—08352, T1—08421, T1—08422
> Men [and] Women [and] Males twelve to twenty [and] Females twelve to twenty [and] Young men [and] Young women
>
> Subdivisions for men and women should be used only for works explicitly emphasizing the sex of the people treated. . .

The Manual note in the example above focuses on a single topic, identification of the sexes. Since this topic applies to the use of several standard subdivisions, it is explained more efficiently in the Manual as opposed to a listing under each applicable subdivision in Table 1.

5.3   NOTES ON PROBLEMS INVOLVING ONLY ONE NUMBER

A second kind of note, on problems involving only one number or a number and its subdivisions, is used to explain certain aspects of a schedule that cannot be done within the regular framework of notes in the schedules and tables. Such a note may be needed due to the length of the explanation, the nature of the problem, and/or the frequency of use of the information. This type of note is also used for general information about a schedule and to introduce major revisions.

For example, there is a Manual note for 280 Denominations and sects of the Christian church that focuses on the topic Biography:

> The kinds of biographies to be classed here are shown in the table of preference for biographies under 230–280: Biography.
> The Decimal Classification Division classifies biographies with the main branch of the denomination rather than with the most specific organization or area. . .

Information on the practices of the Decimal Classification Division is important to users of the Dewey numbers supplied on Library of Congress bibliographic records, but does not belong within the notes in the schedules and tables.

The Manual note for 221 Old Testament (Tanakh) focuses on optional numbers for books of Tanakh. The note includes an alphabetic index to preferred and optional numbers for each book, followed by an optional schedule (222–224).

5.3.1 GENERAL INFORMATION NOTES

An important type of note located at a single number or a number and its subdivisions is the general information or general instructions note. These notes should be read carefully by all users of the Classification, and referred to later as necessary.

One of the most important notes in the Manual is the first—the general note on Table 1 Standard Subdivisions. This note contains important information about standard subdivisions and detailed instruction on their use. Other examples of general notes are the Manual notes on Table 3, Table 3A, Table 3B, and Table 5. Each contains detailed instructions on the use of the table in question, illustrated by sample titles with accompanying DDC numbers. The Manual notes on Table 3A and Table 3B also include flow charts that lead the classifier through each decision point in the table.

Two major revisions introduced in Edition 20, 004–006 Computer science and 780 Music, continue to have lengthy Manual notes in Edition 21. The Manual notes for these schedules contain detailed instructions on their use, and many examples.

General information notes are not limited to main table numbers or main class and division numbers in the schedules. Subdivisions of classes with general information notes may have their own notes. For instance, the Manual note for Table 3B —1 Poetry contains information on preference order illustrated by sample titles with DDC numbers. Likewise, the Manual note for 005 Programs contains many examples to illustrate use of the schedule. Even though there is a major Manual note for 780 Music, 782 Vocal music has its own Manual note complete with a flow chart.

5.3.1.1 NOTES ON MAJOR REVISIONS

Major revisions in each edition of the Classification are introduced and explained by an extensive Manual note. The Manual note addresses the history and reasons for the revision, outlines the basic structure of the schedule, and gives detailed examples on its use with sample titles as illustrations.

In Edition 21, two such revisions have major Manual notes: 351 Public administration and 560–590 Life sciences. The latter is an introductory note and overview of the revision; additional information and instruction notes are included for 560 and 570–590. There are also other Manual notes for numbers or spans within 560–590 discussing topics common to several numbers and differentiating among numbers.

5.4 NOTES DIFFERENTIATING NUMBERS

The most common type of note in the Manual is the note differentiating among numbers, the "versus" note. The numbers may be within the same discipline or in different disciplines. In each case, the "if-in-doubt" number is specified. Two examples follow:

552 vs. 549
> Petrology vs. Mineralogy
>
> Rocks can be defined as aggregates of minerals, the minerals being homogenous, usually crystalline grains (large and small) that give rocks their texture. Petrology encompasses the study of rocks and minerals, or of rocks alone. The homogeneous minerals studied by themselves are classed in 549. If in doubt, prefer 552.

579.165 vs. 616.01
> Harmful organisms vs. Medical microbiology
>
> Class in 579.165 the biology of pathogenic microorganisms. Class in 616.01 the study of the microorganisms in relation to human diseases. If in doubt, prefer 579.165.

5.5 ORGANIZATION OF THE MANUAL

To facilitate its use, the Manual is arranged in the numerical order of the tables and schedules. Notes on the tables precede notes on the schedules. Each Manual note is listed at the preferred or "if-in-doubt" number. For classes with more than one note, the notes are usually arranged in the order listed in 5.1. Within each sequence, the broader span comes before the narrower span (e.g., 583–585 precedes 583–584); however, a note for a single number ending in 0 always comes first in the sequence. A "vs." note always appears last (e.g., 362–363 vs. 364.1 follows 362–363). For example, the sequence of notes beginning with 004 is as follows:

> 004–006
> 004–006 vs. 621.39
> 004 vs. 004.33
> 004 vs. 005

The numbers are accompanied by their corresponding captions from the tables and schedules. The captions appear in boldface type on the line following the numbers. Additional terms are added in square brackets to provide context. For example:

> **340.59 vs. 297.14**
> > **Islamic law vs. [Islamic] Religious and ceremonial laws and decisions**

If the note is narrower than the caption would suggest, a subheading is included (centered in boldface type). For example:

280

Denominations and sects of Christian church
Biography

Subheadings are also used to divide lengthy notes into sections. In several places, sections in notes are divided into subsections. The headings for subsections appear centered in italics. For example, the Manual note for 780 Music includes the following section and subsection:

Examples
Works about music

See-also references link related Manual notes within the Manual. See-also references may be from the full Manual note, or a paragraph or section of the note, to another Manual note (or section thereof). Each reference is listed in italics at the end of the paragraph, section, or note to which it applies. For example, the following reference appears at the end of the "Musicians" section of the Manual note for 780.92 Persons associated with music:

See also 781.6 for discussion on musicians associated with traditions of music other than classical.

5.6 SEE-MANUAL REFERENCES

See-Manual references in the schedules and tables refer the classifier to the entries in the Manual. The reference may be to a full note, several notes, and/or a section of a note. For example, the following see-Manual references appear in the centered entry 571–575 Internal biological processes and structures:

See Manual at 571–575; also at 570–590: Add instructions in 571–575; also at 571–575 vs. 630; also at 571–573 vs. 610

The second reference, "also at 570–590: Add instructions in 571–575," refers to a section of the Manual note for 570–590.

The introduction to Edition 21 contains several references to the Manual note for Table 1 Standard Subdivisions, as does the note at the beginning of Table 1 in volume 1.

See-Manual references appear in the Relative Index under the appropriate index terms for the Manual note or section of the note (see discussion in 6.9).

5.7 APPENDIX

The appendix to the Manual describes the policies and procedures of the Decimal Classification Division of the Library of Congress with respect to segmentation in centrally cataloged records, alternate DDC notation in LC bibliographic records, and the classification of children's books in the Decimal Classification Division.

5.8   SUMMARY

The Manual provides practical advice on selected areas of the Classification. It gives guidance on choosing among numbers for the same topic, detailed instructions on using complicated schedules, and lengthy introductions to major revision. The Manual also contains information on the policies and practices of the Decimal Classification Division at the Library of Congress.

CHAPTER 6
USING THE RELATIVE INDEX

Objectives:

The objectives of this chapter are to explain: the Relative Index; its usefulness and importance; its organization and format; and its use in locating a class number for a given subject.

Outline:

6.0   INTRODUCTION

An index is ordinarily an alphabetically arranged list of concepts occurring in a particular book. The index to the DDC is called the *Relative Index*. It has been a major part of each edition since the first (1876). It is, of course, primarily an adjunct or aid in the use of the schedules, which contain the core of the DDC. Nevertheless, it has always been a feature that transcends the usefulness of a good back-of-the-book index. The reason will be apparent as we proceed. The Relative Index is considered by many to be one of Melvil Dewey's paramount and enduring contributions to library classification and indexing.

6.1   NEED AND IMPORTANCE OF THE RELATIVE INDEX

All terms found in the schedules and in the various auxiliary tables have been arranged logically in whole/part and genus/species relations, in other words, in a systematic order that proceeds from the general to the specific. Such arrangements are designed to mirror the structure of knowledge and its evolution. To locate a desired subject in the schedules, one needs at least a preliminary knowledge of its position in the universe of knowledge. But, as was stated earlier, it is very difficult, if not impossible, for any person, however learned, to have even a preliminary knowledge of all the subjects in the universe of knowledge. Therefore, at one time or another everyone who uses the DDC has to use the Relative Index, the key to the schedules. There are several reasons why.

6.1.1   LIMITED KNOWLEDGE OF THE CLASSIFIER

A classifier at times may not always be familiar with the subject of the work being classified. At other times, the classifier may understand the subject but may not be aware of its location in the overall system. Take, for example, the subject of birthday cards: one may not even be able to guess where its primary class might fall. Some classes, such as engineering, are so crammed with topics that it is no easy matter to locate the desired subject by paging through its schedule. For such reasons, the DDC schedules (volumes 2 and 3) may sometimes seem a formidable fortress that daunts all but the heartiest classifiers.

In some cases, through no fault of the classifier, the hierarchical trail leads to false ends or blind alleys. More determined efforts only incur increased frustration. At such times the Relative Index provides a road to the desired subject.

6.1.2   ILLOGICAL PLACEMENTS OF SOME SUBJECTS IN THE DDC

In addition, in the DDC itself the positions of some subjects are neither logical nor in accord with current scholarly consensus. Although many of the misplacements in the original plan of 1876 have been rectified in later editions, some remain to this day. In later developments of the system some new subjects had to be placed in illogical locations because there were no vacant numbers available at logical places. Again, in these situations, the Relative Index can guide the classifier to the appropriate numbers.

6.2   VALUE OF THE RELATIVE INDEX

There are different views on the use of the Relative Index. One group believes in using the schedules, i.e., the systematic hierarchical ladder, as much as possible. For them the Relative Index should be used minimally and only in hours of difficulty. They believe that the more classifiers rely on the index, the more slowly they will learn the structure of the DDC.

Another view gives prime importance to the Relative Index, even going so far as to suggest that it be consulted every time one assigns a number. For those who hold this view, the Relative Index is the door through which one must pass before entering the house of Dewey numbers. This view is subscribed to by those who perhaps have too much faith in alphabetical arrangement, and who do not care to take the time to learn the logical approach that the schedules provide.

The most reasonable view is that classifiers should use the Relative Index as needed.

Whatever one thinks of the Relative Index and its use, it must be borne in mind that it is an integral part of the system and has always been so. This much is clear from the title: *Dewey Decimal Classification and Relative Index.* Therefore, the index should not be taken as merely an adjunct or a convenient key to the schedules. It complements the schedules by providing an independent approach to the classified structure they embody. Furthermore, the index goes beyond the straightforward alphabetical indexing of terms; through a helpful indexing technique, terms are also listed according to the disciplines in which they appear.

6.3   NOMENCLATURE: RELATIVE INDEX

The index to the DDC has the formal name *Relative Index.* Its approach is the reverse of the approach of the schedules. In the Relative Index all of the indexable terms found in headings and notes plus terms with literary warrant for concepts represented by the schedules have been arranged in an alphabetical sequence, while in the schedules, they are arranged by discipline. The index is called "relative" because it relates subjects to the disciplines in the schedules. Take, for example, the subject amphibians. It has various aspects scattered throughout the schedules. Not all of them are listed in the Relative Index, of course, but we do find the following:

Amphibians	597.8
art representation	704.943 278
commercial hunting	639.13
conservation technology	639.977 8
drawing	743.676
farming	639.378
food	641.396
cooking	641.696
paleozoology	567.8
resource economics	333.957 8
zoology	597.8

As is obvious, many aspects of amphibians have been brought together from their scattered locations in the schedules.

6.4   SCOPE OF THE INDEX

No index can be totally comprehensive or exhaustive. In using the Relative Index, it is important to know what is included and what is not.

6.4.1 WHAT THE INDEX CONTAINS

The index is made up of the following kinds of terms in a single alphabetical sequence:

(1) Indexable terms in the headings and notes of the schedules and tables

(2) Terms with literary warrant for concepts in the schedules or tables

(3) Some useful terms obtained by built numbers

(4) Terms for broad concepts covered in Manual notes

(5) Selected proper names in the following categories:

    (i) Geographic names (names of countries, names of states and provinces of most countries, names of the counties of the United States, names of capital cities and other important municipalities, and names of important geographic features)

    (ii) Names of persons (heads-of-state used to identify historical periods, founders or revealers of religions, and initiators of schools of thought used to identify the schools)

6.4.2 WHAT THE INDEX DOES NOT CONTAIN

The Relative Index is not exhaustive. No index can be expected to contain all names of persons, cities, organizations, minerals, plants, animals, chemical compounds, drugs, manufactured articles, etc. Names are included in the Relative Index selectively. In addition, the following categories of terms are also excluded:

(1) Phrases beginning with the adjectival form of countries, languages, nationalities, and religions, e.g., English poetry, French architecture, Hindu prayer books, Mexican cooking.

(2) Phrases containing general concepts represented by standard subdivisions such as education, history, maintenance, statistics, laboratories, and management; e.g., Art education, History of science, Automobile maintenance, Educational statistics, Medical laboratories, Restaurant management.

A phrase falling in either category listed above may be included if there is strong literary warrant for the heading as a term sought by users, e.g., English literature. One of these headings may also be included if it is a proper name or provides the only form of access to the topic, e.g., English Channel, English horns, English peas.

If a term being sought does not appear in the index, the classifier's first recourse is to look under the index listing for the broader class or term that contains the topic. For example, if the work in hand is a biography of Benjamin Franklin or John Milton or Ludwig van Beethoven—names not found in the Relative Index—the classifier should look instead under the broad class to which each belongs: poets for Milton; composers for Beethoven. With Benjamin Franklin we must first determine the perspective of the work, because Franklin fits in several classes. Similarly, for a work on the Library Association (U.K.) or Oxford University (names not included in the Relative Index), we might look under "library associations" and "universities." If these terms do not help, we can look at terms in the next level up in the hierarchy, i.e., "organizations" and "higher education." The numbers for these terms will not, of course, provide specific numbers for works, but will point to appropriate general areas in the schedules or tables.

6.4.3   INTERDISCIPLINARY NUMBERS

When a topic treated from the perspectives of two or more disciplines is represented by multiple numbers, the class number displayed in the index entry opposite the unindented term for the topic is the number designated for interdisciplinary works. The interdisciplinary number may appear again under the discipline in which the number falls. For example:

Elastomers	678
chemistry	547.842
manufacturing technology	678
equipment manufacture	681.766 8
materials science	620.194
structural engineering	624.189 4

In the entry above, 678 is the interdisciplinary number for elastomers, and also the number for the manufacture of elastomers. A work that discusses elastomers from the viewpoint of materials science and manufacturing would be classed in 678, the interdisciplinary number for elastomers; a work on the manufacturing of elastomers would be classed in the same number. A work limited to the materials science aspects of elastomers would be classed in 620.194.

The Relative Index does not contain interdisciplinary numbers for every entry. The interdisciplinary number is not given in the following cases:

(1)   When the first term in the entry is ambiguous

(2)   When the index term has no disciplinary focus

(3)   When there is little or no literary warrant for the interdisciplinary number

6.5 ORGANIZATION OF THE INDEX

Since Edition 16 (1958), the Relative Index has appeared in a separate volume. In Edition 21, it is found in volume 4. The text of the Relative Index is prefaced by a brief set of guidelines and a list of abbreviations. Detailed guidelines on its use are given in the introduction to Edition 21.[1]

Each page of the index is divided into two columns of entries. An entry is composed of a term, discipline (if any), and a corresponding DDC number. For example:

Food additives	641.3
commercial technology	664.06
preservation	664.028 7
food	641.3
home preservation	641.47
human toxicology	615.954
law	344.042 32
see also Food—product safety	

These entries are to be read as follows:

Food additives, *interdisciplinary works*	641.3
Food additives, commercial *production and use*	664.06
Food additives, *used in* commercial preservation *of food*	664.028 7
Food additives *as* food	641.3
Food additives *used in* home preservation *of food*	641.47
Food additives *as poisons*	615.954
Food additives law	344.042 32

The last line *"see also* Food—product safety" in the index entry shown above displays an instance of an upward *see-also* reference or a *see-also* reference to a related topic. Under the entry referred to, there are additional numbers of possible value.

6.6 READING THE INDEX

Conceptually and typographically the Relative Index is highly structured to yield a maximum of information in a minimum of space. Some points to keep in mind are:

(1)   American spelling is used, e.g., color, catalog, labor

---

[1]Melvil Dewey, *Dewey Decimal Classification and Relative Index*, Ed. 21, edited by Joan S. Mitchell, Julianne Beall, Winton E. Matthews, Jr., and Gregory R. New (Albany, NY: OCLC Forest Press, 1996), v. 1, p. li–liv.

(2)   All terms are arranged in word by word (as distinguished from letter by letter) order. Hyphens are treated as a space. For example:

> Cross County (Ark.)
> Cross-cultural communication
> Cross-cultural psychology
> Cross examination
> Cross River languages
> Cross River State (Nigeria)
> Cross-stitch
> Crossbills
> Crossbreeding

(3)   Entries with the same word or phrase but with different marks of punctuation are arranged in the following order:

> Term
> Term. Subheading
> Term (Parenthetical qualifier)
> Term, inverted term qualifier
> Term as part of phrase

For example:

> Canada
> Canada, Eastern
> Canada, Western
> Canada goose
>
> Georgia
> Georgia (Republic)
> Georgia, Strait of
>
> United Nations
> United Nations. Charter
> United Nations. General Assembly
> United Nations. Security Council
> United Nations (Military alliance)
> United Nations Children's Fund

(4)   Initialisms and acronyms are entered without punctuation and are filed as if spelled as one word.   For example:

> ACTH (Hormone)
> AIDS (Disease)
> CATV systems
> PACS (Action committees)
> SAT (Assessment test)

The punctuation between initials in proper names is retained, e.g., P.K. le Roux Dam (South Africa).

(5)   Most numbers are entered in their spelled out form. For example:

>   Three Rivers (England)
>   Three wise men (Christian doctrines)
>   Twentieth century

Proper names containing Arabic or Roman numerals have not been rewritten, and the number files before a letter in the same position, e.g., the entry "100 Mile House (B.C.)" files before A at the beginning of the index.

(6)   Qualifiers, if needed, are added to differentiate homographs:

>   Biscuits (Breads)
>   Biscuits (Cookies)
>   Foundations (Building elements)
>   Foundations (Organizations)
>   Rays (Fishes)
>   Rays (Nuclear physics)

(7)   The choice of singular versus plural form follows BS 3700:1988, *British Standard Recommendations for Preparing Indexes to Books, Periodicals and Other Documents*. Abstract nouns are usually found in the singular, e.g., Divorce, Immortality, Pathology, Truth. Concrete nouns are usually found in the plural form, e.g., Farmers, Libraries, Pianos, Roads. Parts of the body are in the plural only when more than one occurs in a fully formed organism (e.g., Ears, Hands, Nose).

Plants and animals follow scientific convention in choice of singular versus plural form, with the decision based on whether the taxonomic class has more than one member (e.g., Horses, Lion, Lipizzaner horse). Where usage varies across disciplines, the index entry reflects the form preferred in the discipline where the interdisciplinary works are classed. For example, while there are several kinds of hemp in botany, the index entry is in the singular, because the interdisciplinary number for hemp is 677.12, the number for hemp as a kind of textile fiber.

(8)   Place names and other proper names are generally given in the form specified by *Anglo-American Cataloguing Rules*, 2nd edition, revised (*AACR2R*), based on the names established in the Library of Congress authority files. If the *AACR2R* name is not the common English name, an entry is also included under the common form.

(9)   Plants and animals are indexed under their scientific and common names.

6.6.1 PHRASES/MULTIWORD TERMS

Subjects commonly represented by phrases are usually entered in adjective-noun form. For example:

Agricultural banks
Agricultural credit
Agricultural law
Austrian winter peas
Color television
Indian Ocean
Inorganic chemistry
Islamic calendar
Reinforced concrete

For many other entries, even though a phrase entry could be imagined, such an entry would separate the particular aspect represented by the phrase entry from the other aspects of the base concept. For example, while "Ancient Egypt" and "Wetland ecology" might be useful phrase headings, entering these concepts as phrases would separate these aspects from other aspects of the topics "Egypt" and "Wetlands." For this reason, these concepts are entered as follows:

Egypt	962
	T2–62
ancient	932
	T2–32
Wetlands	551.41
biology	578.768
resource economics	333.952 88
animals	333.954 88
ecology	577.68
geomorphology	551.41
law	346.046 918
public administration	354.34
resource economics	333.918

If the phrase entry for a topic represents a highly sought term, the topic may be entered as entry/subentry as well as phrase entry, e.g., Forest ecology and Forest lands—ecology.

6.6.2 LOOKING UNDER KEY TERMS

As a broad rule: If one term in a phrase refers to an object or a substance and the other refers to a technique or a process or an action, it is better to look under the object/substance, the concrete term, for that is the way most people store information. For example, "Solar flares" is indexed under Solar flares, because "solar" is the adjective pertaining to the sun (an object). Further examples:

Body mechanics
Corporate law
Pipeline processing
Television transmission

6.6.3 USE OF CAPITAL LETTERS

Note that only the main entry has been spelled with an initial capital letter whereas its aspects are spelled with a small letter (which is another device to show superordinate and subordinate relations of subjects and/or disciplines in the index).

6.6.4 ABBREVIATIONS USED IN ENTRIES

AACR2R forms of abbreviations, particularly those used in qualifiers of geographic names, are used in conjunction with entries in the Relative Index. Here are a few examples:

Bras d'Or Lake (N.S.)
Hall Beach (N.W.T)
Liverpool (N.S.)
Liverpool (N.S.W.)
New York (N.Y.)
Nicholas County (W. Va.)
Red Deer (Alta.)

6.6.5 INITIALISMS AND ACRONYMS

Topics that can be expressed as initialisms or acronyms are indexed under both the initialism or acronym and the spelled-out form. For example:

CDs (Compact discs)	384
Compact discs	384
NATO (Alliance)	355.031 091 821
North Atlantic Treaty Organization	355.031 091 821

6.7   DEPICTING RANK RELATIONS

In the Relative Index some entries are direct and stand alone:

Autocracy (Absolute monarchy)	321.6
Autographs	929.88
Chin dynasty	931.04
Lions Bay (B.C.)	T2 −711 33
Sheep dogs	636.737
Siemens process	669.142 2
Theravada Buddhism	294.391
Voodooism	299.675

Many entries, on the other hand, have subentries indicating aspects. At first glance such entries, indeed all the entries taken together, seem to make up an involved and tangled alphabetized web. But the web is more approachable than it appears.

6.7.1   USE OF TYPOGRAPHICAL INDENTIONS

Typographical indentions are used to show the multiplicity of relations and aspects in which a given term figures. Once one learns to read the indentions, there is little difficulty in locating and following the various terms and their relations to one another. Here are two fairly simple entries that tell us a great deal about the nature of the Relative Index:

Rates	
communications industry	384.041
insurance	368.011
transportation services	388.049
Rates (United Kingdom)	336.22
law	343.054 2
public finance	336.22

In the first entry, there is no class number opposite the unindented term "Rates." Rates is a word that appears in many fields of study with a variety of meanings. In the schedules it is a term that is used in the three fields that are indented below its index entry. The actual subjects are communications rates, insurance rates, and transportation rates. Indeed, the term "insurance rates" is so common that it has also been indexed under its natural word order. Rates has no interdisciplinary number opposite its unindented entry because there is no single disciplinary focus for "rates" in its general sense.

Rates (United Kingdom), on the other hand, is a genuine subject: the term means local taxes paid by British property owners. Because Rates (United Kingdom) has a distinct meaning, it is a candidate for an interdisciplinary number.

"Rates" in the sense of local taxes appears in public finance and law. Interdisciplinary works on taxes are classed in public finance; therefore, the interdisciplinary number for rates in the sense of taxes falls in public finance. In the example, 336.22 is listed as the interdisciplinary number for Rates (United Kingdom) opposite the unindented entry for the term. In the Relative Index, the discipline in which the interdisciplinary number falls may be repeated as a subentry if there are several subentries, or if the meaning of the discipline may not be clear. Under "Rates (United Kingdom)," the name of the discipline in which the interdisciplinary number is located, public finance, is repeated as a subentry.

The first "Rates" entry illustrates an important point about the Relative Index: the classifier cannot depend on the Relative Index for a list of all topics covered by the Classification. Section 6.4.2 describes some of the omissions. As a general rule, the schedules and tables are also not recapitulated in the Relative Index. Therefore, "Rates—postal communication" will not be found in the Relative Index. This entry under rates is covered by the broader term Rates—communications industry, of which postal communication is a part.

It is important to keep the foregoing in mind when using the Relative Index. Let us look at a slightly more complicated entry to see what it reveals:

Cotton
agricultural economics	338.173 51
botany	583.685
fiber crop	633.51
textiles	677.21
arts	746.042 1
see also Textiles	

In this entry, an interdisciplinary number is not given for cotton, because it is unlikely that one disciplinary focus can be determined for general works on cotton as a fabric *and* cotton as a plant species (if such works even exist). Notice, however, the subentry for the discipline "textiles" and sub-subentry for "arts." The number 677.21 is to be used for works on the production of cotton fibers and fabric; the number 746.0421 is to be used for works on the use of cotton fibers and fabrics in the arts. The subindention of "arts" under textiles tells us that works on the production of cotton fibers and the use of cotton fibers in the arts should be classed in the technology number, 677.21. The see-also reference is also subindented under the subentry textiles, and leads the classifier to other useful entries under the broader term, Textiles.

Here is another complicated entry:

Divorce	306.89
ethics	173
religion	291.563
Buddhism	294.356 3
Christianity	241.63
Hinduism	294.548 63
Islam	297.563
Judaism	296.363
Judaism	296.444 4
law	346.016 6
social theology	291.178 358 9
Christianity	261.835 89
social welfare	362.829 4
see also Families—social welfare	
sociology	306.89

The interdisciplinary number for divorce is 306.89; it is repeated at the end of this long entry under its disciplinary entry, sociology. The ethics of divorce is classed in 173; the religious ethics of divorce is classed in 291.563. The number for the ethics of divorce in specific religions is listed opposite the name of the religion at the sub-sub-subentry level. The example also shows how aspects have aspects that may in turn have aspects: Divorce—ethics—religion—Buddhism illustrates this. The entry for Judaism is repeated as a subentry directly under Divorce because Judaism has a special rite for divorce. Comprehensive works on divorce in Judaism would be classed in 296.4444, not in 296.363. While the Relative Index discloses this information to the astute user, it is always a good idea to verify the interpretation of the number in the schedules and tables. A final point to note in this example is the indented *see also*—it refers to social welfare, not to divorce. Had the reference been to divorce, it would have fallen directly under the "s" of sociology.

6.8   ENTRIES FROM THE SEVEN TABLES

Index entries from the seven auxiliary tables found in volume 1 have the following format:

(1)   The letter T followed by the number of the Table
(2)   An em dash
(3)   The table number for the concept

For example:

Belarus   T2—478

This entry tells us that the term is from Table 2 (Geographic Areas, Historical Periods, Persons) and its number is —478. The em dash before the number indicates that the number is never to be used alone; it must be appended to another number from the schedules or tables.

6.9   REFERENCES TO THE MANUAL

In Edition 21, the Relative Index includes index entries for Manual notes. They appear as *see* references under appropriate terms and following entries that carry class numbers and see-also references. The "see Manual at" appears in italics, followed by the number of the Manual note. For example:

Theory   T1—01
  see Manual at 1—01

Therapeutics   615.5
  veterinary medicine   636.089 55
  see Manual at 613 vs. 615.8;
  also at 615; *also at* 615.8

Voice
  human physiology   612.78
  music   783
    see Manual at 782
  preaching   251.03
  rhetoric of speech   808.5

The first example, "*see Manual at* 1—01," refers the classifier to the Manual note for —01 in Table 1. The second example refers the classifier to three notes in the Manual pertinent to the topics of therapeutics: 613 vs. 615.8, 615, and 615.8. The reference to the Manual in the third example is subindented under "music," and therefore is limited to a discussion of Voice—music at 782, not voice in general.

6.10   SUMMARY

The Relative Index in volume 4 is a key to the classified (systematic) arrangement of concepts in the schedules and tables. In the Relative Index, the disciplines are subordinated to subject. Therefore, it can be seen at a glance how the various aspects of a subject are scattered by discipline—something that is not possible within the schedules.

The Relative Index contains in a single alphabet and in word-by-word sequence most of the indexable terms found in the schedules and tables, plus some commonly used synonyms and terms with literary warrant for concepts found in the schedules and tables. Subjects in phrase form are usually entered in a direct, not inverted, form; e.g., Civil engineering, not Engineering, Civil. For multiword concepts one should look under all key terms, giving priority to a concrete object over an abstract process, technique, or action. Coordinate and subordinate relations are depicted through indentions and the use of an initial capital letter in the main entry.

Lastly, as a matter of advice, the classifier should not rely too heavily on the Relative Index. Ideally, class numbers should be determined by following the hierarchical structure in the schedules. In reality, most classifiers consult the Relative Index because it provides a shortcut or starting point. However, whenever a number is gleaned from the Relative Index, it must be verified in the schedules.

6.11 EXERCISES

Exercise 1:

Under which terms should you look in the Relative Index for the following subjects?

(1)   Ronald Reagan (the actor)

(2)   American Mathematical Society

(3)   Metropolitan Life Insurance Company of the United States

(4)   John Lennon (the singer-composer of the rock group The Beatles)

(5)   AZT (the anti-AIDS drug)

(6)   Chlorofluorocarbons

(7)   Santa Claus

(8)   Sneakers (tennis shoes)

(9)   Babe Ruth (the baseball player)

(10) Black widow spider

Exercise 2:

Under which terms should you look for the following topics?

(1)   Anthology of one-act plays

(2)   Libraries for children

(3)   Fabian socialism

(4)   Dynamics of particles

(5)   Air-to-air guided missiles

(6)   Modern history

(7)   Modeling pottery

(8)   History of privateering

CHAPTER 7

SYNTHESIS OF CLASS NUMBERS OR
PRACTICAL NUMBER BUILDING

Objective:

The objective of this chapter is to explain how to build or synthesize a class number by adding another number (whole or partial) from the schedules.

Outline:

7.0   INTRODUCTION

In its present form, the DDC falls between the two extremes of enumerative and faceted classification. It began as an enumerative classification scheme. Nonetheless, as A. C. Foskett has pointed out, even in the earlier editions of the DDC, "a very clear facet structure" is discernible in some places, notably Class 400 Philology. However, he goes on to say, "Dewey does not appear to have seen the real significance of this, and it was left to Ranganathan some fifty years later to make explicit and generalize the principle which is implicit and restricted in this example; nevertheless, in this as in many other points, Dewey showed the way ahead at a very early stage."[1] From Edition 18 on, with the introduction of more auxiliary tables and add notes, the DDC has displayed its faceted structure more explicitly.

Edition 21 is even more faceted than earlier editions, with more provisions for the synthesis of class numbers. Needless to say, the DDC has not remained as simple as it was in the beginning, but has become more complex in structure and more sophisticated in its methods. It is now better equipped for the close analysis of knowledge and the subsequent classification of quite narrow (or micro) subjects through synthesis, or number building.

---

[1]A. C. Foskett, *The Subject Approach to Information*, 4th ed. (London: Clive Bingley; Hamden, CT: Linnet Books, 1982), p. 316.

7.1 KINDS OF NUMBER BUILDING IN THE DDC

Most important subjects have ready-made class numbers that are enumerated (listed) in the DDC schedules. Nevertheless, many subjects are still not provided for, and these can be synthesized by the number-building process. Number building is the process of constructing a number by adding notation from the tables or other parts of the schedules to a base number. Broadly speaking, there are two methods of number building in Dewey:

(1) Building a number as appropriate, without specific instructions
(2) Building a number according to instructions found under a particular entry

7.1.1 BUILDING A NUMBER WITHOUT SPECIFIC INSTRUCTIONS

Unless indicated otherwise, any class number in the schedules may be extended by any number taken from Table 1 Standard Subdivisions. In other words, a number or its extension from Table 1 may be used where appropriate without a specific instruction to do so. The only restriction is that the classifier must follow the instructions in Table 1 with regard to the correct application of the numbers. The application of Table 1 is discussed in chapter 8.

7.1.2 NUMBER BUILDING, OR SYNTHESIS, UPON INSTRUCTION

The other kind of number building—what is normally considered to be genuine number building—is done only upon instruction found at an entry in the schedules or tables. When a number is to be extended by any other number, either from the schedules or from Tables 2–7, there are always specific instructions in the form of add notes that are given at the entry. These add instructions or notes are also called number-building notes. They always include one or more examples in order to ensure the note is properly understood. The number to be extended is called the *base number*, which can be as brief as one digit or as long as six or seven. It is the unvarying part of the number upon which many class numbers can be built. A base number may be a number from the schedules or from one of the tables. In the latter case, the built number must then be added to a base number from the schedules to form a complete class number. Chapters 8–12 discuss number building through the use of the auxiliary tables. The remaining part of this chapter explains the process of number building from the schedules only.

7.2 BUILDING CLASS NUMBERS FROM THE SCHEDULES

A complex number may be built by appending a full number or a segment of a class number taken from anywhere in the schedules to a base number, also taken from the schedules, as shown in the example of mathematics libraries in section 7.3 (p. 87).

It should be remembered that a complete class number must contain as the first part, or as the base number, a class number from the schedules. The add instructions may be either limited to a given entry or pertain to a span of class numbers.

7.2.1 CITATION ORDER

In building a number for a complex subject, it is important to determine the proper citation order, i.e., the order in which the parts of the number are strung together into a complete number. In most cases, the base number represents the main focus of the subject. For example, the class number for geology of North America would begin with a base number representing geology; so would the number for a journal of geology. In many other cases, the citation order is less obvious.

Suppose we need a number for a work on mathematics libraries. Two disciplines are involved, library science and mathematics. The first problem is to determine which discipline is to be considered the primary one, which means that it will be cited (given) first in the DDC number. The classifier has to decide which discipline contains the other, whether to consider the work a treatment of the mathematics of libraries or a treatment of libraries specializing in mathematics. In the example at hand, the primary discipline is library science 020. Scanning the 020 section from 021–029 (either in the third summary or directly in the schedules), we find:

026 Libraries, archives, information centers devoted to specific subjects and disciplines

This is the proper section, but it is broader than the subject of our work, so we have to find more specific numbers or notes that will enable us to particularize the base number down to the subject of the item in hand. At 026.001–.999 we find the instruction:

Add to base number 026 notation 001–999, e.g., medical libraries 026.61. . .

We have to determine the number for mathematics, which is easily identified as 510, and this we append to 026, giving us the proper number 026.51.

7.3 ADDING A FULL NUMBER

This is the simplest kind of synthesis. Here a full number from anywhere in the schedules is added to another full class number that has been designated the base number. Usually this kind of number-building note is in the form "Add to base number . . . notation 001–999, e.g., ..." In other words, add any number in the schedules to the base number. The number 026.51 Mathematics libraries results from adding a full class number 510 to another full class number 026.

More examples for 026 are:

(1)	Libraries specializing in the fine arts	026 + 700 = 026.7
(2)	Libraries specializing in folklore	026 + 398 = 026.398
(3)	Libraries specializing in genealogy	026 + 929.1 = 026.9291

Note two things:

(1) Addition means to append the required number to the end of the base number

(2) All final zero digits after the decimal point are discarded

In the last example, note also that only one decimal point has been retained in the proper number; it falls, as it always does, after the third digit if there are more than three digits in the number.

Let us try another subject that has a slightly longer base number, namely, reporting on diplomatic matters. Again, we have two fields: journalism and diplomacy. Does the item treat the diplomacy of journalism or the journalism of diplomacy? The latter is the case; therefore, the primary field of study is journalism. The Relative Index would be the best place to start in this case because it is not immediately apparent where journalism belongs. The index lists Journalism 070.4. Also, in the schedules at 070 we find a summary that tells us that journalism is 070.4. As we read through the entries in 070.4 we encounter features and special topics at 070.44. Perusing 070.44, we find that 070.449 deals with the journalism of specific subjects. The add note follows the standard pattern:

Add to base number 070.449 notation 001–999, e.g., health columns 070.449613

To locate the right number for diplomacy, we can scan the third summary or the Relative Index. The third summary indicates that International relations is found at 327; the Relative Index lists diplomacy at 327.2. So the proper number for our item is:

070.449 + 327.2 = 070.4493272

More examples for 070.449 are:

(1)	Medical journalism	070.449 + 610 = 070.44961
(2)	Legal journalism	070.449 + 340 = 070.44934
(3)	Financial journalism	070.449 + 332 = 070.449332
(4)	Sports journalism	070.449 + 796 = 070.449796

Let us try one final set of items, one dealing with the Bible. The first item deals with astronomy in the Bible. Is the subject the effect of the Bible on astronomy or astronomy as found in the Bible? The latter is the case. Therefore, the number for the Bible serves as the base number. The second summary reveals that the Bible has an entire division to itself; unfortunately for the classifier none of its sections seems to fit our topic. That is indeed the case. Here is an instance where the subject deals with the division itself, i.e., the entire Bible, rather than any of the sections of the division. What must be done here is to look at 220 itself, not 221–229. At the summary for 220.1–220.9 we find 220.8 Nonreligious subjects treated in the Bible. We move to that entry and find among its subdivisions the following:

220.800 1–.899 9   Specific nonreligious subjects
Add to base number 220.8 notation 001–999, e.g., natural sciences in the Bible 220.85 . . .

Astronomy, we learn from the second summary or the Relative Index, is 520. The proper number, therefore, is 220.8 + 520 = 220.852. More examples of the treatment of nonreligious topics in the Bible are:

(1) Women in the Bible   220.8 + 305.4 = 220.83054
(Use the Relative Index to find the number for women.)

(2) UFOs in the Bible   220.8 + 001.942 = 220.8001942
(Use the Relative Index to find the number for UFOs.)

(3) Mother's love in the Bible   220.8 + 306.8743 = 220.83068743
(Another one for the Relative Index; or we can go directly to marriage and the family at 306.8. While "Mother's love" is not in the index, "Mothers—family relationships" is. The third summary's Culture and Institutions for 306 is not much help.)

7.4   ADDING A PART OF A NUMBER

Sometimes we are asked to add only a segment of another number to the designated base number. This segment is considered to be the secondary facet in Dewey, or a secondary aspect of the subject.

Suppose we have a work about wages in textile industries. In this instance our rule of thumb on separating topic and context is not much help. That is, if we ask the question—is this a work about wages in textile industries or a work about textile industries in the context of wages?—we can say either works perfectly well. It is hard to tell which is subsumed under which. So, do we use the number for textile industries (338.47677) or the one for wages (331.21)? Which element of the subject will precede the other?

The schedules do provide assistance in this particular situation. At 330 in the schedules, there is a table of preference. The table directs us to which of two elements of the subject of a work should be preferred over the other when both fall within the same discipline. The table of preference at 330 shows that 331

Labor economics (a factor of production) precedes 338 Production. This means that wages will precede industry. Next we check wages in the Relative Index, which leads us to 331.21 Compensation. Wage is a form of compensation. Reading through the notes in the entry, we encounter a see reference: ". . .for compensation by industry and occupation, see 331.28." We could also get to 331.28 by perusing the summary at 331.2 Conditions of employment, which lists 331.28 Compensation by industry and occupation.

Whichever route (Relative Index vs. summary) we employed to get to 331.28, we must still read the schedules further once we arrive there. At 331.282–.289 Compensation in extractive, manufacturing, construction industries and occupations, we read the add note:

Add to base number 331.28 the numbers following 6 in 620–690, e. g., compensation in the mining industry 331.2822, average factory compensation 331.287
Subdivisions are added for industries, occupations, or both

The note following the add note assures us that we are permitted to build the number for industry; this helpful type of note appears in many places in Edition 21 under multiterm headings. Returning to our number building, we now must find the number for textile manufacturing. The class number for the manufacturing of textiles is 677; this can be found through either the third summary or the Relative Index. In 677 the number following 6 is 77. Thus, as instructed, we add 77 to 331.28, which produces 331.2877, the number for wages in textile industries. Wages in agriculture would be 331.28 + 630 = 331.283.

7.5   ADDITION BY WAY OF A FACET INDICATOR

There are times when a whole number or a segment of a number cannot be attached directly to a base number. When this situation arises, a facet indicator is needed to provide access to the base number. The reason is that if a whole or a partial number were attached directly to a base number, there would be a conflict—the same number would mean two different things. For example:

778.5   Cinematography, video production, related activities
778.52   General topics of cinematography and video production
                  Add to base number 778.52 the numbers following 778.5
                  in 778.53–778.58, e.g., lighting for cinematography and
                  video production

The numbers and captions for some of the numbers in 778.53–778.58 include:

778.53   Cinematography (Motion picture photography)
778.532   Darkroom and laboratory practice

778.534	Specific types and elements of cinematography
778.535	Editing films
778.538	Cinematography of specific subjects
778.55	Motion picture projection
778.56	Special kinds of cinematography
778.58	Preservation and storage of motion picture films

If we were to add the numbers following 778.5 in 778.53–778.58 directly to 778.5 (as we have been doing in number building up to this point), we would come up with 778.535 for editing in cinematography and video production. But this number already means editing films in cinematography alone. Because some numbers that arise from the normal process of number building have already been preempted, a facet indicator is needed before adding on the segment to produce a unique number. In the example above, the 2 following 778.5 is the facet indicator.[2] In many cases, the facet indicator is built into the base number: the classifier does not have to begin with a base number, add zero, and then add something else. In other cases, the classifier must add a facet indicator before proceeding.

Here are two more examples of base numbers with built-in facet indicators:

(1) Housing horses 636.1$\underline{0}$ + 831 = 636.10831

(2) Effect of science and technology 701.$\underline{0}$ + 5 = 701.05
on fine and decorative arts

7.6 COLLECTIVE ADD NOTES

In the print schedules, when all or most of a continuous span of numbers may be expanded by the addition of facets from another continuous span of numbers, the add instruction is given only one time. Since the numbers and the instructions to add to them are found on the same page, all such numbers are asterisked (*), or marked by some other typographical device, and the footnote that corresponds to the asterisk is found at the bottom of the page. For example, on p. 985 of volume 2 we see that the terms in the captions of all of the subdivisions of 546.39 have been marked with an asterisk. The corresponding footnote tells us to add as instructed under 546. This means that once we have chosen the appropriate element, we should turn to 546 where we find an add table, or internal table. An excerpt from the table follows:

---

[2]In the DDC, the facet indicator often indicates that what follows represents a different facet, but it does not always indicate the nature of the facet. For a further discussion of facet indicators in the DDC, see chapter 8.

Add to each subdivision identified by * as follows:

>   1-3   The element, compounds, mixtures
>
>   Class theoretical, physical, analytical chemistry of the element, compounds, mixtures, in 4–6; class comprehensive works in base number for the element in 546.3–546.7

     1   The element

     2   Compounds

           Names of compounds usually end in -ide or one of the suffixes listed in 22 and 24 below

   22   Acids and bases

           Names of acids usually end in -ic or -ous

   24   Salts

           Names of salts frequently end in -ate or -ite

   25   Complex compounds

Suppose we have an item on magnesium salts. Through the index we can find magnesium (546.392). The footnote leads us to the table at 546 where we are told to add the number 24 for salts to the base number (whatever number is to the left of the asterisk). The proper number is:

546.392 + 24 = 546.39224

This brings up an interesting question: if 546.392 + 1 = 546.3921 is the number for the element magnesium studied within the context of inorganic chemistry, what is 546.392 to be used for? Isn't it the number for the element magnesium? The answer is that the number 546.3921 is assigned to a work that deals only with magnesium as an element, whereas the number 546.392 is used for a work on magnesium with respect to more than one aspect enumerated in the table, such as compounds, alloys, etc.

Perhaps the following caveat is not necessary, but it remains a useful admonition: A topic that is not asterisked cannot benefit from the extensions provided by a footnote. The salts of americium remain in 546.411 without further identification because there is no provision that allows adding further notation to the base number.

7.7   SUMMARY

Many DDC class numbers found in the schedules may be extended (subdivided) by another number (or part of it) that has been drawn from the schedules or auxiliary tables. This process of extending class numbers is called number building; in general, it can be done only when there are number-building instructions in the schedules or tables. (An exception is the application of notation from Table 1 Standard Subdivisions, a process that will be dealt with in the next chapter.) Number-building instructions may be found at an entry, in a footnote, or under another number or span of numbers to which the footnote has sent the classifier.

Upon instruction, numbers in the schedules may be added to another number to form complex numbers. When two fields of study or two topics are discussed in a work, finding the add instructions efficiently depends upon the classifier's ability to determine the primary field of study. A general rule is that the primary field of study is the one considered to contain or provide a context for the other. Occasionally, a table of preference will advise the classifier as to which of two fields or subjects is to take precedence over the other. When the context/topic relationship is not obvious, and no preference table is available, the classifier will simply have to look at the numbers for both topics and choose the one that allows extension, i.e., the number with an add note.

In all the activity that the classifier engages in with respect to using the DDC none is so fraught with the possibility of error as the process of number building. When building numbers, we must ascertain that the base number is correct, that a vital digit has not been added or dropped, and that the number being added to the base number is neither more nor less than it should be. After the number is built, it must be checked against the schedules to ensure that the synthesized number does not conflict with any instructions or numbers in the schedules.

Let us put the importance of building the right number in the context of providing access to what has been written. There is a long train of effort behind every work that a classifier encounters. If the classifier gives it an inappropriate number, the work will be stored where a user is unlikely to find it. Its reason for being written is thereby much diminished.

7.8   EXERCISES

Exercise 1:

Build class numbers for the following subjects using whole schedule numbers:

(1)   Library classification for plants and animals

(2)   Special libraries devoted to Judaism

(3)   Production efficiency in the manufacturing of passenger automobiles

(4)   Bibliography of the Dewey Decimal Classification

(5)   Selection and acquisition of art books in libraries

(6)   Bibliography of cool jazz

(7)   Trade in pharmaceutical drugs

(8)   Strikes by professors

(9)   The prices of shoes

Exercise 2:

Build class numbers by adding parts of schedule numbers:

(1) Domestic trade in agricultural products
(2) Trade in diamonds
(3) Labor market for the leather industry
(4) Philosophy based upon Sikhism
(5) Rearing adopted children
(6) The psychology of hyperactive children
(7) A psychological study of slow-learning children
(8) A comprehensive work on the Little Sisters of the Poor (Roman Catholic)
(9) International law regarding credit cards
(10) A library use study of prison libraries

Exercise 3:

Build numbers requiring facet indicators:

(1) Evolution of invertebrates
(2) Teaching mathematics to students with mental retardation
(3) Connective tissues in primates
(4) Contracts for public works projects

Exercise 4:

Build numbers according to collective add instructions:

(1) Physical chemistry of gold
(2) Architectural preservation of warehouses
(3) Routine maintenance and repair of woven rugs
(4) Prevention of malaria by medical personnel
(5) Mass of the planet Venus
(6) Economic utilization of forest lands
(7) Development of arid land
(8) How to manage a supermarket
(9) Protective measures in the use of agricultural chemicals: a social response to a poisonous problem
(10) Abuse of rivers and streams: an economic study

CHAPTER 8
TABLE 1: STANDARD SUBDIVISIONS

Objectives:

The objectives of this chapter are to explain: the concept and need for standard subdivisions in the DDC; the practical use of Table 1; exceptional cases requiring an additional number of zeros in adding standard subdivisions; how to choose between two standard subdivisions for the same work; and when standard subdivisions are not used.

Outline:

8.0   INTRODUCTION

Libraries deal with knowledge found in documents. Library classification deals with the organization of knowledge found in documents. In addition to the primary element of the subject, library classification also considers the characteristics of documents that indicate how the subject is treated. Documents vary by their form of presentation (such as dictionary, data tables, or journal). Their contents also vary according to the particular viewpoint from which they are treated (such as theory, history, or research), and by the medium in which they are published (such as book, videotape, microfilm, or compact disc). Library classification may reflect all these elements. It is defined by the equation:

Library classification = Subject (the primary element) + Form of presentation + Author's viewpoint + Physical medium or form.

In practice, however, these aspects or facets are not always expressed in the class number; some facets are emphasized over others.

8.1 NOMENCLATURE

Standard subdivisions represent nonprimary or nontopical characteristics of documents. The glossary defines standard subdivisions as follows:

> Subdivisions found in Table 1 that represent frequently recurring physical forms (dictionaries, periodicals) or approaches (history, research) applicable to any subject or discipline. They may be used with any number in the schedules and tables for topics that approximate the whole of the number unless there are instructions to the contrary (see glossary, p. 225).

Standard subdivisions were first recognized and listed in the second edition of the DDC (1885). From that edition on they have been a constant feature of the system, though their variety and importance have increased. They were first known as "form divisions," but eventually that phrase became inappropriate. Their present name began in 1965 with Edition 17.

The following two-level summary gives some sense of the scope and nature of Table 1 Standard Subdivisions as found in Edition 21:

Standard Subdivisions

—01	Philosophy and theory
—011	Systems
—012	Classification
—013	Value
—014	Language and communication
—015	Scientific principles
—019	Psychological principles
—02	Miscellany
—021	Tabulated and related materials
—022	Illustrations, models, miniatures
—023	The subject as a profession, occupation, hobby
—024	The subject for persons in specific occupations
—025	Directories of persons and organizations
—027	Patents and identification marks
—028	Auxiliary techniques and procedures; apparatus, equipment, materials
—029	Commercial miscellany
—03	Dictionaries, encyclopedias, concordances
—04	Special topics

—05   Serial publications
—06   Organizations and management
—068   Management
—07   Education, research, related topics
—071   Education
—072   Research; statistical methods
—074   Museums, collections, exhibits
—075   Museum activities and services   Collecting
—076   Review and exercise
—077   Programmed texts
—078   Use of apparatus and equipment in study and teaching
—079   Competitions, festivals, awards, financial support
—08   History and description with respect to kinds of persons
—081   Men
—082   Women
—083   Young people
—084   Persons in specific stages of adulthood
—085   Relatives   Parents
—086   Persons by miscellaneous social characteristics
—087   Persons with disabilities and illnesses, gifted persons
—088   Occupational and religious groups
—089   Racial, ethnic, national groups
—09   Historical, geographic, persons treatment
—0901-0905 Historical periods
—091   Treatment by areas, regions, places in general
—092   Persons
—093-099 Treatment by specific continents, countries, localities; extraterrestrial worlds

8.2   CHARACTERISTICS OF STANDARD SUBDIVISIONS

The general characteristics of standard subdivisions are summarized below:

(1)   Standard subdivisions usually represent (a) recurring nonprimary characteristics of a subject and (b) nontopical characteristics that pertain to the document itself rather than to its primary subject. For instance, the primary element of a history of Japan is Japan, with history a nonprimary element—making the full subject the history of Japan. On the other hand, although a dictionary of Japanese history has as its subject Japanese history, the concept of dictionary-ness does not affect the subject of the item; it pertains to the form the author uses to present the material, not to the information found within the document. Such distinctions may seem eso-

teric, but they are important in subject analysis and in assigning the proper DDC number when standard subdivisions are appropriate.

(2) Standard subdivisions are applicable to any class number (however broad or minute) for any topic that approximates the whole of the number, unless they are disallowed or their use introduces redundancy. Here is an instance that covers both situations. At 540[.28] we see that auxiliary techniques and procedures, apparatus, equipment, materials has been disallowed. The classifier is instructed to proceed to 542 Techniques, procedures, apparatus, equipment, materials. Therefore, for a work on chemical apparatus, the number is 542; adding –028 to 542 would be redundant because the number 542 already means chemical apparatus.

(3) With a few exceptions to be discussed later, standard subdivisions may be attached to any enumerated (listed) or built number without any formal add instructions.

(4) The dash before these numbers in Table 1, e.g., –01, –09, means that standard subdivisions (indeed, notation from any auxiliary table) never stand alone. They convey meaning only when attached to a class number from the schedules.

(5) A standard subdivision consists of at least two digits, of which the initial digit is a zero. In fact, a zero is its constant feature and was the first use of a facet indicator[1] in library classification. In the DDC's standard subdivisions, this featured zero serves as the facet indicator that marks the transition from the primary subject (or primary element of the subject) number to a secondary subject (or a secondary element of the subject) number. For instance, the number 004.09 for a work on the history of computers shows the following elements:

    004   Base number for Computers
    0   Facet indicator
    9   History (the facet specifier)

In this case, the digit 0 after the main number 004 serves as a facet indicator, i.e., a digit that signals a change of facet. The digit 9, the second digit in the standard subdivision, indicates the nature of the facet, i.e., in this case, history.

(6) Standard subdivision notation is a decimal fraction in nature, and, like all notation in Dewey, can be extended decimally.

---

[1]A facet indicator is a symbol in a class number indicating that what follows represents a different characteristic of division. In the DDC, a facet indicator may or may not signify the nature of the facet.

8.3   HOW TO USE STANDARD SUBDIVISIONS

In classifying a document, the classifier's first step is to separate the subject proper from the elements represented by standard subdivisions. Identifying these may not prove easy at first because some standard subdivisions look like subject elements. Moreover, some topics, such as encyclopedias, dictionaries, bibliography, and classification occur both in the schedules and in Table 1. Any initial confusion on this matter soon passes with experience.

The second step is to assign the class number to the subject proper by the usual processes: systematically by way of the summaries and schedules, or alphabetically through the Relative Index.

The third step is to find the notation for the appropriate standard subdivision from Table 1. Because terms in the tables have been included in the Relative Index, notation for a standard subdivision can be located using that route.

The final step is to append the number for the standard subdivision to the schedule number for the subject proper as in any ordinary add operation. For example, suppose we have an encyclopedia of the Hindu religion. Here the subject proper is obviously Hindu religion; its class number is 294.5. An encyclopedia is represented by standard subdivision —03 in Table 1:

$$294.5 + 03 = 294.503$$

Here are a few more examples:

(1) Dictionary of the Koran
$$297.122 + 03 = 297.12203$$

(2) Symbols and abbreviations used in arithmetic
$$513 + 0148 = 513.0148$$

(3) The profession of electrical engineering
$$621.3 + 023 = 621.3023$$

(4) Humor in indexing
$$025.48 + 0207 = 025.480207$$

(5) Research methods in biophysics
$$571.4 + 072 = 571.4072$$

8.4   ADDING A STANDARD SUBDIVISION TO A MAIN CLASS OR A DIVISION

Indicating a standard subdivision for a main class or a division is not as simple as it is for other class numbers in the system because of the terminal zeros that act as space fillers in those numbers. Unless there are contrary instructions, such terminal zeros must be dropped from the class number before appending the standard subdivision, For example, in an encyclopedia of science, science is the core subject; its class number is 500. An encyclopedia is indicated as a standard subdivision by means of the notation —03. Combining the two in the normal fashion would produce the incorrect number: 500 + 03 = 500.03. The correct procedure is indicated by the equation:

$$500 - 00 + 03 = 503$$

Here are a few more examples:

(1) An encyclopedia of philosophy
$$100 - 00 + 03 = 103$$

(2) A journal of philosophy
$$100 - 00 + 05 = 105$$

(3) Computer-assisted instruction in science
$$500 - 00 + 0785 = 507.85$$

However, this formula does not work for the following four main classes:

(1)   000 because there is no significant number to work with, and 003–006 have been preempted by systems and computer science

(2)   200 because 201–209 had been used in editions prior to DDC 21 for standard subdivisions of Christianity

(3)   300 because 301–307 have been preempted by sociology

(4)   700 (The arts) because 701–709 are limited to the standard subdivisions of fine and decorative arts, and iconography

Standard subdivisions for the 200s, 300s, and 700s (The arts) are found at locations that are one digit longer, i.e, at 200.1-200.9, at 300.1-300.9, and at 700.1–700.9.

In the case of division numbers only one zero is available to be dropped from the three-digit number. For example, for an encyclopedia of mathematics:

$$510 - 0 + 03 = 510.3$$

Further examples:

(1) Abbreviations and symbols in mathematics
$$510 - 0 + 0148 = 510.148$$

(2) Formulas in astronomy
$$520 - 0 + 0212 = 520.212$$

(3) History of mathematics
$$510 - 0 + 09 = 510.9$$

(4) History of mathematics in the 20th century
$$510 - 0 + 0904 = 510.904$$

(5) International organizations in chemistry
$$540 - 0 + 0601 = 540.601$$

As was mentioned earlier, there are times when the standard subdivision numbers for main classes require more than one zero. In fact, multiple zeros are required in 30% of the main classes and in about the same percentage of the divisions. The list that follows shows the divisions with irregular standard subdivisions, their headings, and the number of zeros required if more than two. As this list is too long to memorize, the classifier must always consult the schedules when using standard subdivisions. In some cases where there are dual or multiterm headings, only the standard subdivisions for the division as a whole require more zeros. For example, the standard subdivisions for the whole of 760 Graphics arts   Printmaking and prints are in 760.01–760.09, but those for Printmaking and prints alone are in 760.1–760.9.

070 Media, journalism, publishing
180 Ancient, medieval, Oriental philosophy
220 Bible
230 Christianity   Christian theology
    (230.002–230.007 Christianity; 230.01–230.09 Christian theology)
270 Christian church history
280 Denominations and sects of the Christian church
320 Political science
330 Economics
340 Law
380 Commerce, communications, transportation
390 Customs, etiquette, folklore
    (390.001–390.009 Customs, etiquette, folklore; 390.01–390.09 Customs)
430 Germanic (Teutonic) languages
440 Romance languages
460 Spanish and Portuguese languages
470 Italic languages
480 Classical (Greek and Latin) languages
530 Physics
620 Engineering (620.001–620.009)
650 Management
660 Chemical engineering
690 Buildings
730 Plastic arts
760 Graphic arts   Printmaking and prints
790 Recreational and performing arts
830 Literatures of Germanic languages
840 Literatures of Romance languages
860 Literatures of Spain and Portugal
870 Literatures of Italic languages
880 Classical (Greek and Latin) literatures

920   Biography, genealogy, insignia (920.001–920.009)
930   History of ancient world
940   General history of Europe   Western Europe
950   General history of Asia   Orient   Far East
960   General history of Africa
970   General history of North America (970.001–970.009)
980   General history of South America (980.001–980.009)

There are times when more than one zero is required for sections and for numbers longer than three digits. In such cases one simply follows instructions. Here are a few examples of places where, contrary to what one would expect, multiple zeros are required in standard subdivision notation:

(1)   Boots and shoes (685.31001–685.31009)

(2)   History of California (979.4001–979.4009)

(3)   Goats (636.39001–636.39009)

8.5   EXTENDING A STANDARD SUBDIVISION BY AN ADD INSTRUCTION

A few standard subdivisions can be extended according to add instructions. The method for implementing the add instructions in Table 1 is the same as for the schedules. Say that we have a book on the scientific principles of civil engineering. The primary or core element of the subject is civil engineering (624). The secondary element is scientific principles. These are found in Table 1 at –015. Thus:

624 + 015 = 624.015

For the *mathematical* principles of civil engineering, however, we apply the add note under –015 in Table 1:

Add to base number –015 the numbers following 5 in 510–590, e.g., mathematical techniques –0151

Therefore, we arrive at the complete number: 624.0151
       624   Base number for Civil engineering
       015   Scientific principles (Table 1)
       1   Number following 5 in 510 Mathematics, with the final zero being dropped

Further examples:

(1)   Dynamics applied to track and field jumping: 796.4320153111
       796.432   Base number for Jumping
       015   Scientific principles (Table 1)
       3111   Number following 5 in 531.11 Dynamics

(2) Statistical principles of sociology: 301.015195
    301   Base number for Sociology
    015   Scientific principles (Table 1)
    195   Number following 5 in 519.5 Statistical mathematics

(3) Optical principles of photography: 770.1535
    770   Base number for Photography
    015   Scientific principles (Table 1)
    35   Number following 5 in 535 Optics

8.6 VARIATIONS IN THE MEANING OF STANDARD SUBDIVISIONS

Sometimes standard subdivisions are not "standard"; their meanings have been replaced by a subdivision more important in, or unique to, the particular class where the alteration occurs. The new meaning may differ slightly or drastically. For example, standard subdivision —013 Value is still recognizable at 331.013 Freedom, dignity, value of labor. However, —077 means Programmed texts in Table 1, but Coaching under 796. Further examples:

    610.695 Specific kinds of medical personnel
             (Table 1: —06 Organizations and management; —0695 not defined)

    701.9   Methodology of art
             (Table 1: —019 Psychological principles)

Because these altered "standard subdivisions" are unique to their classes, they do not appear in Table 1, but are enumerated in the schedules. The classifier must be careful, therefore, as there are many such altered standard subdivisions in the DDC.

There is one standard subdivision that does not come close to meeting the definition of a standard subdivision; it just happens to share the same span of numbers as legitimate standard subdivisions. Special topics —04 has been provided for those situations where all of the notation available to a class has been used up. When this happens, —04 has been used as a device to provide a place for subdivisions that are needed in the class. For example, suppose that the class number for baseball was subdivided into the present nine team positions. That would mean that xxx.1–xxx.9 would be used one per position, and all the notation would be used up. Suppose next that the baseball league decides to add an extra position—the short left fielder. What notation can be assigned to that position? One possibility would be to squeeze it into the number for an existing position; another, more preferable, possibility would be to use —04. That is the general idea for the existence of —04. It is a fallback to use when a new facet or class of subdivisions arises that must be provided for but for which there is no notation available.

8.7   DISPLACED STANDARD SUBDIVISIONS

Throughout the DDC, there are special developments for standard subdivision concepts that do not use the regular notation found in Table 1. Since Edition 20, however, there has been a major effort to bring many such displaced concepts back to their proper home in the standard subdivision span. This process is called "regularization." Regularization makes the Classification easier to apply, and provides consistent representation of standard subdivision concepts throughout the scheme. The latter is important in subject retrieval.

Some examples of regularization in Edition 21 include:

(1)   370.7 Education, research, related topics now matches the development of –07 in Table 1

(2)   Geographic distribution of temperature at the earth's surface relocated from 551.5252 to 551.52509

(3)   Routine maintenance and repair of drawings relocated from 741.219 to 741.0288; routine safety measures from 741.219 to 741.0289

Because "regularization" must be gradually implemented, there still are many displaced standard subdivisions in the DDC. The classifier must be careful in applying standard subdivision notation. For example:

(1)   Historical, geographic, persons treatment of social welfare problems and services 362.9 should be 362.09;

(2)   One of the most striking displacements can be seen in 666.31–666.39 where the standard subdivisions for pottery-making are found built upon regular subdivision notation.

In each case, there is a do-not-use note under the regular standard subdivision number that leads the user to the displaced one. For example:

> 362.[09]   Historical, geographic, persons treatment
> Do not use; class in 362.9

8.8   CO-OCCURRENCE OF TWO OR MORE STANDARD SUBDIVISION CONCEPTS IN A DOCUMENT

Occasionally a document includes two or more standard subdivision concepts. For example, a journal of political philosophy involves two standard subdivisions: journal (form of presentation) and philosophy (viewpoint). With few exceptions, only one standard subdivision is used in a class number.[2] It is selected on a preferential basis, and the other is ignored. To choose the appropriate standard subdivision, the classifier should consult the table of preference at

---

[2]Melvil Dewey, *Dewey Decimal Classification and Relative Index*, Ed. 21, edited by Joan S. Mitchell, Julianne Beall, Winton E. Matthews, Jr., and Gregory R. New (Albany, NY: OCLC Forest Press, 1996), v. 4, p. 908.

the beginning of Table 1. A subdivision that falls earlier in the table of preference is to be preferred over one that falls later. For instance, —072 Research;
statistical methods is preferred over —01 Philosophy, which itself is preferred
over —03 Dictionaries. Looking at the table we observe that preference is generally based on the following order:

(1) Method
(2) Viewpoint
(3) Form of presentation
(4) Physical medium or form

When selecting one of several standard subdivisions, the classifier should use
the table of preference. For a journal on the teaching of political science, the
primary subject element is political science and the secondary element is teaching. The fact that the work is a journal has nothing to do with the subject, but
everything to do with the document. As —07 Education is preferred over —05
Serial publications, the correct number is 320.07 (political science is one of the
divisions that requires two zeros to signal a standard subdivision). However,
the table of preference should not be used slavishly because it is too easy to
arrive at an incorrect class number. Suppose the work being classified is about
using data processing in Chinese banking. The primary subject is Chinese banking; therefore, the work should be classed with Chinese banking 332.10951,
not data processing in banking 332.10285, the number that would be chosen
according to the table of preference. In summary, if one of the standard subdivisions constitutes an essential or integral part of the primary subject, this subdivision should be chosen, even though the other subdivision may come before it
in the table of preference.

8.9   WHEN STANDARD SUBDIVISIONS ARE NOT USED

Earlier we remarked that standard subdivisions are applicable to almost all of
the class numbers in the schedules and one does not need any add instructions to
use them. However, there are two categories of numbers that should not have
standard subdivisions attached to them.

8.9.1   WHEN A STANDARD SUBDIVISION IS ALREADY IMPLIED IN THE CLASS NUMBER

In some cases a standard subdivision concept is already a part of the class number: —03 is not added to 423 Dictionaries of standard English because 423 already
means dictionaries. Nor is —03 added to 031 for Encyclopedia Americana; the
number already means an American encyclopedia. Similarly, —09 is not added in
class 900 to the number for the history of a place to show the aspect of history
because the nine is already a part of the main number: 973 is a history of the

United States, 973.09 is not. Nor is there any point to adding —072 (Research; statistical methods) to 001.42 Research methods.

8.9.2   WHEN THERE IS NO SPECIFIC CLASS NUMBER FOR THE SUBJECT

Standard subdivisions cannot be used for a subject not provided with a specific class number of its own unless the subject approximates the whole of the contents of the number, or unless there are directions for such addition in the schedules. Classes of items that are considered to approximate the whole are as follows:

(1)   Topics in dual headings

(2)   Topics that are part of unitary terms, e.g., colleges and universities, economic development and growth

(3)   Topics in multiterm headings that are so designated with a standard-subdivisions-are-added note

(4)   Topics in class-here notes

(5)   Topics that represent more than half the content of a heading

(6)   Topics that cover at least three subdivisions of the number (if the number has only three subdivisions, then topics that cover two)

(7)   Topics coextensive with topics that approximate the whole

Topics found in including notes cannot have standard subdivisions added for them; they are considered to be in "standing room" in the number. For instance, for a work on the philosophy and theory of citation indexing, it is against the rules to add —01 Philosophy and theory to 025.48 (the number for Subject indexing). This is because citation indexing does not have its own number (it is found in an including note), nor does it approximate the whole of 025.48 Subject indexing—it is only a small part of it. Adding —01 to the number would be misleading to the user who would expect 025.4801 to be a work on subject cataloging theory as a whole. On the other hand, standard subdivisions can be added to Marxism, which is in a class-here note at 335.4 Marxian systems. At 301 Sociology and anthropology, the first note instructs: "Standard subdivisions are added for either or both topics in heading." Compare this note to the one at 646.3 Clothing and accessories: "Standard subdivisions are added for clothing and accessories together, for clothing alone." This means that a dictionary of accessories would be classed in 646.3, but a dictionary of clothing (or clothing and accessories together) would be classed in 646.303.

8.10 SUMMARY

For the most part, standard subdivisions represent nontopical characteristics of documents. However, at times a standard subdivision may represent a secondary subject. A history of Japanese baseball, for example, has at its core the subject of baseball, but in fact the subject of such a book is Japanese baseball. The next chapter explains how standard subdivisions can be used to indicate baseball in Japan. By and large, however, standard subdivisions represent approaches to a topic that are applicable to all fields of study, such as history, theory, the subject in a place, directories, biography, and so on.

The list of standard subdivisions is found in Table 1 in volume 1 of the DDC. Standard subdivisions normally consist of at least two digits, of which the first is a zero (the facet indicator) and the next (not a zero) usually indicates the nature of the following facet. Like any number in the DDC, notation for standard subdivisions is decimal. Frequently, more than one zero is needed to stipulate a standard subdivision. The proper number of zeros is one, or as many as the instructions indicate.

Unless instructed otherwise, only one standard subdivision is normally used for a document. If two standard subdivisions are applicable to the same work, one is chosen according to the table of preference at the beginning of Table 1 unless an unhelpful collocation results.

A standard subdivision is not added to a class number if the viewpoint or form of presentation is an essential part of the main subject and already represented in the class number. Furthermore, standard subdivisions are not added for topics that do not approximate the whole of the number. Such topics may be part of the heading or in an including note. If the topic represents more than half of the contents of the number, it is said to approximate the whole and may have standard subdivisions added for it.

8.11 EXERCISES

Exercise 1:

Applying standard subdivisions, assign class numbers to the following works:

(1) An encyclopedia of physical and theoretical chemistry

(2) A dictionary of physical chemistry

(3) Teaching methods in dairy technology

(4) Research methods in milk processing technology

(5) A journal of histology

Exercise 2:

Build class numbers for the following topics involving main class or division numbers:

(1)   Science organizations
(2)   Abbreviations and symbols used in science
(3)   History of science
(4)   History of science in the 16th century
(5)   Schools and courses in astronomy
(6)   Research methods in philosophy
(7)   Dictionary of mathematics
(8)   Medical associations
(9)   Encyclopedia of architecture

Exercise 3:

Build class numbers for the following topics requiring multiple zeros:

(1)   Illustrations of human diseases
(2)   A history of naval forces
(3)   An audiovisual presentation on the history of Central Europe
(4)   Tables and formulas in economics
(5)   International organizations on human diseases
(6)   A dictionary of law
(7)   A journal of Christian theology

Exercise 4:

Synthesize numbers for the following subjects:

(1)   Mathematics for biophysics
(2)   The odds of winning in games of chance
(3)   Principles of turbulence in human blood flow
(4)   A journal of military science

Exercise 5:

Assign class numbers to the following subjects, using displaced standard subdivisions:

(1)   Pottery-making in the Middle Ages

(2)   A history of wages

(3)   Apparatus for making plastics

(4)   History of painting (art)

(5)   History of goldsmithing

(6)   Architecture of the modern era

Exercise 6:

Synthesize class numbers for the following topics that involve two standard subdivisions:

(1)   A journal of higher education in public administration

(2)   Encyclopedia of library associations

(3)   A directory of law schools

(4)   A journal of literary history

(5)   A biographical dictionary of musicians

Exercise 7:

Provide class numbers for the following subjects that involve standard subdivision concepts but do not use standard subdivision notation:

(1)   Management of technology

(2)   History of Central Europe

(3)   *Encyclopedia Americana*

(4)   A general periodical in the English language

(5)   Conference on inventorying a library

CHAPTER 9
TABLE 2: GEOGRAPHIC AREAS, HISTORICAL PERIODS, PERSONS

Objectives:

The objectives of this chapter are to explain: the basic structure and coverage of Table 2; how to extend with or without instructions a class number from the schedules by way of an area number taken from Table 2; how to identify the cases where class numbers already imply geographic characteristics; how to include, where possible, two areas in a class number; how to use Tables 1 and 2 simultaneously.

Outline:

9.0   INTRODUCTION

Many subjects, especially in the social sciences and humanities, are best studied in the context of a geographic area. Their intellectual structure in particular differs markedly from place to place. For instance, wages in Canada, the banking system of Hong Kong, libraries in Italy, or the history of science in Sumer are all virtually unique to themselves; they bear the stamp of the place where practiced, and there can be little doubt that geographic location plays a major role in the treatment of the core subjects. Moreover, there are instances in which the area is the subject itself: the history of China is entirely different from the history of Egypt. Equally unlike are the geographies of Saudi Arabia and Alaska.

In the DDC there are times when the area is so important to a class that the geographic facet is built into the division or section of a class. For example:

181	Oriental philosophy
.2	Egypt
.3	Palestine Israel
.4	India
191	[Modern western philosophy of] United States and Canada

Accordingly, there is no further provision for the subdivision of these numbers by way of Table 2 Geographic Areas, Historical Periods, Persons (also called the area table). In all such cases it is difficult to mark the transition of the number from the subject proper to the area table, because there is no facet indicator. However, the arrangement is still helpful.

In other cases, the geographic aspect is expressed by way of adding notation from the area table. This table lists the names and area numbers for all countries, for the provinces and states of many countries, and for the counties and major cities of some countries. Addition of an area number to a class number will help in the complete (close) classification of a document; and it will ultimately help to arrange subjects logically by area and to bring together all studies of a subject within the same area.

9.1   AREA TABLE DEFINITION AND CHARACTERISTICS

The area table may be defined as a table of notation designating historical periods, persons, and geographic areas. It is attached to other notation from the schedules or tables through the use of add notes or through the use of the standard subdivision (ss) —09 from Table 1. Table 2 is the largest of all the auxiliary tables. Not only does it list time periods and areas, but also natural, geographic, and geophysical divisions of the world. The main divisions are political. In addition there are also other sorts of conceptual divisions of the globe: the British Commonwealth, Third World countries, regions where Islam predominates, and so on.

9.2   DIVISIONS OF THE AREA TABLE

The major divisions, or the summary, of the area table are given below:

—001–009	Standard subdivisions [not areas, but placed here for practical number-building purposes]
—01–05	Historical periods [not areas, but placed here for practical number-building purposes]
—1	Areas, regions, places in general
—2	Persons [not areas, but placed here for number-building purposes]
—3	The ancient world

—4	Europe Western Europe
—5	Asia Orient Far East
—6	Africa
—7	North America
—8	South America
—9	Other parts of world and extraterrestrial worlds Pacific Ocean islands

Notation 1 is used for geophysical and conceptually bound but physically scattered areas, such as oceans, temperate zones, and socioeconomic regions. Notation 2 is used for persons regardless of area, region, or place. Notation 3 is used for the ancient world. The modern world is represented by the span —4-9, divided according to internationally accepted geographic and political divisions. Each set of digits has been hierarchically divided into countries, then provinces or states, then counties or similar jurisdictions, then cities in some cases, and even towns in others. Note the following development:

—4	Europe Western Europe
—41	British Isles
—42	England and Wales
—43	Central Europe Germany
—44	France and Monaco
—45	Italian Peninsula and adjacent islands Italy
—46	Iberian Peninsula and adjacent islands Spain
—47	Eastern Europe Russia
—48	Scandinavia
—49	Other parts of Europe

Each of the regions is divided into smaller units:

—43	Central Europe Germany
—431	Northeastern Germany
—432	Saxony and Thuringia
—433	Bavaria (Bayern)
—434	Southwestern Germany
—435	Northwestern Germany
—436	Austria and Liechtenstein
—437	Czech Republic and Slovakia
—438	Poland
—439	Hungary

And each of these is further divided:

—438	Poland
—438 1	Northwestern Poland Polish Pomerania
—438 2	North central Poland
—438 3	Northeastern Poland

−438 4	Central Poland	
−438 5	Southwestern Poland	
−438 6	Southeastern Poland	Polish Galicia

We can go no further in the case of Poland, but we can go further in the case of Hungary: Budapest is −43912.

The geographic divisions of the United States, Canada, the United Kingdom, South Africa, Australia, and New Zealand are more detailed than other areas, with many cities and towns listed for them, because these countries are major users of the English-language standard edition of the DDC. In many countries, the division is down to province only, although several countries have major cities listed. For example, in Japan there are numbers for Tokyo, Yokohama, Nagoya, Osaka, Kyoto, Kobe, Hiroshima, and Nagasaki. In India area numbers can be found for Calcutta, Delhi, New Delhi, and Bombay; Bhopal, Chandigarh, and Madras are mentioned in including notes. In the United States one can sometimes find a number for a relatively small city (for example, Meridian, Mississippi), but not for larger cities (like Pasadena, California). Certain city numbers were probably added at a time when there seemed to be literary warrant for the addition, and the reason may not be obvious now. While, on the whole, there used to be no single, clear criterion for inclusion in Table 2, a policy for establishing criteria has been developed for Edition 21.

9.3 LOCATING AREA NUMBERS IN TABLE 2

Table 2 can be consulted in two ways. One is to proceed systematically and hierarchically. As noted above, the modern world is divided first into continents, then into regions and countries, then into provinces and states, then into counties, and in some cases, into cities and towns. For example, to find a number for Assam, India, the first thing to know is that it is in northeast India, which is a part of south Asia, which is a part of Asia:

−5	Asia	
−54	South Asia	India
−541	Northeastern India	
−5416	Far northeast	
−54162	Assam	

Persons who do not know the general location of Assam can use the Relative Index, where entries for area numbers are simple and direct, and locating a place name delivers a number:

Asia	T2−5
Asia Minor	T2−561
ancient	T2−392
Assam (India)	T2−541 62

The index includes a variety of abbreviations:

Calgary (Alta.)   T2—712 338
Calhoun County (Tex.)   T2—764 121

The abbreviation following Calgary is for the province of Alberta and that following Calhoun County is for the state of Texas. These abbreviations are listed at the beginning of the Relative Index.

Table 2 uses the *AACR2R* form of the name without the qualifier if it is in English; if not, the form found in authoritative Anglophone sources is preferred. The *AACR2R* form is given after the familiar form in parentheses if it differs in spelling other than diacritics. If the form for the type of jurisdiction differs from the English-language form, both are given. For example:

—435 51   Cologne district (Köln Regierungsbezirk)

—482 1   Oslo county (fylke)

The *AACR2R* form of name as determined by the Library of Congress has been used or emulated in the Relative Index. The English form is also listed if the entry term differs significantly in spelling. The index entries for the examples above are as follows:

Cologne (Germany : Regierungsbezirk)
Köln (Germany : Regierungsbezirk)
Oslo fylke (Norway)

9.4   ADDING AREA NUMBERS FROM TABLE 2

As in all number building in the DDC, an area number from Table 2 is attached, not "added" in the mathematical sense, to the class number. An area number can be added in two ways:

(1)   According to add instructions found under numbers to which area notation is to be added directly. In such cases the add note normally appears in the form: "Add to base number . . . notation . . . from Table 2 . . ."

(2)   By way of standard subdivision (ss) —09.

9.5   ADDING AREA NUMBERS ACCORDING TO ADD INSTRUCTIONS

There are times when the geographic treatment of a subject is built directly into the legitimate subdivisions of a class. That is, the span of numbers —.1–.9 has been used to include the standard subdivision concept of place. For instance, under 372.9 Historical, geographic, persons treatment of elementary education, we find the instruction:

Add to base number 372.9 notation 01–9 from Table 2, e.g., elementary education in Brazil 372.981 [372.9 + 81 Brazil from Table 2]

Similarly:

Wages in New Zealand: 331.2993
331.2	Conditions of employment
331.29	Historical, geographic, persons treatment of compensation Add to base number 331.29 notation 001–99 from Table 2, e.g., compensation in Australia 331.2994
93	New Zealand (Table 2)

Observatories in Chile: 522.1983
522.1	Observatories
522.19	Geographic treatment Add to base number 522.19 notation 01–9 from Table 2, e.g., space observatories 522.1919, observatories in China 522.1951
83	Chile (Table 2)

9.5.1 A CLASS, DIVISION, OR SECTION NUMBER DIRECTLY DIVIDED BY AREA

Sometimes a main class, division, or section number, i.e., a one, two, or three-digit figure, is directly divided by area. For example:

History of Wales: 942.9
9	Base number for History
429	Wales (Table 2)

History of Paris: 944.361
9	Base number for History
44361	Paris (Table 2)

Geography of Wales: 914.29
91	Base number for Geography
429	Wales (Table 2)

Geography of Paris: 914.4361
91	Base number for Geography
44361	Paris (Table 2)

Foreign policy of China: 327.51
327	Base number for Foreign policy
51	China (Table 2)

A word of caution is in order here. In the instructions under 327.3–.9 we are asked to add the area notation falling only within the span of −3-9, whereas the full range of the area table is −1-9. This means, of course, that area −1 cannot be added. If it were added it would produce a number that conflicts with the provisions in the schedules for 327.1 Generalities of international relations. So, for a work on the foreign policy of the OPEC countries, we start with 327 and add on the Table 2 notation through the use of ss −09. This process is explained in section 9.6 below.

9.5.2 ADDING A PART OF A NUMBER FROM TABLE 2

There are times when a part of a number from Table 2 is added to the base number. For instance:

> 063   General organizations in Central Europe   In Germany
>   Add to base number 063 the numbers following—43 in
>   notation −431-439 from Table 2, e.g., organizations in
>   Poland 063.8

The number for a work on general organizations in Poland is therefore 063.8:

> 063   Base number for General organizations
> 8   Number following −43 in −438 for Poland in Table 2

Similarly:

> Art galleries in Sweden: 708.85
>
> 708.3-.8   [Galleries, museums, private collections of fine and
>   decorative arts in] Miscellaneous parts of Europe
>   Add to base number 708 the numbers following −4 in
>   notation 43–48 from Table 2, e.g., galleries, museums,
>   private collections in France 708.4
> 85   Number following −4 in −485 for Sweden in Table 2

9.6   ADDING AREA NUMBERS WITHOUT INSTRUCTIONS

Some topics warrant the addition of an area number, but there are no instructions to do so under that entry in the schedules. When this is the case, the area number is added through the use of standard subdivision −09.[1] At ss −09 we have:

> −091   Treatment by areas, regions, places in general
>   Add to base number −091 the numbers following −1 in
>   notation 11-19 from Table 2, e.g., Torrid Zone −0913 . . .
> −093-099   Treatment by specific continents, countries, localities;
>   extraterrestrial worlds
>   Add to base number −09 notation 3-9 from Table 2, e.g.,
>   the subject in North America . . .

---

[1]Note that adding area notation directly takes precedence over adding it through standard subdivision −09. For one thing, adding directly yields a shorter class number.

The add notes under these numbers mean that the area numbers covered by the span −1 or −3-9 may be added. The result, for example −0973, then becomes an extended standard subdivision. Since standard subdivision −09, including its extensions, can be universally added to any number in the schedules, virtually any class number may be subdivided geographically without specific add instructions. For example:

Foreign relations of the OPEC countries: 327.09177

327   Base number for Foreign relations
091   Standard subdivision for treatment by areas, regions, places in general from Table 1
77   Number in Table 2 following −1 in −177 Nations belonging to specific international organizations; OPEC is listed in an including note

To proceed further, take the title *Commercial Banks in Japan*. Here the core subject is commercial banks. Its class number is 332.12. Under this entry there is no provision for geographic treatment. Therefore, we may add area notation through the use of ss −091 or −093-099. The number for Japan in Table 2 is −52. Therefore: 332.120952

332.12   Base number for Commercial banks
09   Standard subdivision (Table 1)
52   Japan (Table 2)

Let us try another:

Female labor in China: 331.40951

331.4   Base number for Women workers
09   Standard subdivision (Table 1)
51   China (Table 2)

9.7   THE DIFFERENCE BETWEEN —09 AND —9

In some cases, geographic treatment may be achieved through two different sets of numbers in the same field of study. The distinctions are explained in the Classification. For example, take the following entries:

330.09   Historical, geographic, persons treatment of economics as a discipline
             For economic situation and conditions, see 330.9

330.9   Economic situations and conditions

330.91   Geographic treatment (Economic geography) by areas, regions, places in general

330.93-.99   Geographic treatment (Economic geography) by specific continents, countries, localities

Here the entry 330.09 pertains to the discipline of economics as studied in various places. The other entries, 330.91–.99, pertain to the economic conditions that exist in various places. For example, 330.0973 means the discipline of economics as studied in the United States; 330.973 stands for economic situations and conditions of the United States. We must be sure not to confuse how place is used in these situations.

Note the difference between the following pairs of numbers:

(1) 720.9   Historical, geographic, persons treatment [of Architecture]
     722–724   Architectural schools and styles

(2) 027.009   Historical and persons treatment [of General libraries,
                    archives, information centers]
     027.01–.09 Geographic treatment [of General libraries,
                    archives, information centers]

(3) 327.093–.099   Treatment [of international relations] by specific con-
                    tinents and localities
     327.3–327.9   Foreign relations of specific nations

9.8   AREA NUMBER INTERPOSED BETWEEN TWO SUBJECT FACETS

There are a few places where an area number is interposed between two subject facets; the major one is law. The citation order for law is:

34 + branch of law + jurisdiction + topic within branch + standard subdivision

For example:

History of evidence in criminal law of the Dominican Republic: 345.72930609
     34   Base number for Law
     5   Criminal law
     7293   Dominican Republic (Table 2)
     06   Evidence (added according to the instruction under 345.3–.9)
     09   History (Table 1)

The first zero that falls between jurisdiction and topic is actually a facet indicator that introduces the specific topic in law subordinate to the branch of law.

9.9   ADDING TWO AREA NUMBERS

There are cases when two areas are considered within a document. This frequently occurs in the 300s in such fields as foreign relations, international commerce, and migration. In these cases there is usually a clarifying explanation in the schedules as to which of the two areas should come first. Normally the two area numbers are joined by a zero. For example, take a work on the foreign relations of the United States with the United Kingdom. It belongs in 327

International relations, specifically at 327.3−.9 Foreign relations of specific nations. The instruction there reads:

Add to base number 327 notation 3−9 from Table 2 . . . then, for relations between that nation and another nation or region, add 0* and to the result add notation 1−9 from Table 2 . . .

Give priority in notation to the nation emphasized. If emphasis is equal, give priority to the nation coming first in Table 2

The asterisk * refers to a footnote in the printed schedules, indicating that in such cases, double zeros are used for standard subdivisions. Implementing the instruction we arrive at the number 327.73041:

327	Base number for Foreign relations
73	United States (Table 2)
0	Facet indicator
41	United Kingdom (Table 2)

The entry also contains an option to give priority in notation to the country requiring local emphasis, e.g., if a library in the United Kingdom wished to gather foreign relations with respect to the United Kingdom as the focus of attention, then 327.41073 would be the proper number.

One more example to show a different notation pattern: Suppose we have a work on trade relations between Canada and tropical countries. Under 382.093−328.099 International commerce in specific continents, countries, localities, the add instructions are as follows:

Add to base number 382.09 notation 3−9 from Table 2 . . .; then, for commerce between two continents, countries, localities or between a continent, country, locality and a region, area, place, add 0† and add notation 1 or 3−9 from Table 2 . . .

Accordingly, the correct number is 382.0971013:

382	Base number for International commerce (Foreign trade)
09	Standard subdivision for Historical, geographic, persons treatment (Table 1)
71	Canada (Table 2)
0	Facet indicator
13	Torrid zone (Tropics) (Table 2)

9.10 EXTENDING A TABLE 2 NUMBER BY ANOTHER TABLE 2 NUMBER

Suppose we want to indicate the deserts of Australia or the forests of Canada. We must realize that in such cases geographic place (namely, Australia and

Canada) is more important than deserts or forests (which can be handled by subject headings). On the other hand, the problem is different for a work dealing with three or more deserts or forests of the world, because for such a work the particular place is not important, but the kind of place is. For instance, deserts of the world obviously belong with deserts, as do deserts of the Southern Hemisphere.

Suppose, then, that the work deals with the coastal regions of California. Coastal regions are represented by —146 in Table 2. Should we attach California to this topic, or the topic to California? Always remember: the particular place is more important when areas are under consideration. In this case California is more important than coastal regions—at least according to the DDC. For a history of the coastal regions of California, then, the number 979.400946 is built in this way:

9	Base number for History
794	California (Table 2)
009	Areas, regions, places in general (internal table under 930–990 in volume 3)
46	Number following —1 in —146 Coastal regions and shorelines (Table 2)

Similarly, place is also transcendent in geography:

Geography of the coastal regions of California: 917.940946

91	Base number for Geography
794	California (Table 2)
09	Areas, regions, places in general (internal table under 913–919)
46	Number following —1 in —146 Coastal regions and shorelines (Table 2)

Even when the first area is represented by standard subdivisions —093–099, the number can be further extended by adding the notation for a second area through the instruction given under —093–099 in Table 1 in volume 1:

Add to base number —09 notation 3–9 from Table 2 . . .; then add further as follows:

01	Forecasts
.	
.	
09	Historical and geographic treatment Add to 09 the numbers following —09 in notation 090–099 from Table 1 . . .Use 093–099 to add notation for a specific

continent, country, locality when first area notation is used to specify area of origin, while second identifies area in which subject is found or practiced . . .

For example:

Urban labor market in the United States: 331.120973091732

331.12	Base number for Labor market
09	Standard subdivision (Table 1)
73	United States (Table 2)
09	Historical and geographic treatment (add table under —093–099 (Table 1)
1732	Urban regions (Table 2)

9.11   ADDING AREA NOTATION TO STANDARD SUBDIVISIONS OTHER THAN —09

There are several places in Table 1 where an area number can be attached to a standard subdivision other than the normal —09:

—0218	Standards
—023	The subject as a profession, occupation, hobby
—025	Directories of persons and organizations
—0272	Patents
—0294	Trade catalogs and directories
—0296	Buyers' guides
—0603–0609	National, state, provincial, local organizations
—0701–0709	Geographic treatment [of Education, research, related topics]
—07101–07109	Geographic treatment [of Education]
—0711	[Geographic treatment of] Higher education
—0712	[Geographic treatment of] Secondary education
—07201–07209	Geographic treatment of research and statistical methods together, of research alone
—074	Museums, collections, exhibits
—079	Competitions, festivals, awards, financial support

Note that in the table of preference in the beginning of Table 1, the span —093–099 takes precedence over —074. The origin of the item being exhibited takes precedence over the place of the exhibition; however, the place of the exhibition may also be shown by using —074 plus area notation instead of —093–099. For example, Australian aboriginal art exhibited in the United States is classed in 704.039915007473, not 704.03991500973 (for an explanation of the valid number, see 12.2).

9.12   USING STANDARD SUBDIVISIONS AFTER AN AREA NUMBER

We have just seen how certain standard subdivisions may be extended by a number from Table 2. At times the converse is true—but only upon instruction. Here are a few instances. First, however, let us add the reminder that any number that is built in the Classification may have a standard subdivision added to it so long as: 1) there are no instructions to the contrary; 2) the added notation is not redundant; and 3) the built number does not already have a standard subdivision attached to it.[2]

A journal of elementary education in South Africa: 372.96805

372.9	Historical, geographic, persons treatment of elementary education
68	South Africa (Table 2)
05	Serial publications (Table 1)

A journal of higher education in Ghana: 378.66705

378	Base number for Higher education
667	Ghana (Table 2)
05	Serial publications (Table 1)

Research on Japanese economy: 330.95200722

330.9	Base number for Economic situation and conditions
52	Japan (Table 2)
0072	Research (Table 1)

A history of French foreign policy: 327.44009

327	Base number for Foreign policy
44	France (Table 2)
009	History (Table 1)

Note in the last two examples that two zeros are used for standard subdivisions. There are instructions in the schedules to this effect in both cases. In the last example we have to use two zeros because a single zero is used to introduce the second area in those cases where two areas are involved.

9.13   SUMMARY

Table 2 in volume 1 contains the area notation. Here the entire world has been covered by the digits —1-9. The world and regions in general are denoted by —1 and its subdivisions. The digit —3 denotes the ancient world. The modern world is denoted by the digits —4-9; it has been divided first

---

[2]For more information about adding standard subdivisions to synthesized numbers, see the Manual note on Table 1 in Melvil Dewey, *Dewey Decimal Classification and Relative Index*, Ed. 21, edited by Joan S. Mitchell, Julianne Beall, Winton E. Matthews, Jr., and Gregory R. New (Albany, NY: OCLC Forest Press, 1996), v. 4, pp. 905–9.

into continents, then into regions, countries, provinces, states, and so on down in a few cases to counties and cities (especially in the United States, the United Kingdom, Canada, South Africa, Australia, and New Zealand). These hierarchical divisions are based on geographic divisions accepted by geographers and historians.

Area numbers are given in the Relative Index. They are preceded by the symbol "T2."

The dash before the area number indicates that it is not to be used alone, but is to be combined with a class number from the schedules. The combining can be done in two ways. The first is to add an area number when told to do so in the schedules. Such an instruction is usually found in the form "Add to base number . . . notation 1–9 from Table 2 . . ." If instructions are absent and a topic has its own number, the classifier may add an area number by way of standard subdivision —09 (which acts as a connecting symbol between the class numbers from the schedules and the area number from Table 2).

Two area numbers may be added upon instructions, usually with the interposition of a zero. Sometimes a Table 2 number is added to a standard subdivision other than —09, the normal facet indicator for area.

9.14 EXERCISES

Exercise 1:

In the Relative Index identify the area numbers for the following areas, and then locate and verify them in Table 2.

(1) Genesee County, Michigan
(2) Punjab, Pakistan
(3) Chad
(4) North Carolina
(5) Ghana
(6) Unaligned countries
(7) Eastern Hemisphere
(8) Indian Ocean
(9) Antarctic Ocean
(10) Arctic Ocean
(11) Christian countries
(12) Rural regions

Exercise 2:

Classify the following with direct subdivision by place:

(1) Adult education in Singapore
(2) Education policy in India
(3) General statistics of Finland
(4) General geology of Athens
(5) History of Jammu and Kashmir
(6) History of Jammu and Kashmir during the reign of Aurangzeb
(7) General organizations in Liverpool, England
(8) Journalism and newspapers in Finland
(9) Art galleries in Sweden
(10) Public administration in Papua New Guinea

Exercise 3:

Assign class numbers to the following, using extensions of area number −1:

(1) Social welfare programs in developing countries
(2) Democratic political systems in unaligned countries
(3) Health insurance systems in the Pacific region

Exercise 4:

Assign class numbers to the following, using standard subdivision −09 and area numbers −3–9:

(1) Social services to families in Washington State
(2) Child labor in Southeast Asia
(3) Taxes in Kuwait
(4) Costume in Wales
(5) Prices in France: an economic study
(6) Sexual division of labor, a case study in Chicago, Illinois
(7) Broadway musicals: a theatrical history

Exercise 5:

Classify the following subjects requiring area notation between two subject facets:

(1) Physical geography of Mexico
(2) Law of property in Nigeria
(3) Public health law of Mozambique
(4) The lower house of the British Parliament
(5) Communist parties of Eastern Europe

Exercise 6:

Classify the following subjects requiring two area numbers:

(1) Migration from Vietnam to the United States: a sociological study
(2) Trade agreements between India and Italy (emphasizes India)
(3) Trade between India and Italy (emphasizes India)
(4) Foreign relations between India and countries of the Pacific Rim
(5) U.S. economic aid to developing countries
(6) Foreign relations between Japan and South Korea

Exercise 7:

Class the following topics using an area notation extended by another area notation:

(1) Civil rights in francophone countries of Africa
(2) Male costume in rural Austria
(3) Economic conditions in rural England

Exercise 8:

Classify the following, using a standard subdivision (other than —09) extended by an area notation:

(1) Research in economics in Scotland
(2) Library science as a profession in the United States
(3) The teaching of law in Asia
(4) Colleges and universities teaching law in Latin America
(5) Higher education in Spain in public administration
(6) Athletic instruction in U.S. colleges

Exercise 9:

Classify the following, using a standard subdivision after an area notation:

(1) Journal of Indian geography
(2) Women in the Church of England
(3) Foreign policy of Germany in the 1990s
(4) Sickness and health: Canadian statistics at a glance
(5) Ancient Roman coins [minted in Rome] in the Hobart Classics Museum (Hobart, Tasmania)
(6) A journal of housing services in Argentina

CHAPTER 10
USING TABLE 3 WITH
INDIVIDUAL LITERATURES AND OTHER CLASSES

Objectives:

The objectives of this chapter are to explain: the classification of creative literature in all languages and forms of expression; the classification of collections and critical appraisal of literature; and the use of Tables 3A–3C with main class 800 Literature and other classes.

Outline:

10.0   INTRODUCTION

Main class 800 was originally designed for literary works of the imagination by known authors. That is still its basic cast. However, it also contains other types of works. For instance, anonymous classics, such as the *Mabinogion* and *Tales of the Arabian Nights*, could be classed in folk literature, but in the DDC they are classed in 800. Section 808 includes topics that are not strictly literature. For example, it includes material on how to use language to express ideas. We do not mean only material on how to write poetry or prose or fiction or drama, but also material on how to write a legal brief, a medical report, an engineering analysis, or a teacher's lesson plan. Section 808 also includes editorial techniques.

For literature, the 800 class includes both literary texts and works about literature. When dealing with individual authors, Table 3A is used. When dealing with works by or about more than one author, Tables 3B and 3C are used. The use of Table 3 is described at length below, but, first, a general discussion of class 800 may be helpful.

10.1 DIVISION OF MAIN CLASS 800 LITERATURE

Main class 800 begins with generalia, in 801-809. The remaining notation, 810-890, is divided among the literatures of the world. Sections 801-807 represent standard subdivisions of literature; 808-809 have been extended to accommodate Rhetoric and texts and criticisms from more than two literatures. Following is the outline for 801-809:

800 Literature (Belles-lettres) and rhetoric
801 Philosophy and theory
802 Miscellany
803 Dictionaries, encyclopedias, concordances
805 Serial publications
806 Organizations and management
807 Education, research, related topics
808 Rhetoric and collections of literary texts from more than two literatures
809 History, description, critical appraisal of more than two literatures

Classes 801-809 deal with literature in general: 808.8 and 809 are particularly important for several reasons. Class 808.8 contains provisions for collections of texts from more than two literatures, as well as criticism of more than two literatures when a sufficient amount of literary text is present. This makes 808.8 one of the major units in main class 800.

Class 809 deals with history, description, and critical appraisal of more than two literatures. There are many such works, and their classification requires careful handling. We will treat 808.8 and 809 at length later.

10.1.1 FACETS OF LITERATURE

The 800 class is one of the most faceted of all the main classes. The main facets represented in the classification of literature are language, literary form (subdivided by kind of form[1]), and literary period. Beyond these main facets are other aspects such as bibliographic form (i.e., collection or history/critical appraisal), literary features (such as naturalism, plot, characters), themes (such as love, friendship, everyday life), and persons (such as for or by women or children).

The general citation order for a class number in literature consists of *language* (except for American literature, which has its own span), *literary form* (such as poetry) or *kind of form* (such as mystery fiction), *period* in which the work is written, and *standard subdivisions*. Literary features, themes, and persons are extensions of standard subdivisions —08 and —09. This citation order varies slightly when dealing with literary works not limited to a particular language.

---

[1]Kind of form does not apply to works by individual authors.

10.1.1.1 LANGUAGE

The literatures of individual languages are classed in 810-899. Each language that at one time was considered to be of importance to western scholars has been allotted a division in 810-880. Consequently, many other important literatures are classed as subdivisions of 890 Literatures of other languages, and thus have long numbers; still other national literatures receive only scant treatment. Furthermore, some national literatures, although written in a western language, are not treated as well as the mother nation of the tongue. That is, Spanish literature from Spain is treated fully, but literature from Mexico in Spanish is not. British literature can be gathered by periods, but Australian literature cannot. This is a serious shortcoming in Dewey that cannot be rectified soon, because it would require a major restructuring of the 800s. Options have been provided throughout the 800s to address these shortcomings.

The divisions of the 800s follow:

810 American literature in English
820 English and Old English (Anglo-Saxon) literatures
830 Literatures of Germanic (Teutonic) languages   German literature
840 Literatures of Romance languages   French literature
850 Literatures of Italian, Sardinian, Dalmation, Romanian, Rhaeto-Romanic languages   Italian literature
860 Literatures of Spanish and Portuguese languages   Spanish literature
870 Literatures of Italic languages   Latin literature
880 Literatures of Hellenic languages   Classical Greek literature
890 Literatures of other specific languages and language families

10.1.1.2 FORM

Most literature is written in a particular form or genre such as poetry or drama. At the head of Tables 3A and 3B in volume 1, there is a list of the literary forms of literature that the DDC recognizes. The forms are placed in their order of preference and the table should be consulted when two or more forms are involved in a work.

Let us recapitulate the preference table from Tables 3A and 3B:

Drama   −2
Poetry   −1
    Class epigrams in verse in −8
Fiction   −3
Essays   −4
Speeches   −5
Letters   −6
Miscellaneous writings   −8
Humor and satire   −7 (Table 3B only)

The form subdivision —7 Humor and satire poses a special problem. These are not true literary forms or genres; they are literary devices to make a point. The subdivision —7 does not exist in Table 3A for individual authors. Because a work of humor and/or satire must be written in a particular literary form, it is classed with the form, e.g., satirical poem —1, humorous fiction —3, etc. Humor or satire without identifiable form is classed under —8, as is a collection of satire or humor by an individual author written in more than one form. Subdivision —7 is used only for collections and criticism of works in two or more literary forms by more than one author.

The literary forms represented by —1-3 and —5 are further subdivided into kinds of forms which are subgenres of literature. These include epic poetry, lyric poetry, comedy, melodrama, historical fiction, science fiction, oratory, recitation, etc. These numbers for subgenres are used only with collections and critical appraisal of works by more than one author, and are not used for individual authors.

10.1.1.3 PERIOD

Because literary styles vary in different time periods, the time or period facet is an important consideration in classifying literature. The literature in each major language is divided into recognized time periods. These period subdivisions are found in the schedules under the numbers for individual literatures. For works containing collections from, or critical appraisal of, more than two literatures, the period subdivisions follow those defined in Table 1.

10.1.1.4 FEATURE/THEME/PERSONS

Many literary works have identifiable themes or manifest specific features, such as style, mood, and perspective, and literature for and by specific kinds of persons. In Dewey, features, themes, and persons are represented in the class numbers for works by or about more than one author. They are not represented in class numbers for works by or about individual authors.

10.2 INTRODUCTION TO TABLE 3

Few class numbers in literature are found ready-made in the schedules. Most numbers have to be synthesized by way of Tables 3A, 3B, and 3C. For this reason class 800 is rightly considered to be one of the most faceted main classes in the DDC. The notation from Tables 3A–3C is to be used only when so instructed in the schedules or tables, and only with base numbers for individual literatures that are listed with add instructions (or a note or asterisk leading to add instructions). The base number may be identified in a note, e.g., in the note at 899: "899.969 Georgian"; otherwise it is the number given for the literature, e.g., *Dutch literature 839.31.

As mentioned earlier, Table 3A is used with works by or about individual authors, and Table 3B with works by or about more than one author written in the same language. Table 3C contains notation representing aspects of literature other than language and form.

10.3   TABLE 3A: WORKS BY AND ABOUT INDIVIDUAL AUTHORS

Class numbers assigned to works by or about individual authors normally contain four component parts in the following citation order:

main class + language + form + period

The procedures for building numbers for individual authors are outlined at the beginning of Table 3A. Detailed explanations of building numbers for individual authors also are found in the Manual notes for Table 3 and Table 3A. In addition, a flow chart is included in the Manual note for Table 3A as an aid to show the step-by-step process.

Table 3A is easy to use primarily because once the form of a literary work and the period during which an author wrote are determined, the classifier's work is essentially completed. There are pitfalls: forms are not always apparent, or a work may be juvenilia, or it may have been written in the time before the period or periods in which an author is known to have produced his or her major works.

Let us take an example of an individual work:

Cress Delehanty by Jessamyn West

Jessamyn West is an American writer whose work began to be published in the late 1940s. Because she is an American writer, the base number for her work is 81. Next we have to determine the literary form or genre. *Cress Delehanty* is a series of short stories that are combined to make a novel. We go to Table 3A and look for form, which in this case is −3 Fiction. As we said earlier, kind of form (e.g., historical fiction) is not used for individual authors. Under −31–39 Specific periods [for fiction] in Table 3A, we are told to add to −3 notation from the period table for the specific literature in 810–890. Period numbers are found in the schedules under each of the literatures described in section 10.1.1.1. Jessamyn West's fits nicely in 1945–1999, for which the number 54 is found under 810 American literature in the schedules. Adding the period notation to −3 results in −354, which is then added to base number 81, resulting in the correct number 813.54. That is the end of our number building, because there are no instructions to continue further.

Book numbers based on Cutter numbers take care of the rest of the needed information. Cutter numbers are devices to subarrange a class—alphabetically by author or subject, or chronologically by date, whatever the occasion demands.

In the case of *Cress Delehanty* the number might be W52cr, W52 for West and cr for *Cress Delehanty*. Using such a method to gather works of an author together alphabetically is a help to users. (Cutter numbers are treated in detail in two books, one by John P. Comaromi[2] and the other by Donald J. Lehnus.)[3]

We repeat here a point made earlier: once the form of the work and the period of an individual author have been selected, the work of the classifier is done.

In the DDC, works by an individual author and critical appraisal of works about the author in general or about a particular work by the author are classed in the same number. In other words, the class number for a work of criticism about *Cress Delehanty* will be the same as the class number for the book itself. Their call numbers will differ slightly through adjustments to book numbers; different libraries follow different practices in this regard.

Here are a few more examples:

Works by individual authors

Newspaper days by Theodore Dreiser [1871–1945]. 813.52

81	Base number for American literature
3	Notation for fiction from Table 3A
52	Period notation for 1900–1945 from the schedules

Stories, poems, and other writings by Willa Cather [1873–1947]. 813.52

81	Base number for American literature
3	Notation for fiction from Table 3A
52	Period notation for 1900–1945 from the schedules

The nondramatic works [poems] *of John Ford* [1586-ca.1640] edited by L.E. Stock et al. 821.3

82	Base number for English literature
1	Notation for poetry from Table 3A
3	Period notation for Elizabethan period, 1558–1625, from the schedules

The dragon and the dove: the plays of Thomas Dekker [1572–1632] by Julia Gasper. 822.3

82	Base number for English literature
2	Notation for drama from Table 3A
3	Period notation for Elizabethan period, 1558–1625, from the schedules

---

[2]John P. Comaromi, *Book Numbers: A Historical Study and Practical Guide to Their Use* (Littleton: CO: Libraries Unlimited, 1981).

[3]Donald J. Lehnus, *Book Numbers: History, Principles, and Application* (Chicago: American Library Association, 1980).

Essays: first and second series by Ralph Waldo Emerson [1803–1882]. 814.3

81	Base number for American literature
4	Notation for essays from Table 3A
3	Period notation for 1830–1861 from the schedules

Note that collected works of individual authors receive the same class numbers as individual works providing that the author worked in the same form.

Works about individual authors

A critical appraisal of an individual author with emphasis on a particular literary form is classed in the same number as the author's works in that form. Table 1 number —092 for biography is not used with works about individual authors. For example:

Henry James [1843–1916]: *a study of the short fiction* by Richard A. Hocks. 813.4

81	Base number for American literature
3	Notation for fiction from Table 3A
4	Period notation for 1861–1899 from the schedules

If the critical appraisal does not emphasize a particular form, it is classed with the notation for the form with which the author is chiefly identified.

Salem is my dwelling place: a life of Nathaniel Hawthorne [1804–1864] by Edwin Haviland Miller. 813.3

81	Base number for American literature
3	Notation for fiction from Table 3A
3	Period notation for 1830–1861 from the schedules

In the footsteps of Hans Christian Andersen [1805–1875] by Kai Chr. Rasmussen. 839.8136

839.81	Base number for Danish literature
3	Notation for fiction from Table 3A
6	Period notation for 1800–1899 from the schedules

Charles Baudelaire [1821–1867] *revisited* by Lois Boe Hyslop. 841.8

84	Base number for French literature
1	Notation for poetry from Table 3A
8	Period notation for 1848–1899 from the schedules

Works about individual works

Works about individual literary works are assigned the same class numbers as the works themselves:

New essays on White noise [a novel by Don DeLillo, late 20th-century American author] edited by Frank Lentricchia. 813.54

81	Base number for American literature
3	Notation for fiction from Table 3A
54	Period notation for 1945–1995 from the schedules

Tristan in the underworld: a study of Gottfried von Strassburg's [13th cent.] *Tristan together with the Tristan of Thomas* by Neil Thomas. 831.21

83	Base number for German literature
1	Notation for poetry from Table 3A
21	Period notation for 1100–1249 from the schedules

Love and social contracts: Goethe's [1749–1832] *Unterhaltungen deutscher Ausgewanderten* by Robin A. Clouser. 833.6

83	Base number for German literature
3	Notation for fiction from Table 3A
6	Period notation for classical period 1750–1832 from the schedules

Authors who write in the same language, form, and period share the same class number; for example, poetry by Tennyson and Browning, both being Victorian authors, is assigned the same class number: 821.8.

The language and form of literature are ordinarily obvious to the classifier. The author's period occasionally causes some difficulty. Reference tools, such as the *Oxford Companion to English Literature*, will prove helpful when the classifier is in doubt.

Form subdivision —8 Miscellaneous writings presents a special case. It is used for authors not limited to or chiefly identifiable with one specific form, and also for diaries, journals, notebooks, and reminiscences. Such works are classed with —8 in Table 3A plus period subdivision plus subdivisions —02–09 under —81–89. This results in the citation order of 8 + language + 8 + period + special form, as shown in the following examples:

A movable feast by Ernest Hemingway. 818.5203

81	Base number for American literature
8	Notation for Miscellaneous writings fromTable 3A
52	Period notation for 1900-1945 from the schedules
03	Diaries, journals, notebooks, reminiscences (under —81-89 in Table 3A)

Henry and June: from a journal of love: the unexpurgated diary of Anaïs Nin, 1931-1932. 818.5403

81	Base number for American literature
8	Notation for Miscellaneous writings from Table 3A
54	Period notation for 1945–1999 from the schedules
03	Journals (under —81-89 in Table 3A)

Translations of works by individual authors are classed in the same numbers as the original works. For example:

Souvenirs intimes de David Copperfield: De grandes espérances/Dickens. 823.8

82	Base number for English literature
3	Notation for Fiction from Table 3A
8	Period notation for English literature, Victorian period, 1837-1899, from the schedules

10.3.1 A WORD OF CAUTION

If a literature does not have a designated base number, i.e., the name of the literature is not listed with add instructions (or a note or asterisk leading to add instructions), it cannot be extended beyond the base number, i.e., form and literary period cannot be added. For example, the number for the collected works of a Livonian writer (Livonian is a Finnic language found at 894.54) cannot be extended beyond 894.54 because it is not a base number to which Table 3A notation can be added.

For some writers it is permissible to add form but not period. Period notation is not added to works by most writers who do not live in the ancestral continent of their mother tongue. That is to say, the periods listed under French literature are not used for authors writing in French who reside in Africa, Canada, or the Caribbean; only French writers living in France or elsewhere in Europe receive numbers for such periods. The optional period tables for French under 840.1–848 are just that—options. The Decimal Classification Division at the Library of Congress does not use them. Similarly, a novel by the Australian writer Nevil Shute is classed in 823, and there the number ends, because the periods for England are not appropriate for Australia. A collection of poems by the Nobel Prize winning Mexican author Octavio Paz is classed in 861; no period is added for him because the periods for Spain are not appropriate for Mexico.

10.4   USING TABLES 3B AND 3C

Class numbers for general works on literature, such as literary anthologies, literary histories, and critical appraisals of literature, are considerably more difficult to build than those for one author from one literature. However, the introduction to Table 3B, outlining the procedure for number building in eight steps, should ease some of the difficulties in classifying literary anthologies and critical appraisals. Unlike class numbers for works by and about individual authors, which show language, form, and period, class numbers for general collections and criticism also express other facets, such as kind of literary form, bibliographic form, scope, media, and feature/theme/persons wherever applicable.

10.4.1 TABLE 3B: SUBDIVISIONS FOR WORKS BY OR ABOUT MORE THAN ONE AUTHOR

Table 3B contains subdivisions for works by or about more than one author, arranged first by standard subdivisions —01-07 as provided in Table 1 and subdivisions —08 and —09 and then by literary forms —1-8. Subdivisions —08 and —09 warrant special mention.

Subdivision —08 is used to indicate whether the work in hand is a collection. Through Edition 18 of the DDC, —08 Collections was a standard subdivision applicable to all subjects. Beginning with Edition 19, —08 in Table 1 has been assigned a different meaning: History and description with respect to kinds of persons, with the exception that it remains a subdivision for collections in Table 3B. Subdivision —09 in Table 3B is used to indicate whether the document in hand is a work about literature. Since Edition 20, —9 has been expanded to History, description, or critical appraisal (hereafter also referred to as "criticism"). Subdivisions —08 and —09 may be further extended by notation from Table 1 or Table 3C to accommodate additional facets.

To assist in the complex number building needed for collections or critical appraisals of literature written by more than one author, the Manual note for Table 3B includes a detailed discussion with two flow charts showing the decisions the classifier must make at each step of the number-building process. The flow charts are followed by many examples in the notes for several subdivisions of Table 3B.

10.4.2 TABLE 3C: NOTATION TO BE ADDED WHERE INSTRUCTED IN TABLE 3B, 700.4, 791.4, 808–809

Table 3C contains subdivisions used as extensions of the notation in Table 3B and of certain numbers in the schedules. The four main subdivisions in Table 3C are listed below in their order of preference (also listed in the Manual note for Table 3B under "Preference order"):

Themes and subjects	—3
Elements	—2
Qualities	—1
Persons	—8-9

Each is further divided into greater detail.

10.5 GENERAL COLLECTIONS OF LITERARY TEXTS AND CRITICISM: MORE THAN TWO LITERATURES

If we have a general anthology or criticism of world literature or an anthology or criticism of material from literatures in more than two languages,[4] we

---

[4]Works in two languages are classed with the language that predominates or that comes first in numerical order.

begin with the main class number 800. The first thing to recognize is that, for a collection or criticism of literature in more than two languages, we cannot enter the span 810–899, which is used for literatures of a specific language.[5] Works of literature not limited to a particular language are classed in 800–809. Note that the second digit after main class number 8 is a zero, which indicates that the language facet is absent. Sections 801–807 carry regular standard subdivisions. Literary texts and criticism are classed in 808.8–809.[6] These numbers can be extended to accommodate literary facets such as literary form, period, and feature/theme/persons. In such cases, the citation order is:

808.8 or 809 + form + period + feature/theme/persons

10.5.1 GENERAL COLLECTIONS AND CRITICISM WITH ONE FACET

The class number for a literary work that manifests only one facet—form, period, or feature/theme/persons—follows the citation order: 808.8 *or* 809 + facet.

10.5.1.1 FORM

Suppose we are classifying a collection of world poetry. 808.81, the number for collections of poetry, is divided into the spans 808.812–808.818 for specific kinds of poetry. In such situations we are told to add to base number 808.81 the numbers following −10 in −102–108 from Table 3B. For example:

A collection of epic poetry: 808.8132

808.81	Collections of poetry
32	Number following −10 in −1032 Epic poetry (Table 3B)

Cosmos and epic representation: Dante, Spenser, Milton, and the transformation of Renaissance heroic poetry by John G. Demaray. 809.132

809	Base number for History, description, critical appraisal of more than two literatures
1	Number following 808.8 in 808.81 Poetry
32	Number following −10 in −1032 Epic poetry (Table 3B)

10.5.1.2 PERIOD

Suppose that we are classifying a work entitled "20th-century literature: a collection." At 808.8 Collections of literary texts from more than two literatures we have the subdivisions:

---

[5]The Decimal Classification Division uses 810–899 for works in multiple related languages, e.g., Germanic languages. See Manual note at 800: Language: *Literature of two or more languages* in Melvil Dewey, *Dewey Decimal Classification and Relative Index,* Ed. 21, edited by Joan S. Mitchell, Julianne Beall, Winton E. Matthews, Jr., and Gregory R. New (Albany, NY: OCLC Forest Press, 1996), v. 4, p. 1186.

[6]Notation 808.001–808.7, the span that might have been used for a general collection of literature, has been assigned to works of Rhetoric.

808.8001–.8005 Collections from specific periods
Add to base number 808.800 the numbers following —090 in notation
0901–0905 from Table 1, e.g., collections of 18th century literature
808.80033

The number for the 20th century in Table 1 is —0904. Discarding 090 as instructed results in the number 808.8004. Note that the period numbers used are taken from Table 1, not from the periods found under 810–890 for individual literatures. The reason is simple: there is no pattern that works for literature in general, so the pattern of Table 1 is used.

Criticism of world literature by period falls into 809.01–809.05; a single zero is used instead of double zeros. Thus the history of literature in the 19th century falls at 809.034:

Exotic memoires: literature, colonialism, and the fin de siècle by Chris Bongie. 809.034

809	Base number for History, description, critical appraisal of more than two literatures
0	Facet indicator for 809.01–.05 Literature from specific periods
34	Period notation: number following —090 in —09034 19th century (Table 1)

10.5.1.3 FEATURE/THEME/PERSONS

Suppose we have an anthology of literature that features King Arthur. We begin with 808.80 and then look in Table 3C. Numbers —1-3 in Table 3C express specific features such as style, mood, perspective, themes, and subjects. A person as a character in, or subject of, literature is classed in —351 Literature dealing with specific persons. The number for a collection of literature featuring King Arthur, therefore, is 808.80351:

808.80	Base number for Collections of literature displaying specific features
351	Specific persons (Table 3C)

For works about literature, notation for specific themes and subjects are added to the base number 809.93 without intervening zeros. One simply adds to 809.93 the appropriate number from 3C. Therefore, criticism of Arthurian literature is 809.93351; compare this with the number for the Arthurian anthology in our earlier example.

Example of an anthology displaying specific features:

The love of cats: an illustrated anthology about our love for cats. 808.803629752

808.80	Base number for Collections of literature displaying specific features
362	Animals (Table 3C)
9752	Cats (from 599.752)

Example of a work about literature displaying specific qualities:

Abyss of reason: cultural movements, revelations, and betrayals by Dan Cottom. 809.91

809	Base number for History, description, critical appraisal of more than two literatures
9	Literature displaying specific features
1	Literature displaying specific qualities of style, mood, viewpoint (Table 3C)

Numbers —8–9 in Table 3C are used for literature for and by specific kinds of persons. For example, a collection of literature by women authors is classed in 808.899287.

10.5.2 GENERAL COLLECTIONS AND CRITICISM WITH TWO FACETS

The class number for a work that is either a general collection or criticism, and contains two facets, has one of the following citation orders:

(1) 808.8 or 809 + form + period
(2) 808.8 or 809 + form + feature/theme/persons
(3) 808.8 or 809 + feature/theme/persons (period is ignored) or 808.8 or 809 + period if emphasized (feature/theme/persons is ignored)

10.5.2.1 FORM AND PERIOD

When a literary work combines form and period, the period notation follows the form notation. For example:

Travels of a genre: the modern novel and ideology by Mary N. Layoun. 809.304

809	Base number for History, description, critical appraisal of more than two literatures
3	Number following 808.8 in 808.83 Fiction
0	Historical periods (added to 808.83 as instructed under 808.81–808.88)
4	Number following —090 in —0904 20th century (Table 1)

10.5.2.2 FORM AND FEATURE/THEME/PERSONS

A collection of poetry that features King Arthur is classed in base number 808.819, where we are instructed to add notation from Table 3C. As we saw above, King Arthur is classed in —351; therefore, a collection of poems from more than two literatures about King Arthur or the Arthurian ideal is classed in 808.819351. (Of course, the number is shared with a number of other heros from many times and climes.) Another example:

The landscapes of alienation: ideological subversion in Kafka, Céline, and Onetti by Jack Murray. 809.39353

809 Base number for History, description, critical appraisal of more than two literatures

39 Number following 808.8 in 808.839 Fiction displaying specific features

353 Human characteristics and activities (Table 3C)

10.5.2.3 PERIOD AND FEATURE/THEME/PERSONS

Suppose we have a collection or criticism of literature from a particular period on a specific theme or quality. What do we do? Here is as good a place as any to introduce the rule of fewest zeros. When a work contains several facets but there is no instruction in the DDC to combine them, the classifier is faced with the problem of choosing among several single-facet numbers. Given a series of numbers that share the first few digits, the classifier should choose the class number that has the least number of zeros following the common digits. For example, anthologies from more than two literatures have the base number 808.8 to which other facets are added. Anthologies by period are introduced by two zeros, e.g., 808.8004. Anthologies by theme or feature are introduced by one zero, e.g., 808.8036 and therefore are to be preferred before an anthology by period. For example:

A collection of 18th-century world literature about friendship: 808.80353

808.80 Base number for Collections displaying specific features

353 Friendship (Table 3C)

The number 808.80353, meaning a collection of world literature about friendship, is preferred to the number 808.80033 meaning a collection of 18th-century literature because the former has fewer zeros. However, 808.80033 would be chosen if the period were emphasized. Furthermore, the standard subdivision —09033 18th century cannot be added after 808.80353 to bring out the period because the theme "friendship" is in an including note and therefore does not approximate the whole meaning of —353 in Table 3C.

10.6 ANTHOLOGIES OF AND CRITICISM OF LITERATURE IN A SPECIFIC LANGUAGE

When we deal with literature written in a specific language, we turn to 810–899. Moreover, both anthologies and criticism partake of subdivision —08 (collections) and standard subdivision —09 (historical treatment), when appropriate. For example, an anthology of English literature is classed in base number 82 plus —08 for collections, resulting in 820.8. Similarly, a history or criticism of English literature is classed in 820.9, and a history of Polish literature in 891.8509 (891.85 + 09). Further examples:

From sea to shining sea [a collection of American songs, tales, poems, and stories]. 810.8

81 Base number for American literature

08 Collections of literary texts in more than one form (Table 3B)

Imitating the Italians: Wyatt, Spenser, Synge, Pound, Joyce by Reed Way Dasenbrock. 820.9

82 Base number for English literature

09 History, description, critical appraisal of works in more than one form (Table 3B)

10.6.1 ANTHOLOGIES OF AND CRITICISM OF LITERATURE IN A SPECIFIC LANGUAGE AND ANOTHER FACET

The number for a collection or study of literature in a specific language that contains one other facet follows one of the citation orders:

8 + language + (form *or* period) + (−08 or −09)

8 + language + (−08 *or* −09) + feature/theme/person

10.6.1.1 FORM

For an anthology of literature in a specific form written in a specific language, the notation for the form (−1 for poetry, −2 for drama, etc.) with the subdivision −008 or −009 as displayed in Table 3B is added to the base number for the individual literature. For example:

An anthology of German poetry: 831.008

83 Base number for German literature

100 Poetry (Table 3B) (includes facet indicator 00)

8 Collections of literary texts (internal table under −1-8 in Table 3B)

A study of Japanese drama: 895.62009

895.6 Base number for Japanese literature

200 Drama (Table 3B) (includes facet indicator 00)

9 History, description, critical appraisal (internal table under −1-8 in Table 3B)

A history of Spanish fiction: 863.009

86 Base number for Spanish literature

300 Fiction (Table 3B) (includes facet indicator 00)

9 History, description, critical appraisal (internal table under −1-8 in Table 3B)

10.6.1.1.1 KIND OF FORM

Some works contain specimens of or deal with the literature of a specific language and a kind of literary form, i.e., a subgenre such as lyric poetry or historical fiction. Table 3B provides specific numbers for these kinds of literary forms. For example:

An anthology of English epic poetry: 821.03208

82	Base number for English literature
1032	Epic poetry (Table 3B)
08	Collections of literary texts (internal table under −102-108 in Table 3B)

A critical study of American historical fiction: 813.08109

81	Base number for American literature
3081	Historical and period fiction (Table 3B)
09	History, description, critical appraisal (internal table under −102-108 in Table 3B)

Standard subdivisions −01-07 may be added to a kind of literary form if the work consists equally of literary texts and history, description, critical appraisal. For example:

A journal of English dramatic poetry: 821.0205

82	Base number for English literature
102	Dramatic poetry (Table 3B)
05	Serial publications (Standard subdivision −05 as instructed in internal table under −102-108 in Table 3B)

10.6.1.2 PERIOD

A history of 20th-century English literature brings us to −09001-09009 in Table 3B, which provides us with numbers to attach to base number 82. The instructions say to add to −0900 notation for the appropriate period for each specific literature given in the schedules. The number for the 20th century under 820 English literature is 91, thus yielding −090091. The result is therefore 82 + 0900 + 91 = 820.90091. Another example:

German literature from the classical period: a collection: 830.8006

83	Base number for German literature
080	Collections of literary texts in more than one form (Table 3B) (includes facet indicator 0)
0	Additional facet indicator for −01-09 Specific periods (Table 3C)
6	Classical period (Period table under 830 German literature)

10.6.1.3 FEATURE/THEME/PERSONS

Table 3C enables us to extend —08 anthology and —09 criticism to represent specific themes, features, and persons. For example:

An anthology of English literature illustrating Romanticism: 820.80145

82	Base number for English literature
080	Collections of literary texts in more than one form (Table 3B) (includes facet indicator 0)
145	Romanticism (Table 3C)

For literature written for and by specific kinds of persons, numbers —8-9 from Table 3C are used. For example:

An anthology of Polish literature for children: 891.850809282

891.85	Base number for Polish literature
080	Collections of literary texts in more than one form (Table 3B) (includes facet indicator 0)
9282	[Literature for and by] Children (Table 3C)

Similarly, for a criticism or history of the literature in a specific language displaying specific features, themes, or persons, notation 09 from Table 3B may be extended by adding notation from Table 3C to express such themes and features. For example:

Language in her eye : views on writing and gender by Canadian women writing in English. 810.99287

81	Base number for Canadian literature
09	History, description, critical appraisal of works in more than one form (Table 3B)
9287	Women (Table 3C)

Similarly:

A critical appraisal of Romanticism in English literature: 820.9145

A critical appraisal of English literature for children: 820.99282

In Table 3C, under —93-99 Literature for and by persons resident in specific continents, countries, localities, there is an instruction to add to —9 numbers —3-9 from Table 2. For example:

An anthology of American literature by residents of New England: 810.80974

81	Base number for American literature
080	Collections of literary text in more than one form (Table 3B) (includes facet indicator 0)
9	Literature for and by persons resident in specific continents, countries, localities (from —93-99 in Table 3C)
74	New England (Table 2)

10.6.2 ANTHOLOGIES OF AND GENERAL CRITICISM OF LITERATURE IN A SPECIFIC LANGUAGE WITH TWO OTHER FACETS

The class number for a literary work in a specific language that contains two other facets has one of the following citation orders:

8 + language + form + period + —08 or —09
8 + language + form + —08 or —09 + feature/theme/persons
8 + language + —08 or —09 + feature/theme/persons + —09 +period
(from Table 1)

10.6.2.1 FORM AND PERIOD

The following examples illustrate the number-building process:

An anthology of 20th-century French poetry: 841.9108

84	Base number for literature
1	Poetry (Table 3B)
91	1900–1999 (Period table under 840.1–848)
0	Facet indicator as instructed under —11-19 in Table 3B
8	Collections of literary texts (internal table under —1-8 in Table 3B)

Similarly:

A critical study of 20th-century French poetry: 841.9109

10.6.2.2 FORM AND FEATURE/THEME/PERSONS

If the anthology or criticism focuses on a particular literary form, the form is expressed before adding the subdivision —008 or —009. In Table 3B, under —1-8 Specific forms, both —008 and —009 can be further extended by adding notation from Table 3C to express specific features, themes, or persons. The instructions indicate that the subdivisions —008 and —009 shown in the examples in section 9.6.1.1 may be further extended by adding —001-99 from Table 3C:

An anthology of German poetry illustrating classicism: 831.0080142

83	Base number for German literature
100	Poetry (Table 3B) (includes facet indicator 00)
80	Collections of literary texts displaying specific features (internal table under —1-8 in Table 3B)
142	Classicism (Table 3C)

Similarly, for poems written for or by specific kinds of persons, notation 1008, 1009, 2008, etc. from Table 3B may be extended by —8–9 from Table 3C:

American drama written for teenagers: a critical study: 812.0099283

81	Base number for American literature
200	Drama (Table 3B) (includes facet indicator 00)
9	History, description, critical appraisal (internal table under —1–8 in Table 3B)
9283	Literature for and by young people twelve to twenty (Table 3C)

An anthology of American poetry by residents of New England: 811.0080974

81	Base number for American literature
100	Poetry (Table 3B) (includes facet indicator 00)
80	Collections displaying specific features or emphasizing specific subjects, for and by specific kinds of persons (internal table under —1–8 in Table 3B) (includes facet indicator 0)
9	Literature for and by persons resident in specific continents, countries, localities (from —93–99 in Table 3C)
74	New England (Table 2)

A critical study of American poetry by residents of New England: 811.009974

If the work is in a particular kind of literary form, the number for collections —08 requires only one zero as instructed under —102–108 in Table 3B. For example:

Tales of the diamond: selected gems of baseball fiction [short stories] by William Price Fox [et al.]. 813.0108355

81	Base number for American literature
301	Short stories (Table 3B)
08	Collections of literary texts (internal table under —102–108 in Table 3B)
355	Sports (Table 3C)

10.6.2.3 PERIOD AND FEATURE/THEME/PERSONS

If the collection or criticism of literature in one language relates to a period and a feature, a theme, or is for and/or by specific kinds of persons, but is not in a particular form, the citation order in the class number varies slightly from those for other combinations. For example:

An anthology of 16th-century British literature on Ireland: 820.93241509031

82	Base number for English literature
09	History, description, critical appraisal (Table 3B)
32	Literature dealing with places (Table 3C)
415	Ireland (Table 2)
09031	16th century, 1500–1599 (Table 1)

In this case, because Tables 3B and 3C do not have provision to combine period and feature/theme/persons under −09, the feature/theme/persons facet takes precedence because the number 820.932415 contains fewer zeros than the number 820.9003 study of 16th-century English literature. The period is then added through the standard subdivision −09.

10.6.3 LITERATURE IN A PARTICULAR LANGUAGE WITH ALL FACETS

For works involving all facets (language, form, period, and feature/theme/persons), the citation order for the class number is:

> 8 + language + form (Table 3B) + period (from period tables under the base number in the schedules) + −08 or −09 + feature/theme/persons (Table 3C)

For example:

An anthology of 20th-century French poetry depicting seasons: 841.9108033

84	Base number for French literature
1	Poetry (Table 3B)
91	1900–1999 (Period table under 840.1-848)
0	Facet indicator as instructed under −11-19 (Table 3B)
80	Collections of literary texts displaying specific features (internal table under −1-8 in Table 3B) (includes facet indicator 0)
33	Times (Table 3C)

A critical study of 20th-century French poetry depicting seasons: 841.910933

84	Base number for French literature
1	Poetry (Table 3B)
91	1900–1999 (Period table under 840.1-848)
0	Facet indicator as instructed under −11-19 (Table 3B)
9	History, description, critical appraisal of texts displaying specific features (internal table under −1-8 in Table 3B)
33	Times (Table 3C)

Narrative time/descriptive time: lying, forgetting, and beyond in the [19th century] *French realist novel* by James H. Reid. 843.70912

84	Base number for French literature
3	Fiction (Table 3B)
7	19th century (Period table under 840.1-848)
0	Facet indicator as instructed under −31-39 (Table 3B)
9	History, description, critical appraisal of texts displaying specific features (internal table under −1-8 in Table 3B)
12	Realism (Table 3C)

10.7   USING TABLE 3C WITH OTHER CLASSES

Table 3C was originally designed for use with main class 800. Beginning with Edition 20, it has also been used with certain base numbers from main class 700. In Edition 21, its use has been extended to more numbers in 700. For example:

The grotesque in the arts: 700.415

700.41	Base number for Arts displaying specific qualities of style, mood, viewpoint
5	Number following —1 in —15 Symbolism, allegory, fantasy, myth (Table 3C—the grotesque is in an including note at —15)

Urban themes in the arts: 700.421732

700.4	Base number for Arts displaying specific themes and subjects
2	Number following —3 in —32 Places (Table 3C)
1732	Urban regions (Table 2)

Comedy films: 791.43617

791.4361	Base number for Films displaying specific qualities
7	Number following —1 in —17 Comedy (Table 3C)

Films portraying the Bible: 791.436822

791.436	Base number for Films dealing with specific themes and subjects
82	Number following —3 in —382 Religious themes (Table 3C)
2	Number following 2 in 220 Bible

10.8   SUMMARY

Literary works of the imagination are classed in main class 800. Collections of literary texts from more than two literatures are classed in 808.8, and the history, description, and critical appraisal (criticism) of such literature are classed in 809. Literatures written in specific languages are classed in 810–890. Most of these numbers may be extended by adding notation from Tables 3A–3C on instruction. Each literature that may be extended is listed with add instructions (or a note or asterisk leading to add instructions). Tables 3A–3C are not used with numbers for literatures lacking such instructions. Tables 3A–3C provide notation for bibliographic forms (e.g., collections); approaches (e.g., history); literary forms (e.g., poetry, drama) and kinds of literary forms (e.g., narrative poetry, comedy); and specific features (symbolism, plot) and themes (e.g., chivalry, travel), or persons (e.g., for and by children, women).

Class numbers for works of individual authors reflect the facets of language, form, and period. The base number for a literature is taken from the schedules, and is followed by the form notation from Table 3A, and the period notation that is given in the schedules under the base number for the specific literature in 810–890. Literary works by and literary criticism of individual authors (including criticism about their individual works) that are written in the same language, the same form, and the same period share the same number. Subdivisions —08 and —09 are not used for works by and about individual authors.

Collections and critical appraisal of literature in a particular language written by more than one author reflect the facets of language, form, period, and feature, theme, or persons. Notation for form and kind of form come from Table 3B, and the period notation is given in the schedules under the base number for the individual language in 810–890. Subdivisions —08 and —09 given in Table 3B many be extended by notation representing feature, theme, and persons from Table 3C, which in turn may be further extended by notation from other tables.

Notation from Table 3C may also be added directly to certain numbers in 808.8–809 and in main class 700 The arts.

10.9   EXERCISES

Exercise 1:

Classify the following works by or about individual authors:

(1)   Poems of Charles Baudelaire (French poet, 1821–1867)
(2)   A biography of Hans Christian Andersen (Danish writer of fairy tales, 1805–1875)
(3)   A critical study of Thomas Dekker's plays (British, 1572–1632)
(4)   Selected poetry of William Butler Yeats (Irish author, 1865–1939, writing in the English language)
(5)   Dramatic works of Eugene O'Neill (American, 1888–1953)
(6)   *Peter Pan*, an English novel by J.M. Barrie (1860–1937)
(7)   *The Adventures of Huckleberry Finn* by the American novelist Mark Twain (1835–1910)
(8)   A biography of Claus Silvester Dörner (German writer not limited to or chiefly identifiable with one specific form, 1913–   )
(9)   A collection of jokes by the American author Nancy Gray (1959–   )

Exercise 2:

Classify the following works from or on more than one literature:

(1)   A collection of sonnets
(2)   A collection of poetry by women
(3)   An anthology of nineteenth-century literature
(4)   A critical appraisal of lyric poetry
(5)   A collection of poetry displaying realism
(6)   A collection of poetry with marriage as the theme
(7)   A critical appraisal of romantic literature

Exercise 3

Classify the following works about one literature:

(1)   A study of symbolism in French literature
(2)   A history of twentieth-century English literature
(3)   A study of French women authors
(4)   A study of social themes in 15th-century English literature
(5)   A study of Portuguese literature by African authors
(6)   Discourses of salvation in English literature: an historical study

Exercise 4:

Classify the following works from one literature and in a particular form:

(1)   Collection of English lyric poetry on love
(2)   An anthology of English allegorical narrative poetry
(3)   A critical study of plots in American historical fiction
(4)   A study of English horror tales
(5)   A study of heroism in the English novel

Exercise 5:

Classify the following works from one literature with multiple facets:

(1)   Collection of Elizabethan English poetry
(2)   Love in twentieth-century American drama: a critical study
(3)   Collection of late twentieth-century American drama by teenagers
(4)   A study of the Berlin wall in East German fiction
(5)   A bibliography of English romantic poetry by women authors, 1770–1835

Exercise 6:

Classify the following works, using Table 3C with numbers from class 700:

(1) Fantasy films
(2) Horror programs on television
(3) Werewolves in the arts
(4) Atlantis in art and literature

CHAPTER 11
TABLE 4: SUBDIVISIONS OF INDIVIDUAL LANGUAGES AND TABLE 6: LANGUAGES

Objectives:

The objectives of this chapter are to explain: the basic structure and coverage of Tables 4 and 6; the classification of works relating to linguistics and languages that require the use of Table 4; and those cases in the schedules or tables that require the use of Table 6.

Outline:

11.0   INTRODUCTION

Tables 4 and 6 are treated together in this chapter because they both deal with languages. Table 4 is used with a limited span of numbers, 420–490 Specific languages. It provides notation for specific aspects, such as etymology and grammar, of individual languages. Table 6, on the other hand, is used throughout the Classification. It provides notation for groups of languages (such as Hellenic languages and Bantu languages) and for individual languages (such as Spanish and Zulu) as an aspect of a subject. The relationship of Table 6 with Table 5 Racial, Ethnic, National Groups is discussed in chapter 12.

11.1   INTRODUCTION TO TABLE 4

Table 4 Subdivisions of Individual Languages and Language Families is the simplest auxiliary table in the DDC. Simple in structure and application, it is used exclusively with the main numbers for individual languages and language families (420–490) in class 400 Language. Notation in this table, paralleling that for subdivisions under the general topic 410 Linguistics, has considerably eased number building in main class 400. In Table 4, linguistic elements, problems, and other aspects of linguistics are provided for separately. A summary of Table 4 is reproduced below:

Summary of Table 4

—01–09	Standard subdivisions
—1	Writing systems, phonology, phonetics of the standard form of the language
—2	Etymology of the standard form of the language
—3	Dictionaries of the standard form of the language
—5	Grammar of the standard form of the language
—7	Historical and geographic variations, modern nongeographic variations
—8	Standard usage of the language (Prescriptive linguistics) Applied linguistics

Notation from this table for recurring aspects such as etymology and grammar is to be combined, on instruction, with designated base numbers for individual languages in the schedules. The base number in this context is a compound number comprised of the main class digit 4 followed by the language number for that particular language. For example, in base number 42 English, 4 is the main class digit and 2 is the notation for English. For such reasons, 400 Language is considered to be one of the most highly faceted classes in the DDC. The base numbers for all the major languages of the world are enumerated and listed with add instructions (or a note or asterisk leading to add instructions). With a few minor exceptions, there is a close parallel between the base numbers for languages in main classes 400 Language and 800 Literature:

Language	Base number Language 400	Base number Literature 800
English	42	82
German	43	83
French	44	84
Hindi	491.43	891.43
Bengali	491.44	891.44

A base number from main class 400 combined with notation from Table 4 results in the complete class number. However, only those numbers that are listed with add instructions (or a note or asterisk leading to add instructions) may be extended by notation from Table 4.

Table 4 and Table 6: Languages / 153

11.2   DIVISION OF MAIN CLASS 400

The division of main class 400 Language is also similar to that of class 800 Literature. A single major exception is 410–419, designated for Linguistics in general, regardless of language. For example:

Etymology	412
Dictionaries	413
Grammar	415

Classes 401–409 are generalities of languages resulting from adding standard subdivisions (Table 1) to base number 400. For example:

401	Philosophy and theory [of language]
402	Miscellany
405	Serial publications

Specific Indo-European languages (except for East Indo-European and Celtic languages) are accommodated in the span 420–480. Within this span, each major Indo-European language is assigned its own division represented by a three-digit number with two meaningful digits:

420	English language
430	German language
440	French language
450	Italian language
460	Spanish and Portuguese languages
470	Latin language
480	Greek language

East Indo-European, Celtic, Oriental, and other languages have been grouped together at 490 Other languages. Examples include 491.7 Russian, 492.4 Hebrew, 492.7 Arabic, and 495.1 Chinese.

11.3   USING TABLE 4

As in the case of all the tables, notation in Table 4 Subdivisions of Individual Languages and Language Families is never used alone, but may be used as required with the base numbers for individual languages that are listed with add instructions (or a note or asterisk leading to add instructions) under 420–490.

Numbers from Table 4 and their subdivisions can be combined with base numbers in the schedules according to instruction under 420–490. The citation order of 420–490 is straightforward and regular:

Language + language subdivision from Table 4 + standard subdivision from Table 1

11.3.1 USING TABLE 4 WITH DESIGNATED BASE NUMBERS

In the print schedules, the asterisk by a number in the 400 class leads us, through the footnote at the bottom of each page, to the instructions under 420–490 Specific languages. The relevant instruction at 420–490 reads:

> Except for modifications shown under specific entries, add to base number for each language identified by * notation 01–8 from Table 4, e.g., grammar of Japanese 495.65. The base number is the number given for the language unless the schedule specifies a different number

Some examples of base numbers include:

429	*Old English (Anglo-Saxon)
469	*Portuguese
495.7	*Korean

In these cases, the base number for the language is the one shown in the number column.

In other cases, the use of Table 4 with the base number is explained through an add instruction:

> 491.701–.75 Standard subdivisions, writing systems, phonology, phonetics, etymology, dictionaries, grammar of Russian
> Add to base number 491.7 notation 01–5 from Table 4, e.g., grammar of Russian 491.75

In each case, it is the specified base number to which notation from Table 4 is added. For example, to build a number for a work on Portuguese grammar, we begin with the asterisked base number 469, since the language is the main subject. "Grammar" is a linguistic aspect whose number in Table 4 is −5. Hence the complete class number for our work is: 469.5, analyzed as follows:

| 469 | Base number for Portuguese |
| 5 | Grammar (Table 4) |

The following table, showing the use of different notation from Table 4 with different base numbers, illustrates its simple but efficacious use:

Language Elements

Language	Base Number	Etymology −2	Dictionary −3	Grammar −5
English	42	422	423	425
German	43	432	433	435
French	44	442	443	445
Hindi	491.43	491.432	491.433	491.435
Bengali	491.44	491.442	491.443	491.445

Table 4 and Table 6: Languages / 155

Further examples:

    Foreign words in English: 422.4

42	Base number for English
24	Foreign elements (Table 4)

    A study of Russian spellings: 491.7152

491.7	Base number for Russian
152	Spelling (Table 4)

    Hausa dialects: 493.727

493.72	Base number for Hausa
7	Dialects (Table 4)

    German dictionary of synonyms: 433.1

43	Base number for German
31	Specialized dictionaries (Table 4)

In the 420–490 schedules, some of the numbers show composites that either result from using Table 4 or are extensions of notation from Table 4:

421.52	Spelling (Orthography) and pronunciation [of standard English]
421.54	Standard American (U.S.) spelling and pronunciation
425	Grammar of standard English
427	Historical and geographic variations, modern nongeographic variations [of English]
451–453	Writing systems, phonology, phonetics, etymology, dictionaries of standard Italian
465	Grammar of standard Spanish

Note that a dictionary of the standard form of the language is classed in —3 instead of ss —03, e.g., dictionary of Italian 453. Some composite numbers can be further extended by notation from Table 2. For example:

427.1–.8	Geographic variations [dialects of English] in England Add to 427 the numbers following —42 in notation 421–428 from Table 2, e.g., dialects of London 427.1

    North Yorkshire dialect of English: 427.84

427	Historical and geographic variations [of English]
84	Number following —42 in —4284 for North Yorkshire (Table 2)

Variations in English in other parts of the world are classed in 427.9, which may be further subdivided by area:

    Indian English: 427.954

427	Historical and geographic variations [of English]
9	Geographic variations in other places
54	India (Table 2)

African English: 427.96

427	Historical and geographic variations [of English]
9	Geographic variations in other places
6	Africa (Table 2)

As usual, these built numbers may be further extended by standard subdivisions from Table 1:

An outline of German grammar for foreigners written in the 17th century: 438.2409032

43	Base number for German
824	Structural approach to expression for those whose native language is different (Table 4)
09032	Standard subdivision for 17th century (Table 1)

11.3.2 NUMBERS THAT CANNOT BE EXTENDED

It follows that a number in 420–490 without add instructions in the entry or an asterisk leading to add instructions cannot be extended by Table 4. For example:

A grammar of Middle English: 427.02

427.02 is in fact the number for Middle English proper. The notation for grammar from Table 4 cannot be added, because there is no add instruction for 427.02 Middle English. In other words, any language aspect of Middle English will get the number 427.02. For example, a work on the etymology of Middle English is also classed in 427.02.

Some of the subdivisions in Table 4 can be further extended by notation from Table 6. Such cases will be taken up later in the chapter in section 11.4.4.

11.4   INTRODUCTION TO TABLE 6

Table 6 Languages contains notation designating specific languages. Notation from this table may be added, when instructed, to numbers from the schedules or from other tables. The most important use of Table 6 is to provide the basis for building numbers in 490 and 890 for specific languages and literatures. In addition, numbers from Table 6 are used to extend Table 2 number —175 Regions where specific languages predominate; to extend Table 5 notation to represent languages spoken by specific peoples; and in combination with various numbers scattered throughout the tables and schedules.

Table 6 consists of a systematic list of various languages of the world grouped according to language family. Its summary is reproduced on the opposite page:

Table 4 and Table 6: Languages / 157

—1	Indo-European languages
—2	English and Old English (Anglo-Saxon)
—3	Germanic (Teutonic) languages
—4	Romance languages
—5	Italian, Sardinian, Dalmatian, Romanian, Rhaeto-Romanic
—6	Spanish and Portuguese
—7	Italic languages
—8	Hellenic languages
—9	Other languages

Each of these families is further subdivided hierarchically. The existence of this language table has made possible the representation of language as an aspect of a subject; examples are general serial publications in a particular language, or translations of the Bible in a particular language.

The main outline of the notation in Table 6 parallels that of the main numbers for languages in class 400 and for literatures in class 800. However, further subdivisions under each language may not correspond exactly to those in classes 400 and 800. For example, although the base number for the German language in 420–490 is 43 and for German literature is 83, the number for German in Table 6 is --31, not —3.

11.4.1 USING TABLE 6

Unlike Tables 3 and 4 which are used only with specific spans of numbers from the schedules, Table 6 is applicable in many places throughout the schedules and auxiliary tables. However, like other tables (except Table 1), notation from Table 6 is used only with explicit instruction in the schedules or other tables. For example, for a Bible in languages other than English, we follow the instruction given under 220.53–.59:

220.53–.59   Versions in other languages [other than English]
              Add to base number 220.5 notation 3–9 from Table 6

Following this instruction, we can build the following numbers:

Bible in the Ibo language: 220.596332
    220.5   Base number for Bible versions in other languages [other than English]
    96332   Ibo language (Table 6)

Bible in the French language: 220.541
    220.5   Base number for Bible versions in other languages [other than English]
    41   French language (Table 6)

Similarly:

> The New Testament in the Chinese language: 225.5951
>
> | | |
> |---|---|
> | 225 | Base number for the New Testament |
> | 5 | The number following 220 in 220.5 Modern versions and translations (with 220.53–.59 for versions in other languages [other than English]) |
> | 951 | Chinese language (Table 6) |
>
> Talmudic literature in English: 296.120521
>
> | | |
> |---|---|
> | 296.12 | Base number for Talmudic literature |
> | 05 | Translations (from internal table under 296.12–296.14) |
> | 21 | English language (Table 6) |

11.4.2 TABLE 6 NOTATION IN THE RELATIVE INDEX

Table 6, enumerating almost all the languages of the world, is a relatively long table. The world of languages is indeed exotic and large; the name of a particular language may often be unfamiliar. In such cases, the Relative Index can be of great assistance. In the index the numbers for all entries from Table 6 are preceded by the designation T6. For example:

> Mon-Khmer languages   495.93
>   T6—959 3

This means that in addition to the number in main class 400, Mon-Khmer languages also have a number in Table 6, —9593. In addition, the Relative Index also lists many built language numbers not enumerated in main class 400. For example:

> Mambwe language   496.391
>   T6—963 91

11.4.3 EXAMPLES ILLUSTRATING THE USE OF TABLE 6

The numbers 031–039 General encyclopedic works in specific languages and language families are divided on the basis of language. Class numbers for some general encyclopedias in major languages have been given ready-made numbers:

031	American English-language encyclopedias
032	General encyclopedic works in English
034	General encyclopedic works in French, Provençal, Catalan

These and other numbers in this span can be further specified with notation from Table 6. For example, the schedules list the number 036 for General

Table 4 and Table 6: Languages / 159

encyclopedias in Spanish and Portuguese, with the instruction to add to base number 036 the numbers following −6 in Table 6 numbers −61-69. Hence:

General encyclopedia in Spanish: 036.1
036   Base number for General encyclopedic works in Spanish and Portuguese
1   Spanish (from −61 in Table 6)

General encyclopedia in Portuguese: 036.9
036   Base number for General encyclopedic works in Spanish and Portuguese
9   Portuguese (from −69 in Table 6)

General encyclopedias[1] in languages other than those provided for in 031-038 are classed in 039, which may be further extended by Table 6. For example:

General encyclopedia in Chinese: 039.951
039   Base number for General encyclopedic works in Italic, Hellenic, other languages
951   Chinese (Table 6)

Similarly, 051-059 General periodicals in specific languages and language families are divided by language patterned after 031-039 General encyclopedias:

General periodical in Spanish: 056.1
General periodical in Chinese: 059.951

Table 6 is also used with 305.7, 372.65, and 398:

A social study of English-speaking people: 305.721
305.7   Base number for [Social] Language groups
21   English (Table 6)

French as a second language in elementary schools: 372.6541
372.65 Base number for Foreign languages in elementary education
41   French language (Table 6)

Judeo-Spanish folktales: 398.20467
398.204 Base number for Folk literature by language
67   Judeo-Spanish (Table 6)

English proverbs: 398.921
398.9   Base number for Proverbs
21   English (Table 6)

---

[1]It should be noted that while general encyclopedias are classed in 031-039, subject encyclopedias are classed with their respective subjects further extended by ss −03 from Table 1. For example, an encyclopedia of mathematics is classed at 510.3.

11.4.4 USING PARTIAL NOTATION FROM TABLE 6

Sometimes instead of adding a full number from Table 6 we are instructed to add only a part of a number from this table. For example:

Chinese calligraphy: 745.619951

745.6199 Base number for Other styles [of Calligraphy]
51 Number following 9 in −951 Chinese (Table 6)

One of the most important uses of Table 6 is to provide the basis for building certain specific language numbers in 490 Other languages and to provide the basis for building certain specific literature numbers in 890 Literature of other specific languages and language families.

Main class 400 provides many broad numbers for language families. In order to specify comparatively minor languages from a family group, the main numbers given in the schedules are extended with the use of notation from Table 6. For example:

496.33 Igboid, Defoid, Edoid, Idomoid, Nupoid, Oko, Ukaan-Akpes languages; Kwa languages; Kru languages
Add to 496.33 the numbers following −9633 in notation 96332–96338 from Table 6 . . .

Therefore:

The Ewe language: 496.3374

496.33 Base number for Igboid, Defoid . . . languages
74 Number following −9633 in −963374 Ewe (Table 6)

Similarly, under 495.92-.95 Viet-Muong, Mon-Khmer, Munda, Hmong-Mien (Miao-Yao) languages we are instructed to add to the base number 495.9 the numbers following −959 in numbers −9592-9597 from Table 6. The number for Munda languages in Table 6 is −9595. Hence a work about Munda languages is classed in 495.95.

Following the same pattern we can build class numbers in 800 for literatures in minor languages:

Swazi literature: 896.3987

11.4.4.1 CAUTION

The class number for a language or literature built by using notation from Table 6 cannot be further extended by Table 4 (or Table 3 as the case may be) unless the built number is listed with add instructions (or a note or asterisk

Table 4 and Table 6: Languages / 161

leading to add instructions) in the schedule. For example, the following numbers cannot be further extended:

Elamite languages:	499.93
Elamite grammar:	499.93
Elamite etymology:	499.93

On the other hand, in cases where the synthesized number for a particular language resulting from the combination of a base number and a notation from Table 6 is enumerated (precombined) in the schedules and listed with add instructions (or a note or asterisk leading to add instructions), the number may be further extended through the use of Table 4. For example:

494   Altaic, Uralic, Hyperborean, Dravidian languages
       Add to 494 the numbers following −94 in notation 941–948
       from Table 6, e.g., Mongolian 494.23, Altai 494.33; then to
       the number given for each language listed below add notation
       01–8 from Table 4, e.g., grammar of Mongolian 494.235

       .

       .

       .

       494.83 Brahui

Therefore:

Brahui grammar
       494.83 + 5 (Table 4) = 494.835

Brahui dictionary
       494.83 + 3 (Table 4) = 494.833

Similarly, in literature, a number resulting from the use of Table 6 may be further subdivided by notation from Table 3 as long as there are add instructions (or a note or asterisk leading to add instructions). For example:

896   African literatures
      Add to 896 the numbers following −96 in notation 961–965
      from Table 6 . . . then to the number given for each literature
      listed below add further as instructed at beginning of Table 3

      .

      .

      .

      896.3985 Xhosa

Xhosa poetry: 896.39851
  896   Base number for African literatures
  3985   Number following —96 in —963985 Xhosa (Table 6)
         (896.3985 is also enumerated in the schedule)
  1   Poetry (Table 3A or 3B)

11.5   USING TABLE 6 WITH TABLE 4: CLASSIFYING BILINGUAL DICTIONARIES

Upon instruction, Table 6 may also be used in combination with other tables. Its notation is often combined with notation from Table 4 to represent subjects that manifest two languages, as do bilingual dictionaries in which the entry words are given in one language and their meanings in another. The number-building formula for representing such dictionaries is:

Base number for first language + 3 (dictionaries from Table 4) + number for second language from Table 6

The first language is the one with entry words arranged alphabetically; its base number is found in main class 400 in the schedules. The number for the second language (the one in which meanings are given) is taken from Table 6. For example, for an English-French dictionary, English is the primary language, and the base number is taken from main class 400 Language. French, the language in which meanings are given, is taken from Table 6. Hence:

English-French dictionary: 423.41
  42   Base number for English from the schedules
  3   Dictionaries (Table 4)
  41   French (Table 6)

Similarly:

French-English dictionary: 443.21
English-Dutch dictionary: 423.3931
French-Korean dictionary: 443.957
Ibo-English dictionary: 496.332321

In fact, to build the number shown in the last example, Table 6 was used twice. The following analysis of the number illustrates the number-building process:

  496   Base number for African languages
  332   Number following 96 in —96332 Ibo (Table 6)
        (496.332 is also enumerated in the schedule)
  3   Dictionaries (Table 4)
  21   English language (Table 6)

Table 4 and Table 6: Languages / 163

As instructed under −32–39 in Table 4, a bilingual dictionary with entry words in both languages is classed with the language in which it will be more useful, with the addition of the notation for the second language after −3. For example, in most libraries in English-speaking regions, an English-Spanish, Spanish-English dictionary is classed with Spanish in 463.21. If classification with either language is equally useful, preference is given to the language coming later in the 420–490 sequence, for example, a French-Korean, Korean-French dictionary: 495.7341.

In addition to its use with numbers −32–39 in Table 4, Table 6 is also used with the following Table 4 numbers:

−042   Biligualism
−24   Foreign elements
−802   Translation to and from other languages
−824   Structural approach to expression for those whose native
        language is different
−834   Audio-lingual approach to expression for those whose native
        language is different
−864   Readers for those whose native language is different

The following examples illustrate the use of Table 6 with these numbers:

French words and phrases used in the Italian language: 452.441

45   Base number for Italian language
24   Foreign elements (Table 4)
41   French (Table 6)

Similarly:

Latin elements in the French language: 442.471
German grammar for English-speaking people: 438.2421
Audio-lingual approach to German for English-speaking people:
  438.3421
German reader for English-speaking people: 438.6421

11.6   USING TABLE 6 WITH OTHER TABLES

In addition to its use with Table 4, Table 6 may also be used in conjunction with other tables. For example, Table 6 notation is used to extend Table 2 number −175 Regions where specific languages predominate to define an area where a particular language predominates. Thus, regions of the world where English is spoken is represented by −17521, i.e., −175 (Table 2) + −21 (Table 6). As shown in the following cases, this subdivision can be used whenever there is any instruction to add area number −1:

Wages in English-speaking countries of the world: 331.2917521

331.29	Historical, geographic, persons treatment of compensation
175	Regions where specific languages predominate (Table 2)
21	English (Table 6)

General libraries in the French-speaking world: 027.017541

027.0	Base number for Geographic treatment [of General libraries] (final 0 is facet indicator)
175	Regions where specific languages predominate (Table 2)
41	French (Table 6)

The use of Table 6 with Table 5 is discussed in chapter 12.

11.7 SUMMARY

Tables 4 and 6 have been treated together in this chapter because of the complementary relationship between the two. Table 4 contains numbers representing various problems, aspects and tools of linguistics as they relate to individual languages; it is patterned after sections 411–419 of the schedules. It is used exclusively with 420–490 Specific languages. Only those entries in 420–490 that contain add instructions, or a note or asterisk leading to add instructions, may be extended by notation from Table 4. The divisions 420–490 represent almost all the languages of the world. Class numbers for some minor languages that are not enumerated in 420–490 can be built with the use of Table 6. In application, Table 4 is the simplest of all the seven auxiliary tables in the DDC. In some cases Table 4 can be further extended by Table 6, e.g., for classifying bilingual dictionaries.

Table 6 contains a systematic listing of all the major and minor languages of the world grouped according to language families. The outline of Table 6 parallels that of 420–490, but it provides greater detail for individual languages. Used with many numbers in the schedules as well as with other auxiliary tables, notation from Table 6 is applied on instruction only. In many cases, it is added to a base number to specify the language in which a subject is treated in a document. In other cases, it may be used to extend a number from another table.

Table 4 and Table 6: Languages / 165

11.8 EXERCISES

Exercise 1:

Classify the following topics with the use of Table 4:
(1) Phonology of Slovak
(2) An introduction to Middle Dutch
(3) Norwegian grammar
(4) English verb tables for ESL (English as a second language) speakers
(5) Grammar of Portuguese language

Exercise 2:

Classify the following topics with the use of Table 6:
(1) German-language encyclopedia
(2) A study of Ojibwa (a North American native language)
(3) Arabic folktales from Israel
(4) English-speaking people in Africa: a social study
(5) General encyclopedia in Thai
(6) General periodicals in Norwegian (New Norse)
(7) Spanish quotations
(8) Introduction to Huambisa (a South American native language)

Exercise 3:

Classify the following topics with the use of both Table 4 and Table 6:
(1) Chinese-English dictionary
(2) Finnish-English dictionary
(3) Spanish reader for English-speaking people
(4) Latin words in the German language
(5) Conversational English for Russian-speaking people

Exercise 4:

Classify the following topics with the use of Table 6 through Table 2:
(1) School enrollment in the French-speaking world
(2) Conservation of national resources in the Spanish-speaking world

CHAPTER 12

TABLE 5: RACIAL, ETHNIC, NATIONAL GROUPS AND TABLE 7: GROUPS OF PERSONS

Objectives:

The objectives of this chapter are to explain: the basic structure and coverage of Tables 5 and 7; the classification of works relating to groups of persons identified by different characteristics; those cases in the schedules or tables that require the use of Tables 5 and 7; and the use of Tables 5 and 7 in conjunction with another table.

Outline:

12.0   INTRODUCTION

Tables 5 and 7 are treated together here because both deal with persons identified by specific characteristics. Use of Table 5 or 7 is not exclusive to any class; either one may be used upon instruction with numbers from many classes throughout the schedules. Furthermore, numbers from either one may be added to certain notation from other Tables. When they are added to standard subdivision —088 or —089 from Table 1, their use becomes universal because a standard subdivision may be added whenever appropriate.

12.1   INTRODUCTION TO TABLE 5

Table 5 lists persons systematically according to their racial, ethnic, and national origins. It is usually applied via an add instruction given in the schedules. Its notation can also be added to any class number through the ss —089 Specific racial, ethnic, national groups. Here the ss —089 works as a facet indicator. This

Table 5 and Table 7: Groups of Persons / 167

provision (made for the first time in Edition 19) has universalized the use of Table 5, because notation from Table 1 is applicable to any number in the schedules without specific instructions. Thus, a class number can be built for any subject studied amongst or in relation to any racial, ethnic or national group, even when there is no explicit instruction to this effect. However, adding Table 5 notation directly to a base number, if allowed, is preferred over using ss —089.

A summary of Table 5 is reproduced below:

—03-04   [Basic races, mixtures of basic races]
—1   North Americans
—2   British, English, Anglo-Saxons
—3   Nordic (Germanic) people
—4   Modern Latin peoples
—5   Italians, Romanians, related groups
—6   Spanish and Portuguese
—7   Other Italic peoples
—8   Greeks and related groups
—9   Other racial, ethnic, national groups

Each division listed above is further divided hierarchically. The name of each racial, ethnic, and national group enumerated in the table is indexed in the Relative index, where each notation from Table 5 is preceded by the symbol T5. For example:

African Americans	T5—96073
Asians	T5—95
Caucasoid race	T5—034
Russians	T5—917 1
Swedes	T5—397

In Table 5, "ethnic group" normally refers to a group with linguistic ties; it can also mean a group with cultural or racial ties. The numbers for basic races —034-036 are used only for works that treat race very broadly. For example, T5—036 is used for Black peoples wherever they originated, while T5—96 is used for Black peoples of African origin.

12.1.1 CITATION AND PREFERENCE ORDER IN TABLE 5

Because some people can be categorized by more than one characteristic as in the case of national groups of foreign origins and noncitizen residents, a citation order (when numbers can be combined to show multiple facets) and preference order (when numbers cannot be combined and a choice must be made between two or more numbers) are needed to maintain consistency in treatment. In Table 5, the generally preferred citation order is (1) ethnic group, (2) nationality, and (3) basic races. For example, T5—13 means people of the United States, but T5—68073 means Spanish Americans in the United States (where —68 means Spanish Americans and —73 [from Table 2] means United States). In a few cases, however, the citation order is reversed to nationality over ethnic group, for example, T5—114 Canadians of French origin, where —11 denotes Canadians and —4 (from Table 2) denotes France.

When choosing between two ethnic groups, preference is given to the group for which the notation is different from that of the nationality of the people. For example, a work treating equally the Hispanic and native American heritage of bilingual Spanish-Guaraní mestizos of Paraguay is classed in —983820892 Guaraní-speaking people in Paraguay (not —68892 Paraguayans as a Spanish-American national group). When choosing between two national groups, preference is given to the former or ancestral national group instead of the current national group. For example, a work dealing with people from Ukraine who have become United States citizens is classed in —91791073 Ukrainians in the United States (not —13 People of the United States).

12.2   USING TABLE 5 ON SPECIFIC INSTRUCTIONS

Upon instruction, Table 5 notation may be added directly to a base number. Let us take an example: Ethnopsychology of the Jewish people. The class number for ethnopsychology given in the Relative Index is 155.82. Upon consulting the schedules, we find that the ethnopsychology of specific racial and ethnic groups is classed in 155.84.

155.84   [Ethnopsychology of] Specific racial and ethnic groups
              Add to base number 155.84 notation 03–99 from Table 5,
              e.g., ethnopsychology of African Americans 155.8496073

The notation for Jews in Table 5 is —924. Hence the complete class number is: 155.84924. Further examples:

A sociological study of the German people: 305.831
      305.8   Base number for [Sociology of] Racial, ethnic, national groups
      31   Germans (Table 5)

Australian native art: 704.039915
      704.03   Base number for History and description [of Fine and
                decorative arts] with respect to racial, ethnic, national groups
      9915   Australian native peoples (Table 5)

Polish folk music: 781.629185
      781.62   Base number for Folk music of specific racial, ethnic, national
                groups
      9185   Polish people (Table 5)

Table 5 and Table 7: Groups of Persons / 169

A history of twentieth-century literature by African authors: 809.8896

809.889	Base number for Literature for and by persons of other racial, ethnic, national groups
6	Number following −9 in −96 Africans and people of African descent (Table 5)

The result of synthesis may be further extended by adding a standard subdivision. For example:

Australian aboriginal art exhibited in the United States: 704.039915007473

704.03	Base number for History and description [of Fine and decorative arts] with respect to racial, ethnic, national groups
9915	Australian native peoples (Table 5)
00	Facet indicator to introduce standard subdivisions (double zeros used according to instructions at beginning of Table 5)
74	Standard subdivision for Museums, collections, exhibits (Table 1)
73	United States (Table 2)

12.3 EXTENDING TABLE 5 NUMBERS BY NOTATION FROM TABLES 2 AND 6

Numbers from Table 5 may be extended by area notation from Table 2 and partial notation from Table 6. Extensions using area notation can be achieved in two ways:

(1) through 0 (zero) as instructed in a general note at the beginning of Table 5;

(2) by adding an area notation directly to a Table 5 notation when specifically instructed. In such cases there is no need of a zero as a facet indicator.

12.3.1 EXTENDING TABLE 5 NOTATION USING ZERO AS A FACET INDICATOR

Instructions given at the beginning of Table 5 indicate that each number from this table may be further extended by adding a notation from Table 2, unless there is specific instruction to do otherwise or unless it is redundant. The general instruction at the beginning of Table 5 reads:

Except where instructed otherwise, and unless it is redundant, add 0 to the number from this table and to the result add notation 1 or 3–9 from Table 2 for area in which a group is or was located . . . If notation from Table 2 is not added, use 00 for standard subdivisions . . .

As a result, almost any number in Table 5 may be extended by area notation through 0, and there is no need for any specific instruction under the particular number. For example, the number for the Chinese in Brazil is —951081: —951 (Table 5) + 0 + 81 (Table 2). On the other hand, the number for the Chinese in China is —951, since adding —051 here would be redundant.

Now let us take some examples:

A study of the social status of Jews in Germany: 305.8924043

305.8	Base number for [Sociology of] Racial, ethnic, national groups
924	Jews (Table 5)
0	Facet indicator (as instructed at the beginning of Table 5)
43	Germany (Table 2)

Jews as a minority in Germany: a political study: 323.11924043

323.11	Base number for [Civil rights and political rights of] Specific racial, ethnic, national groups
924	Jews (Table 5)
0	Facet indicator (as instructed at the beginning of Table 5)
43	Germany (Table 2)

Similarly:

A social study of German nationals in the United States: 305.831073

Civil rights of African Americans in the United States: a political study: 323.1196073

12.3.2 EXTENDING TABLE 5 NOTATION BY OTHER MEANS

Some of the numbers in Table 5 may be further subdivided directly by notation from Table 2, without using the facet indicator 0. For example, under —687-688 [Spanish-American] National groups, we are instructed to add to base number —68 Table 2 numbers —7-8 to get the number for a specific national group. Therefore, for Chilean nationals we have: —68 (Table 5) + 83 (Table 2) = —6883.

Under 909.04 [World] History with respect to racial, ethnic, national groups, we find the following instruction:

Add to base number 909.04 notation 03-99 from Table 5, e.g., world history of Jews 909.04924; then add 0 and to the result add the numbers following 909 in 909.1-909.8, e.g., world history of Jews in 18th century 909.0492407

Table 5 and Table 7: Groups of Persons / 171

Therefore:

World history of Romany people in the 20th century: 909.0491497082

909.04	Base number for World history with respect to racial, ethnic and national groups
91497	Romany people (Table 5)
0	Facet indicator as instructed under 909.04
82	The number following 909 in 909.82, 20th century

12.3.3 EXTENDING TABLE 5 NOTATION BY TABLE 6

Table 5 numbers —94, —96, —97, —98, and —99 may be extended on instruction with notation from Table 6 to represent peoples who speak, or whose ancestors spoke, specific languages. In this way, the detailed development for languages in Table 6 does not have to be repeated in Table 5. For example:

—98	South American native peoples Add to base number —98 the numbers following —98 in notation 982–984 from Table 6, e.g., Quechua —98323; then add further as instructed at beginning of Table 5, e.g., Quechua in Bolivia —98323084

Therefore:

Arawakans in Colombia: —98390861

—98	Base number for South American native peoples (Table 5)
323	Number following —98 in —98323 Arawakan languages (Table 6)
0	Facet indicator for area notation
861	Colombia (Table 2)

Note that notation for a people built using Table 5 + Table 6 may be further extended by Table 2 as explained above.

12.4 ADDING A PART OF A NUMBER FROM TABLE 5

In some cases, a part of a Table 5 number is added to a base number. For instance, some of the lesser known religions are not enumerated under 290–299 in the schedules but are built by using a portion of Table 5 notation. For example, in the schedules we find:

299.1–.4	Religions of Indo-European, Semitic, North African, North and West Asian, Dravidian origin Add to base number 299 the numbers following —9 in notation 91–94 from Table 5, e.g., Druidism 299.16

Hence:

Mithraism, an ancient Iranian religion: 299.15

| 299 | Base number for Religions of Indo-European, Semitic, North African, North and West Asian, Dravidian origin |
| 15 | Number following —9 in —915 Iranians (Table 5) |

12.5 USING TABLE 5 THROUGH STANDARD SUBDIVISION —089

In Edition 18 the use of Table 5 was restricted in the sense that it could be used only according to specific instructions in the schedules. Since Edition 19 its use has been universalized through use with standard subdivision —089. The combination of Table 1 and Table 5 notation can be freely added to any class number in the schedules when appropriate:

—089 03–089 9 [History and description with respect to] Specific racial, ethnic, national groups

> Add to base number —089 notation 03–9 from Table 5, e.g., the subject with respect to Chinese —089951, with respect to Chinese in United States —089951073

For example:

Dolls made by Hopi Indians: 745.592210899745

745.59221	Base number for Dolls
089	Standard subdivision for Specific racial, ethnic, national groups (Table 1)
9745	Hopi (Table 5)

Reading habits of Spanish Americans in the United States: 028.908968073

028.9	Base number for Reading interests and habits
089	Standard subdivision for Specific racial, ethnic, national groups (Table 1)
68	Spanish Americans (Table 5)
0	Facet indicator as instructed at the beginning of Table 5
73	United States (Table 2)

12.6 USING TABLE 5 THROUGH TABLE 3C

In Table 3C the subdivision —8 Literature for and by persons of racial, ethnic, national groups is further subdivided by using notation from Table 5 to specify individual groups. For example:

Table 5 and Table 7: Groups of Persons / 173

A collection of African American literature: 810.80896073

81	Base number for American literature
080	Collections of literary texts in more than one form (Table 3B) (includes facet indicator 0)
8	Literature for and by persons of racial, ethnic, national groups (Table 3C)
96073	African Americans (United States) (Table 5)

12.7   INTRODUCTION TO TABLE 7

Table 7 Groups of persons contains notation designating persons by specific occupational and other characteristics. Its most important use is to provide subdivisions under standard subdivisions —024 Works for specific types of users and —088 History and description with respect to occupational and religious groups in Table 1. Notation from Table 7 is also used with 305.909–.999 Sociology of occupational groups as well as with various other numbers throughout the schedules.

Two main categories of people are defined in Table 7:

(1)   persons denoted by —01-08 categorized by gender, kinship, age, social, economic, physical, mental, and other individual and personal characteristics; and

(2)   persons characterized by their subject expertise/profession, denoted by the spans —091–097 and —1-9. For example, in Table 7, —092 means persons occupied with library and information science; —093 means encyclopedists. The divisions of —1-9 Specialists parallel main classes 100-900. This mnemonic feature facilitates greatly the task of locating a notation for a given group of people. For example, physicians are represented by —61, a parallel of 610 Medicine in the schedules. Similarly mathematicians in Table 7 are denoted by —51.   One must consult Table 7 for the exact notation; there are some differences between Table 7 and the schedules, e.g., students are classed in 371.8 in 370 Education, and —375 in Table 7.

The summary of Table 7 is reproduced below:

—01-09	[Persons by various nonoccupational characteristics; generalists, novices]
—1	Persons occupied with philosophy, parapsychology and occultism, psychology
—2	Persons occupied with or adherent to religion
—3	Persons occupied with the social sciences and socioeconomic activities

−4	Persons occupied with languages, linguistics, lexicography
−5	Persons occupied with natural sciences and mathematics
−6	Persons occupied with applied sciences (Technologists)
−7	Persons occupied with the arts Persons occupied with fine and decorative arts
−8	Persons occupied with creative writing and speaking
−9	Persons occupied with geography, history, related disciplines and activities

Note that −2 pertains to persons as scholars of religion, as religious officials/ leaders, and as the followers of a religion.

12.7.1 USING TABLE 7

Like Table 5, Table 7 is also used in two ways:

(1) adding Table 7 notation on specific instructions in the schedules or in another table

(2) adding Table 7 notation to ss −088 in Table 1 and using the combination as a standard subdivision

12.8 USING TABLE 7 ON SPECIFIC INSTRUCTIONS

As in the case of Table 5, notation from Table 7 may be added directly, on instruction, to a base number. For example, in the schedules we find:

704.04−.87   History and description [of the fine and decorative arts] with respect to miscellaneous kinds of persons
Add to base number 704 notation 04−87 from Table 7, e.g., women as artists 704.042 . . .

As a result:

Muslim artists: 704.2971

704	Base number for History and description [of the fine and decorative arts] with respect to miscellaneous kinds of persons
2971	Islam (Table 7)

In 174 ethics, after enumerating ethics for some of the professions, ethics for the rest of the professions is classed at 174.9. There we are asked to add to the base number 174.9 the appropriate notation from Table 7. For example:

Ethics of librarianship: 174.9092

174.9	Base number for [Ethics of] Other professions and occupations
092	Person occupied with library and information science (Table 7)

Table 5 and Table 7: Groups of Persons / 175

12.8.1 ADDING A PART OF A NUMBER FROM TABLE 7

Sometimes we are instructed to add a part of a number from Table 7. For example, in the schedules, we find:

> 305.6   [Social group:] Religious groups
> > Add to base number 305.6 the number following −2 in notation 21–29 from Table 7, e.g., Christian Scientists 305.685 . . .

As a result:

Social status of Roman Catholics: 305.62

| 305.6 | Base number for [social status of] Religious groups |
| 2 | Number following −2 in −22 Roman Catholic Church (Table 7) |

Social status of Buddhists: 305.6943

| 305.6 | Base number for [social status of] Religious groups |
| 943 | Number following −2 in −2943 Buddhism (Table 7) |

12.9 USING TABLE 7 IN CONJUNCTION WITH OTHER TABLES

As in the case of Tables 2, 5, and 6, notation from Table 7 may be used as extensions of notation from other tables.

12.9.1 USING TABLE 7 WITH TABLE 1 STANDARD SUBDIVISIONS

Certain numbers in Table 1 may be extended by notation from Table 7. Among these, the most frequently used standard subdivision is −088. Whenever a situation warrants using Table 7 Persons but there is no official instruction to add directly, we can still express the persons aspect by adding a notation from Table 7 through ss −088 [History and description with respect to] Specific occupational and religious groups. For example:

Nonordained ministry in the Catholic Church: 262.1508822

262.15	Base number for Laity
088	Standard subdivision for [History and description with respect to] Specific occupational and religious groups (Table 1)
22	Number for Roman Catholic Church (Table 7)

History of the Puritans in seventeenth-century England: 942.0608825

942.0	Base number for a history of England, 1603– (includes facet indicator 0)
6	Number following 941.0 in 941.06 for House of Stuart and Commonwealth periods, 1603–1714
088	Standard subdivision for [History and description with respect to] Specific occupational and religious groups (Table 1)
25	Number for Puritanism (Table 7)

Another standard subdivision that can be extended by adding notation from Table 7 is —024.

> —024 The subject for persons in specific occupations
> Add to base number —024 notation 09–9 from Table 7,
> e.g., the subject for engineers —02462

The combination of —02462 can then be used as a standard subdivision with a main number. For example:

Internal medicine and surgery for dentists: 616.00246176

> 616 Base number for Internal medicine
> 0024 Standard subdivision for The subject for persons in specific occupations (Table 1)
> 6176 [Persons occupied with] Dentistry (Table 7)

Note that the ss —024 has been added with an extra zero as prescribed under 616. Similarly:

Geometry for sculptors: 516.0024731

> 516 Base number for Geometry
> 0024 Standard subdivision for The subject for persons in specific occupations (Table 1)
> 731 [Persons occupied with] Sculpture (Table 7)

12.9.2 USING TABLE 7 WITH TABLE 2 GEOGRAPHIC AREAS

Table 2 number —176 can be extended by adding notation from Table 7. For example, in Table 2, we find:

> —176 Regions where specific religions predominate
> —176 2–176 9 Other religions
> Add to base number —176 the number following —29 in notation 292-299 from Table 7, e.g., regions where Islam predominates —17671

Similarly, the area notation for regions where Buddhism predominates is represented by —17643 (43 is the number following —29 in —2943 Buddhism from Table 7). The combinations formed according to these instructions can then be used whenever area number —176 applies. For example:

General libraries in Islamic countries: 027.017671

> 027.0 Base number for Geographic treatment [of General libraries]
> 176 Regions where specific religions predominate (Table 2)
> 71 The number following —29 in —2971 Islam (Table 7)

Table 5 and Table 7: Groups of Persons / 177

When area notation cannot be added directly to a number in the schedules, the combination of Table 2 notation with Table 7 notation can be achieved through ss —09. For example:

Civil and political rights in Buddhist countries: 323.0917643

323	Base number for Civil and political rights
09	Standard subdivision 09 (Table 1)
176	Regions where specific religions predominate (Table 2)
43	The number following —29 in —2943 Buddhism (Table 7)

Here we are using three auxiliary tables simultaneously.

12.9.3 USING TABLE 7 IN CONJUNCTION WITH TABLE 3

In Table 3C under —352 Specific kinds of persons [as themes and subjects of arts and literature], we are instructed to add to —352 numbers —03-99 from Table 7, e.g., women —352042.

The following examples show the use of Table 7 in conjunction with Table 3 in numbers built for literary works.

Portrayal of women in German literature: a critical evaluation: 830.9352042

83	Base number for German literature
09	Critical appraisal (Table 3B)
352	Literature dealing with specific kinds of persons (Table 3C)
042	Females (Table 7)

Also in Table 3C under —9204–9279 [Literature for and by] Persons of specific occupational and miscellaneous characteristics, there is an instruction to add numbers —04–79 from Table 7 to base number —92. For example:

English poetry by scientists: a collection: 821.0080925

82	Base number for English literature
100	Poetry (Table 3B) (includes facet indicator 00)
80	Collections for and by specific kinds of persons (internal table under —1–8 in Table 3B)
92	For and by persons of specific classes (Table 3C)
5	Persons occupied with natural sciences and mathematics (Table 7)

12.10   ORDER OF PREFERENCE IN TABLE 7

In Table 7, under —03-08 Persons by various nonoccupational characteristics, there is the following note:

> Unless other instructions are given, class a subject with aspects in two or more subdivisions of Table 7 in the number coming last, e.g., gifted upper middle-class Jewish male young adults —0829 (*not* —0622, —0562, —041, or —03924)

For example:

Upper-class retired persons
     —0696 Retired persons; *not* —0621 Upper classes

Upper-class middle-aged persons
     —0621 Upper classes; *not* —0564 Middle adulthood

Applying the notation above to full numbers results in:

Upper-class retired persons as artists
     704.0696 *not* 704.0621

Upper-class middle-aged persons as artists
     704.0621 *not* 704.0564

12.11   SUMMARY

Table 5 contains a list of persons categorized by their racial, ethnic or national characteristics. Table 7 lists persons characterized primarily by their occupations and professions. It also includes groups of persons characterized by certain personal and social traits such as age, health, economic and family status. Subdivisions —091–097 designate persons occupied with generalia subjects, and subdivisions —1–9 designate persons occupied with major disciplines. Divisions of —1–9 in Table 7 closely and mnemonically parallel the divisions of main classes 100–900 in the schedules. This parallelism facilitates the location or identification of numbers in Table 7.

Tables 5 and 7 are used throughout the schedules and other tables, and are not exclusive to any one class. Both tables may be used upon instruction in two ways: directly with numbers in the schedules or tables, and through standard subdivisions —089 for Table 5 and —024 and —088 for Table 7. Thus the universalization of the use of Tables 5 and 7 has made possible the classification of very minute subjects, bringing out the aspect of persons with regard to a particular subject.

Table 5 and Table 7: Groups of Persons / 179

12.12   EXERCISES

Exercise 1:

Classify the following topics with the use of Table 5:

(1)   Folksongs of the Romany people

(2)   The Dutch people (a social study)

(3)   Jewish art

(4)   Religion of the Hittites

(5)   Traditional religion of Zulus (an African ethnic group)

(6)   Contemporary Australian aboriginal paintings

Exercise 2:

Classify the following topics with the use of Table 7:

(1)   Jain artists

(2)   Ethics of social scientists

(3)   Church work with Catholic college students

(4)   Reader advisory services for scientists in libraries

(5)   Statistical mathematics for librarians

(6)   Introduction to law for police officials

Exercise 3:

Classify the following topics with the use of Table 7 through Table 2:

(1)   Islamic decorative arts

(2)   Economic conditions in Islamic countries

(3)   Adult education in Islamic countries

CHAPTER 13
NUMBER BUILDING FOR COMPLEX SUBJECTS

Objectives:

The objectives of this chapter are to explain: multiple synthesis; and multiple synthesis in various subject areas.

Outline:

13.0   INTRODUCTION

In the DDC, multitopical or multi-aspect subjects are referred to as *complex subjects*. Because of its provisions for building numbers, Dewey is able to accommodate many such subjects. Although the system is neither totally faceted nor does it allow for unlimited synthesis, many aspects of a subject can be expressed through number building. Previous chapters discussed and illustrated the number-building processes that use notation from the schedules and from one or two tables simultaneously. This chapter discusses cases where multiple elements taken from both the schedules and the tables are put together to form complex numbers.

With each edition of the DDC, especially since Edition 17, we have witnessed the progressive use of *multiple synthesis*, in other words, the combining of multiple elements to form complex numbers. Multiple synthesis has been made possible both by the increasing number of "add" notes in the schedules, and by the provision of separate auxiliary tables. Theoretically speaking, multiple synthesis is a simple extension of add instructions or number building (discussed in chapter 7 and elaborated in chapters 8–12). The basic problem again is how to identify the correct base number, locate the notation to be added, and decide on the citation order. In a complex subject, many aspects may seem equal contenders for the base number. Choice of the appropriate one will depend upon the classifier's knowledge of the structure of the Classification and his or her perception of the facet of primary importance. This is a somewhat elusive skill which improves constantly with practice; at times, however, it requires intuitive insight. One simple test is that the correct base number is often followed by an add note, except, of course, for those cases in which standard subdivisions are appropriate. In building numbers, one must proceed slowly and make sure to follow instructions carefully. At times it may be necessary to move forward and backward among different parts of the DDC schedules and tables. Once a number is built, the schedules must be checked again to ensure that the resulting number does not conflict with any number or instructions in the schedules.

The following sections illustrate complex number building with multiple notation from the schedules and tables. The discussion and examples are loosely grouped by subject area.

13.1   MULTIPLE SYNTHESIS IN THE SOCIAL SCIENCES

In the topic Administration of science libraries, there are two main facets:

(1)   Library administration
(2)   Science library

The second facet in turn comprises two subfacets:

(1)   Special libraries
(2)   Science

In the schedules, we find:

> 025.19   Administration of specific types of institutions [i.e. libraries, archives, information centers]

We also find:

> 026   Libraries, archives, information centers devoted to specific subjects and disciplines

Number 025.19 can be extended by type of library; 026 can be extended by the subject or discipline of the library. Under 026.001–.999 the instruction reads:

> Add to base number 026 notation 001–999, e.g., medical libraries 026.61; however, do not add notation 068 from Table 1 for organizations and management; class in 025.19

Since our work is on administration (management), the second part of the add instruction leads us back to 025.19. At 025.19, we encounter the following instruction:

> Add to base number 025.19 the numbers following 02 in 026–027

This leads us back 026. Adding the number for science (500) without the zero fillers (00) to 6 (the number following 02 in 026) results in:

6 + 500 = 65 (the number for libraries devoted to science subjects)

Adding this to 025.19 results in the correct class number: 025.1965. The number may also be analyzed as:

025.19	Base number for Administration of specific types of libraries
6	Number following 02 in 026 Libraries devoted to specific subjects and disciplines
5	Number 500 Science with the zeros removed

This number can be extended further by standard subdivisions from Table 1:

Journal of administration of science libraries

025.1965 + 05 (Table 1) = 025.196505

Let us take another case:

International law for trade in agricultural products: 341.75471

341.7547	Base number for [International law of] Trade in specific commodities and groups of commodities
1	Number following 380.14 in 380.141 Products of agriculture

To proceed further, say to classify a work on international law pertaining to trade in wheat, under 380.141 we are instructed to add the number following 63 in 633–638. Following the instruction, we arrive at the number for the specific commodity wheat:

International law for trade in wheat: 341.75471311

341.75471	Number built previously
311	Number following 63 in 633.11 Wheat

News coverage of coal miners' strikes in the United States: 070.4493318928223340973

070.449	Base number for [Journalism relating to] Specific subjects
3318928	Number for Strikes in extractive, manufacturing, construction industries and occupations
2233	Number following 6 in 622.33 [Mining of] Coal, graphite, solid and semisolid bitumens
4	Number following 553.2 in 553.24 Bituminous and semibitumenous coal
0973	Standard subdivision for the United States (Table 1 + Table 2)

International trade of Rouen, France, 1950–1990: 382.450009442509045

382.4	Base number for International commerce by products and services
5	Number following 380.14 in 380.145 Products of secondary industries and services
0009	Standard subdivision for Historical, geographic, persons treatment (Table 1) (extra zeros from 380.1450001–.1450009)
4425	Area notation for Rouen (Table 2)
09	Notation for Historical and geographic treatment (internal table under −093–099 in Table 1)
045	Number following −09 in −09045 [late 20th century] (Table 1)

A pictorial work portraying Turks in Vorarlberg, Austria:
943.645004943500222

9	Base number for History of specific localities (internal table at 930–990)
43645	Vorarlberg province, Austria (Table 2)
004	Racial, ethnic, national groups (internal table under 930–990)
943	Turkic peoples (Table 5)
5	Number following −943 in notation 9435 Turkish (Table 6)
00222	Standard subdivision for pictorial works

13.1.1 PUBLIC ADMINISTRATION

The schedule for public administration has been completely revised in Edition 21. Public administration still occupies 351-354, but the subdivisions and citation order have been changed, and U.S. bias in wording and structure reduced. The citation order is reversed from jurisdiction/topic to topic/jurisdiction. The schedule features significant use of facet indicators and notational synthesis. The basic structure of the schedule is as follows:

351 Public administration
352 General considerations of public administration
353 Specific fields of public administration
354 Public administration of economy and environment

At 352-354, the classifier is instructed to class a subject with aspects in two or more subdivisions of 352-354 in the number coming last unless there are instructions to the contrary. The schedule also features a "retroactive" citation order in number building; in general, one starts with a number coming later in the schedule as the base number, and then adds as instructed from numbers earlier in the sequence. For example:

Personnel administration in provincial governments in Canada: 352.62130971

352.6	Base number for Personnel administration
21	Jurisdictional level (internal table under 352-354)
3	Number following 352.1 in 352.13 State and provincial administration
09	Historical, geographic, persons treatment (Table 1 notation as instructed in internal table under 352.13-352.19)
71	Canada (Table 2)

Environmental administration in state governments in the U.S.:
354.32130973

354.3	Base number for Administration of environmental and natural resources
21	Jurisdictional level (internal table under 352–354)
3	Number following 352.1 in 352.13 State and provincial administration
09	Historical, geographic, persons treatment (Table 1 notation as instructed in internal table under 352.13–352.19)
73	United States (Table 2)

In both examples, the topic precedes the jurisdiction. Though not listed as such in the number-building steps, the initial digit (2) of the notation for jurisdictional level is a facet indicator for general considerations in public administration. Also, in both examples one is instructed to add notation from a number earlier in the sequence to a base number later in the sequence. The Manual note for 351 Public administration contains detailed instructions on the schedule and many examples illustrating its application.

13.2 MULTIPLE SYNTHESIS IN SCIENCES AND TECHNOLOGY

Because scientific and technical studies in a particular field or discipline often borrow concepts and techniques from other fields and disciplines, the basic concepts and techniques enumerated under the basic sciences in the DDC are often used to build numbers in related fields. For example:

Thermochemistry of uranium: 546.43156

546.431	Base number for Uranium
5	Number for Physical chemistry (internal table under 546)
6	Number following 541.3 in 541.36 Thermochemistry

Molecular structure of aliphatic hydrocarbons: 547.410442

547.41	Base number for Hydrocarbons
044	Number for Theoretical chemistry (internal table under 547)
2	Number following 541.2 in 541.22 Molecular structure

Animal pests of apple orchards: 634.1196

634.11	Base number for Apple orchards
9	Injuries, diseases, pests (internal table under 633–635)
6	Number following 632 in 632.6 Animal pests

As instructed further under 632.6 the particular kind of pests can be specified by adding to 632.6 the number following 59 in 592–599, hence:

Worms as pests of apple orchards: 634.119623
634.11	Base number for Apple orchards
9	Injuries, diseases, pests (internal table under 633–635)
6	Number following 632 in 632.6 Animal pests
23	Number following 59 in 592.3 Worms

Further examples:

Anatomy of horses: 636.10891
636.10	Base number for Horses (includes facet indicator 0)
89	Number following 636.0 in 636.089 Veterinary sciences
1	Number following 61 in 611 Anatomy

Anatomy of the lungs of horses: 636.1089124
636.10	Base number for Horses (includes facet indicator 0)
89	Number following 636.0 in 636.089 Veterinary sciences
124	Number following 61 in 611.24 Anatomy of the lungs

Diseases of the digestive system of horses: 636.108963
636.10	Base number for Horses (includes facet indicator 0)
89	Number following 636.0 in 636.089 Veterinary sciences
63	Number following 61 in 616.3 Diseases of the digestive system

13.2.1 LIFE SCIENCES

The life sciences have also been revised in Edition 21. The 570 schedule has been completely revised, along with 583 Dicotyledons. The rest of 560–590 has been extensively revised. The citation order for internal biological processes has been switched from organism/process to process/organism, and facet indicators are used to introduce the organism. As in 351 Public administration and 780 Music, 570 features retroactive citation order in number building.

T cells in mammals: 571.96619
571.966	Base number for T cells
1	Facet indicator for animals (Number following 571 in 571.1 Animals) (from instruction in internal table under 571.5–571.9)
9	Number following 59 in 599 Mammals

Circulation in monkey brains: 573.8621198
573.86	Base number for Brain
21	Circulation in the system (internal table under 573)
1	Facet indicator for animals (Number following 571 in 571.1 Animals)
98	Number following 59 in 599.8 Monkeys

In both examples, the process precedes the organism, and the organism (an animal) is introduced by the facet indicator for Animals (1). The facet indicator is derived from a schedule earlier in the sequence (571.1). In the second example, intermediate number building takes place using retroactive citation order to specify the process. There are several Manual notes in volume 4 of Edition 21 providing detailed instructions and examples on revised schedules 560–590.

13.3 MULTIPLE SYNTHESIS IN THE HUMANITIES

In certain fields in the humanities such as fine arts, music, and language and literature, class numbers must accommodate various facets such as forms and genres, themes, and performing agents. Number building can therefore be rather complicated. The following examples illustrate number building in these fields.

13.3.1 ARTS

Christmas in Renaissance art: 704.9485309409024

704.94853	Base number for Jesus Christ [in art] (Manual note at 704.9 instructs to prefer iconography over historical and geo-graphic treatment; note also instructs that standard subdivisions may be added for topics that do not approximate the whole)
09	Standard subdivision for Historical, geographic, persons treatment (Table 1)
4	Area notation for Europe (Table 2)
09	Notation for Historical and geographic treatment (internal table under −093–099 in Table 1)
024	Number following −09 in −09024 15th century (Table 1)

Exhibition of book illustrations at Yale Center for British Art: 741.6409410747468

741.64	Base number for [Graphic design, illustration, commercial art for] Books and book jackets
09	Standard subdivision for Historical, geographic, persons treatment (Table 1)
41	Area notation for Great Britain (Table 2)
074	Museums, collections, exhibits (internal table under −093–099 in Table 1)
7468	Area notation for New Haven, Connecticut [the location of the exhibit] (Table 2)

The portrayal of journalists in motion pictures: 791.43652097

791.436	Base number for Films dealing with specific themes and subjects
52	Number following −3 in −352 Specific kinds of persons (Table 3C)
097	Persons occupied by publishing and journalism (Table 7)

125 years of musical theatre in New York City: an exhibition at the IBM Gallery of Science and Art in New York City: 792.60974710747471

792.6	Base number for Musical plays
09	Standard subdivision for Historical, geographic, persons treatment (Table 1)
7471	Area notation for New York City (Table 2)
074	Museums, collections, exhibits (internal table under −093−099 in Table 1)
7471	Area notation for New York City (Table 2)

13.3.2 MUSIC

In Edition 20, the schedule for 780 Music was completely revised. The schedule for 780 Music represents one of the most faceted classes in the DDC. Number building in 780 Music is often complicated. To assist classifiers, the Manual note for 780 in volume 4 offers a detailed discussion with examples.

In building numbers for musical works, the classifier should bear in mind the following citation order that is also listed in the Manual note for 780 in volume 4:

Voices and instruments	782–788
Musical forms	781.8
Sacred music	781.7
Traditions of music	781.6
Kinds of music	781.5
Techniques of music	781.4
Composition	781.3
Elements of music	781.2
Basic principles of music	781.1
Standard subdivisions	780.1–.9

Notice that this citation order is the reverse of the order in which these elements are listed in the schedules. In building numbers in music, always begin with the later number and work backwards. The following examples illustrate this retroactive citation order:

American (U.S.) popular songs: 782.421640973

782.42	Songs
1	Facet indicator for General principles (internal table under 782.1–782.4)
64	Number following 781 in 781.64 Western popular music
09	Standard subdivision for geographic treatment (Table 1)
73	United States (Table 2)

Rhythm of the barrio: Mexican-American music in Los Angeles:
781.626872079494

781.62	Base number for Folk music of specific racial, ethnic, national groups
68	Spanish Americans (Table 5)
72	Mexico (Table 2)
0	Facet indicator for geographic subdivision (instructions in note at beginning of Table 5)
79494	City of Los Angeles (Table 2)

Sound recordings of rock ballet music: 781.6615560266

781.66	Rock (Rock 'n' roll)
1	Facet indicator for General principles (internal table under 781.63–781.69)
556	Number following 781 in 781.556 Ballet music
0266	Modified standard subdivision for Sound recordings of music (as modified at 780.266)

13.3.3 LITERATURE

Numbers for literary works and works about literature are built with the use of Tables 3A–3C. In many cases, these numbers are extended with notation from other tables. Chapter 10 contains examples illustrating number building for works of and about literature. The following examples illustrate more complicated numbers:

A collection of African American poetry: 811.0080896073

81	Base number for American literature
100	Poetry (Table 3B) (includes facet indicator 00)
80	Collections for and by specific kinds of persons (internal table under −1-8 in Table 3B) (includes facet indicator 0)
8	Literature for and by persons of racial, ethnic, national groups (Table 3C)
96073	African Americans (United States Blacks) (Table 5)

A critical study of African American fiction: 813.009896073

81	Base number for American literature
300	Fiction (Table 3B) (includes facet indicator 00)
9	History, description, critical appraisal (internal table under −1-8 in Table 3B)
8	Literature for and by persons of racial, ethnic, national groups (Table 3C)
96073	African Americans (United States Blacks) (Table 5)

American gay and lesbian literary heritage: 810.9920664

81	Base number for American literature
09	History, description, critical appraisal of works in more than one form (Table 3B)
92	Literature for and by persons of specific classes (Table 3C)
06	Persons by miscellaneous social characteristics (Table 7)
64	Number following —086 in —08664 Gays (Table 1)

Portrayal of Berlin in late 19th-century German fiction: 833.8093243155

83	Base number for German literature
3	Fiction (Table 3B)
8	1856–1899 (period table under 830)
0	Facet indicator as instructed under —31–39 (Table 3B)
9	History, description, critical appraisal (internal table under —1-8 in Table 3B)
32	[Literature dealing with specific] Places (Table 3C)
43155	Berlin (Table 2)

Similarly, in 400 Language, numbers may be built with the use of multiple tables, as illustrated in the following example showing the use of four tables:

Conversational Spanish for English-speaking library employees: 468.3421024092

46	Base number for Spanish
834	Audio-lingual approach to expression for those whose native language is different (Table 4)
21	English (Table 6)
024	[Standard subdivision for] The subject for persons in specific occupations (Table 1)
092	Persons occupied with library and information science (Table 7)

13.4 SUMMARY

The term multiple synthesis has not been used in a formal sense in the DDC. We may define it as a process requiring the addition of two or more facets, one after the other, to the same base number. There are many situations and provisions in the DDC where the classifier follows the add operation more than once to arrive at the synthesized number. It is this feature of Dewey that provides for the close classification of many minute and specific subjects.

To repeat: The first task for classifying a complex subject is to identify the base number; the second is to follow the instructions for adding segments from auxiliary tables and/or other parts of the schedules to the number chosen. This operation can be long and involved, requiring considerable manipulation of the schedules and tables. It is extremely important to keep track of each step in the number-building process to ensure that notation is assembled in the correct citation order.

Examples in this chapter are restricted to multiple synthesis through the addition of two or more subdivisions to the same base number, deriving one add instruction from another. In such cases, the first and foremost step is the choice of the appropriate base number. The citation formula is generally entity/operation/agent; choosing the correct base number enables the classifier to combine maximum facets through add instructions. It is important to follow such instructions step-by-step. The operation, though sometimes long and involved, uses the same technique as simple synthesis. Proficiency comes with practice.

With the exception of Table 1 Standard Subdivisions, all other number building in Dewey must be performed according to instructions.

13.5 EXERCISES

Exercise 1:

Classify the following topics in science and social sciences involving multiple synthesis:

(1) Social reform movement for heroin addicts in the United States

(2) African-American college students

(3) Behavior of chipmunks

(4) Administration of medical libraries in New York State

(5) Paratroop training in France

(6) Annual administrative reports on proposed budgets of New York State

(7) Viral diseases in maize

Exercise 2:

Classify the following topics in the humanities involving multiple synthesis:

(1) Jewish art in the Victoria and Albert Museum (South Kensington, London)

(2) A critical study of women in British comedy

(3) A study of late nineteenth-century German novels about Berlin

(4) A list of journals on German literature for children

(5) Discography of bluegrass songs

(6) German opera in the eighteenth century

ANSWERS TO EXERCISES

CHAPTER 4

Exercise 1:

Answers to Exercise 1:

Identify the class numbers for the
following subjects:

(1) Aves: a zoological study
(2) Heart diseases
(3) Surgery for diseases of the gums
(4) 20th-century sculpture
(5) Reign of Elizabeth I (of England)

(1) 598
(2) 616.12
(3) 617.632
(4) 735.23
(5) 942.055

Exercise 2:

Answers to Exercise 2:

Classify the following subjects by using
the appropriate table of preference:

(1) Preparing luncheon for schools
(2) Deportation for political offenses
(3) Decorative lighting for weddings
(4) Miniature portraits of women
    (paintings)
(5) Compensation of working
    mothers

(1) 641.571 (not 641.53)
(2) 364.68 (not 364.131)
(3) 747.92 (not 747.93)
(4) 757.7 (not 757.4)

(5) 331.44 (not 331.21)

Exercise 3:

Answers to Exercise 3:

Identify the class numbers for the
following subjects:

(1) Educational service in adult
    women prisons
(2) Veteran immigrant labor
(3) Production (economic) efficiency
    in agriculture
(4) Maladjusted young people

(1) 365.66 (not 365.43)

(2) 331.52 (not 331.62)
(3) 338.16

(4) 362.74 (not 364.36)

CHAPTER 4 *(Continued)*

Exercise 4:

Identify the class numbers for the following subjects:

(1) Evaluation of curricula in elementary schools

(2) Color printing by photo mechanical techniques

(3) Metallic chairs

(4) Atomic weight of curium (chemical element)

(5) Breeding of Oriental horses

(6) Diseases of arrowroot

Answers to Exercise 4:

(1) 372.19 (not 375.006)

(2) 686.232 (not 686.23042)

(3) 684.13 (not 684.105)

(4) 546.442 (not 541.242)

(5) 636.11 (not 636.082)

(6) 633.68 (not 632.3)

CHAPTER 6

Exercise 1:

Under which terms should you look in the Relative Index for the following subjects?

(1) Ronald Reagan (the actor)

(2) American Mathematical Society

(3) Metropolitan Life Insurance Company of the United States

(4) John Lennon (the singer-composer of the rock group The Beatles)

(5) AZT (the anti-AIDS drug)

(6) Chlorofluorocarbons

(7) Santa Claus

(8) Sneakers (tennis shoes)

(9) Babe Ruth (the baseball player)

(10) Black widow spider

Answers to Exercise 1:

(1) Actors

(2) Societies or Organizations

(3) Insurance companies

(4) Rock musicians

(5) AIDS (Disease)— medicine

(6) Chlorine or fluorine or carbon

(7) Christmas

(8) Shoes

(9) Baseball players

(10) Spiders

CHAPTER 6 *(continued)*

Exercise 2:

Under which terms should you look for the following topics?

(1) Anthology of one-act plays
(2) Libraries for children
(3) Fabian socialism
(4) Dynamics of particles

(5) Air-to-air guided missiles
(6) Modern history
(7) Modeling pottery
(8) History of privateering

Answers to Exercise 2

(1) One-act plays
(2) Children's libraries
(3) Fabian socialism
(4) Dynamics—particles or Particles (Matter)—classical mechanics

(5) Air-to-air guided missiles
(6) Modern history
(7) Modeling pottery
(8) Privateering

CHAPTER 7

Exercise 1:

Build class numbers for the following subjects using whole schedule numbers:

(1) Library classification for plants and animals
(2) Special libraries devoted to Judaism
(3) Production efficiency in the manufacturing of passenger automobiles
(4) Bibliography of the Dewey Decimal Classification
(5) Selection and acquisition of art books in libraries
(6) Bibliography of cool jazz
(7) Trade in pharmaceutical drugs

(8) Strikes by professors

(9) The prices of shoes

Answers to Exercise 1:

(1) $025.46 + 570 = 025.4657$

(2) $026 + 296 = 026.296$

(3) $338.456 + 29222$ (from $6[29.222] = 338.45629222$

(4) $016 + 025.431 = 016.025431$

(5) $025.27 + 700 = 025.277$

(6) $016 + 781.655 = 016.781655$

(7) $380.145 + 615.1 = 380.1456151$

(8) $331.89281 + 378.12 = 331.8928137812$

(9) $338.43 + 685.31 = 338.4368531$

CHAPTER 7 *(Continued)*

Exercise 2:

Build class numbers by adding parts of schedule numbers:

(1) Domestic trade in agricultural products

(2) Trade in diamonds

(3) Labor market for the leather industry

(4) Philosophy based upon Sikhism

(5) Rearing adopted children

(6) The psychology of hyperactive children

(7) A psychological study of slow-learning children

(8) A comprehensive work on the Little Sisters of the Poor (Roman Catholic)

(9) International law regarding credit cards

(10) A library use study of prison libraries

Answers to Exercise 2:

(1) 381.4 + 1 (from 380.14[1]) = 381.41

(2) 380.142 + 82 (from 553.[82]) = 380.14282

(3) 331.129 + 75 (from 6[75]) = 331.12975

(4) 181.0 + 46 (from 29[4.6]) = 181.046

(5) 649.14 + 5 (from 155.44[5]) = 649.145

(6) 155.45 + 3 (from 371.9[3]) = 155.453

(7) 155.45 + 26 (from 371.9[26]) = 155.4526

(8) 255.9 + 5 (from 271.9[5]) = 255.95

(9) 341.751 + 765 (from 332.[765]) = 341.751765

(10) 025.58 + 7665 (from 02[7.665]) = 025.587665

Exercise 3:

Build numbers requiring facet indicators:

(1) Evolution of invertebrates

(2) Teaching mathematics to students with mental retardation

(3) Connective tissues in primates

(4) Contracts for public works projects

Answers to Exercise 3:

(1) 592 + 1 (from table under 592–599) + 38 (from 591.[38]) = 592.138

(2) 371.9280 + 4 (from 371.904[4]) +7 (from 372.[7]) = 371.928047

(3) 571.56 + 1 (from 571.[1] + 98 (from 59[9.8]) = 571.56198

(4) 352.77 + 2 (from table under 352–354) + 53 (from 352[.53]) = 352.77253

CHAPTER 7 *(Continued)*

Exercise 4:

Build numbers according to collective add instructions:

(1) Physical chemistry of gold

(2) Architectural preservation of warehouses

(3) Routine maintenance and repair of woven rugs

(4) Prevention of malaria by medical personnel

(5) Mass of the planet Venus

(6) Economic utilization of forest lands

(7) Development of arid land

(8) How to manage a supermarket

(9) Protective measures in the use of agricultural chemicals: a social response to a poisonous problem

(10) Abuse of rivers and streams: an economic study

Answers to Exercise 4:

(1) 546.656 + 5 (from table under 546) = 546.6565

(2) 725.35 + 0288 = 725.350288

(3) 746.72 + 0288 = 746.720288

(4) 616.9362 + 05 (from table under 616.1–616.9) = 616.936205

(5) 523.42 + 1 (from 523.3[1]) = 523.421

(6) 333.75 + 13 (from table under 333.7) = 333.7513

(7) 333.736 + 15 (from table under 333.7) = 333.73615

(8) 381.148 + 068 = 381.148068

(9) 363.1792 + 72 (from table under 362–363) = 363.179272

(10) 333.9162 + 137 (from table under 333.7) = 333.9162137

CHAPTER 8

Exercise 1:

Applying standard subdivisions, assign class numbers to the following works:

(1) An encyclopedia of physical and theoretical chemistry

(2) A dictionary of physical chemistry

(3) Teaching methods in dairy technology

(4) Research methods in milk processing technology

(5) A journal of histology

Answers to Exercise 1:

(1) 541.03

(2) 541.303

(3) 637.071

(4) 637.1072

(5) 571.505

CHAPTER 8 *(Continued)*

Exercise 2:

Build class numbers for the following topics involving main class or division numbers:

Answers to Exercise 2:

(1) Science organizations

(1) 506

(2) Abbreviations and symbols used in science

(2) 501.48

(3) History of science

(3) 509

(4) History of science in the 16th century

(4) 509.031

(5) Schools and courses in astronomy

(5) 520.71

(6) Research methods in philosophy

(6) 107.2

(7) Dictionary of mathematics

(7) 510.3

(8) Medical associations

(8) 610.6

(9) Encyclopedia of architecture

(9) 720.3

Exercise 3:

Build class numbers for the following topics requiring multiple zeros:

Answers to Exercise 3:

(1) Illustrations of human diseases

(1) 616.00222

(2) A history of naval forces

(2) 359.009

(3) An audiovisual presentation on the history of Central Europe

(3) 943.000208

(4) Tables and formulas in economics

(4) 330.021

(5) International organizations on human diseases

(5) 616.00601

(6) A dictionary of law

(6) 340.03

(7) A journal of Christian theology

(7) 230.05

CHAPTER 8 *(Continued)*

Exercise 4:

Synthesize numbers for the following subjects:

(1) Mathematics for biophysics

(2) The odds of winning in games of chance

(3) Principles of turbulence in human blood flow

(4) A journal of military science

Answers to Exercise 4:

(1) 571.40151

(2) 795.0151952

(3) 612.1181 (Since blood flow does not have its own number, standard subdivisions cannot be added for it. See section 8.9.2 in chapter 8.)

(4) 355.005

Exercise 5:

Assign class numbers to the following subjects, using displaced standard subdivisions:

(1) Pottery-making in the Middle Ages

(2) A history of wages

(3) Apparatus for making plastics

(4) History of painting (art)

(5) History of goldsmithing

(6) Architecture of the modern era

Answers to Exercise 5:

(1) 666.3902

(2) 331.29

(3) 668.41

(4) 759

(5) 739.227

(6) 724

Exercise 6:

Synthesize class numbers for the following topics that involve two standard subdivisions.

(1) A journal of higher education in public administration

(2) Encyclopedia of library associations

(3) A directory of law schools

(4) A journal of literary history

(5) A biographical dictionary of musicians

Answers to Exercise 6:

(1) 353.60711 (not 353.605)

(2) 020.6 (not 020.3)

(3) 340.0711

(4) 809.005

(5) 780.922

CHAPTER 8 *(Continued)*

Exercise 7:

Answers to Exercise 7:

Provide class numbers for the following subjects that involve standard subdivision concepts but do not use standard subdivision notation:

(1) Management of technology

(1) 658

(2) History of Central Europe

(2) 943

(3) *Encyclopedia Americana*

(3) 031

(4) A general periodical in the English language

(4) 052

(5) Conference on inventorying a library

(5) 025.82

CHAPTER 9

Exercise 1:

In the Relative Index identify the area numbers for the following areas, and then locate and verify them in Table 2.

Answers to Exercise 1:

(1) Genesee County, Michigan

(2) Punjab, Pakistan

(1) −77437

(3) Chad

(2) −54914

(4) North Carolina

(3) −6743

(5) Ghana

(4) −756

(6) Unaligned countries

(5) −667

(7) Eastern Hemisphere

(6) −1716

(8) Indian Ocean

(7) −1811

(9) Antarctic Ocean

(8) −165

(10) Arctic Ocean

(9) −167

(11) Christian countries

(10)−1632

(12) Rural regions

(11)−1761

(12)−1734

CHAPTER 9 *(Continued)*

Exercise 2:

Classify the following with direct
subdivision by place:

(1) Adult education in Singapore

(2) Education policy in India

(3) General statistics of Finland

(4) General geology of Athens

(5) History of Jammu and Kashmir

(6) History of Jammu and Kashmir
during the reign of Aurangzeb

(7) General organizations in
Liverpool, England

(8) Journalism and newspapers in
Finland

(9) Art galleries in Sweden

(10) Public administration in Papua
New Guinea

Answers to Exercise 2:

(1) 374.95957

(2) 379.54

(3) 314.897

(4) 554.9512

(5) 954.6

(6) 954.60258

(7) 062.753

(8) 078.97

(9) 708.85

(10) 351.953

Exercise 3:

Assign class numbers to the following,
using extensions of area notation 1:

(1) Social welfare programs in
developing countries

(2) Democratic political systems in
unaligned countries

(3) Health insurance systems in the
Pacific region

Answers to Exercise 3:

(1) 362.91724

(2) 321.8091716

(3) 368.3820091823

CHAPTER 9 *(Continued)*

Exercise 4:

Assign class numbers to the following, using standard subdivision —09
and area numbers 3–9:

(1) Social services to families in
Washington State

(2) Child labor in Southeast Asia

(3) Taxes in Kuwait

(4) Costume in Wales

(5) Prices in France: an economic
study

(6) Sexual division of labor, a case
study in Chicago, Illinois

(7) Broadway musicals: a theatrical
history

Answers to Exercise 4:

(1) 362.82809797

(2) 331.310959

(3) 336.20095367

(4) 391.009429

(5) 338.520944

(6) 306.36150977311

(7) 792.6097471

Exercise 5:

Classify the following subjects
requiring area notation between two
subject facets:

(1) Physical geography of Mexico

(2) Law of property in Nigeria

(3) Public health law of Mozambique

(4) The lower house of the British
Parliament

(5) Communist parties of Eastern
Europe

Answers to Exercise 5:

(1) 917.202

(2) 346.66904

(3) 344.67904

(4) 328.41072

(5) 324.247075

CHAPTER 9 *(Continued)*

Exercise 6:

Classify the following requiring two area numbers:

(1) Migration from Vietnam to the United States: a sociological study

(2) Trade agreements between India and Italy (emphasizes India)

(3) Trade between India and Italy (emphasizes India)

(4) Foreign relations between India and countries of the Pacific Rim

(5) U.S. economic aid to developing countries

(6) Foreign relations between Japan and South Korea

Answers to Exercise 6:

(1) 304.8730597

(2) 382.954045

(3) 382.0954045

(4) 327.5401823

(5) 338.917301724

(6) 327.5195052

Exercise 7:

Class the following topics using an area notation extended by another area notation:

(1) Civil rights in francophone countries of Africa

(2) Male costume in rural Austria

(3) Economic conditions in rural England

Answers to Exercise 7:

(1) 323.0960917541

(2) 391.109436091734

(3) 330.9420091734

CHAPTER 9 *(Continued)*

Exercise 8:

Classify the following, using a standard subdivision (other than —09) extended by an area notation:

(1) Research in economics in Scotland

(2) Library science as a profession in the United States

(3) The teaching of law in Asia

(4) Colleges and universities teaching law in Latin America

(5) Higher education in Spain in public administration

(6) Athletic instruction in U.S. colleges

Answers to Exercise 8:

(1) 330.0720411

(2) 020.2373

(3) 340.07105

(4) 340.07118

(5) 351.0711046

(6) 796.071173

Exercise 9:

Classify the following, using a standard subdivision after an area notation:

(1) Journal of Indian geography

(2) Women in the Church of England

(3) Foreign policy of Germany in the 1990s

(4) Sickness and health: Canadian statistics at a glance

(5) Ancient Roman coins [minted in Rome] in the Hobart Classics Museum (Hobart, Tasmania)

(6) A journal of housing services in Argentina

Answers to Exercise 9:

(1) 915.4005

(2) 283.42082

(3) 327.43009049

(4) 614.4271021

(5) 737.493760749461

(6) 363.58098205

CHAPTER 10

Exercise 1:

Classify the following works by or about individual authors:

(1) Poems of Charles Baudelaire (French poet, 1821–1867)

(2) A biography of Hans Christian Andersen (Danish writer of fairy tales, 1805–1875)

(3) A critical study of Thomas Dekker's plays (British, 1572–1632)

(4) Selected poetry of William Butler Yeats (Irish author, 1865–1939, writing in the English language)

(5) Dramatic works of Eugene O'Neill (American, 1888–1953)

(6) *Peter Pan*, an English novel by J.M. Barrie (1860–1937)

(7) *The Adventures of Huckleberry Finn* by the American novelist Mark Twain (1835–1910)

(8) A biography of Claus Silvester Dörner (German writer not limited to or chiefly identifiable with one specific form, 1913–   )

(9) A collection of jokes by the American author Nancy Gray (1959–   )

Answers to Exercise 1:

(1) 841.8

(2) 839.8136

(3) 822.3

(4) 821.8

(5) 812.52

(6) 823.912

(7) 813.4

(8) 838.91409

(9) 818.5402

CHAPTER 10 *(Continued)*

Exercise 2:	Answers to Exercise 2:
Classify the following works from or on more than one literature:	
(1) A collection of sonnets	(1) 808.8142
(2) A collection of poetry by women	(2) 808.810082
(3) An anthology of nineteenth-century literature	(3) 808.80034
(4) A critical appraisal of lyric poetry	(4) 809.14
(5) A collection of poetry displaying realism	(5) 808.81912
(6) A collection of poetry with marriage as the theme	(6) 808.8193543
(7) A critical appraisal of romantic literature	(7) 809.9145

Exercise 3	Answers to Exercise 3:
Classify the following works about one literature:	
(1) A study of symbolism in French literature	(1) 840.915
(2) A history of twentieth-century English literature	(2) 820.90091
(3) A study of French women authors	(3) 840.99287
(4) A study of social themes in 15th-century English literature	(4) 820.935509024
(5) A study of Portuguese literature by African authors	(5) 869.0996
(6) Discourses of salvation in English literature; an historical study	(6) 820.938234

CHAPTER 10 *(Continued)*

Exercise 4:

Answers to Exercise 4:

Classify the following works from one literature and in a particular form:

(1) Collection of English lyric poetry on love

(1) 821.04083543

(2) An anthology of English allegorical narrative poetry

(2) 821.0320815

(3) A critical study of plots in American historical fiction

(3) 813.0810924

(4) A study of English horror tales

(4) 823.0873809

(5) A study of heroism in the English novel

(5) 823.009353

Exercise 5:

Answers to Exercise 5:

Classify the following works from one literature with multiple facets:

(1) Collection of Elizabethan English poetry

(1) 821.308

(2) Love in twentieth-century American drama: a critical study

(2) 812.5093543

(3) Collection of late twentieth-century American drama by teenagers

(3) 812.540809283

(4) A study of the Berlin wall in East German fiction

(4) 833.91409358

(5) A bibliography of English romantic poetry by women authors, 1770–1835

(5) 016.8216080145082

CHAPTER 10 *(Continued)*

Exercise 6:

Classify the following works, using Table 3C with 700 numbers:

(1) Fantasy films

(2) Horror programs on television

(3) Werewolves in the arts

(4) Atlantis in art and literature

Answers to Exercise 6:

(1) 791.43615

(2) 791.456164

(3) 700.474

(4) 700.472

CHAPTER 11

Exercise 1:

Classify the following topics with the use of Table 4:

(1) Phonology of Slovak

(2) An introduction to Middle Dutch

(3) Norwegian grammar

(4) English verb tables for ESL (English as a second language)speakers

(5) Grammar of Portuguese language

Answers to Exercise 1:

(1) 491.8715

(2) 439.317

(3) 439.825

(4) 428.24

(5) 469.5

Exercise 2:

Classify the following topics with the use of Table 6:

(1) German-language encyclopedia

(2) A study of Ojibwa (a North American native language)

(3) Arabic folktales from Israel

(4) English-speaking people in Africa: a social study

(5) General encyclopedia in Thai

(6) General periodicals in Norwegian (New Norse)

(7) Spanish quotations

(8) Introduction to Huambisa (a South American native language)

Answers to Exercise 2:

(1) 033.1

(2) 497.3

(3) 398.204927095694

(4) 305.72106

(5) 039.95911

(6) 058.83

(7) 086.1

(8) 498.372

CHAPTER 11 *(Continued)*

Exercise 3:

Classify the following topics with the use of both Table 4 and Table 6:

(1) Chinese-English dictionary

(2) Finnish-English dictionary

(3) Spanish reader for English-speaking people

(4) Latin words in the German language

(5) Conversational English for Russian-speaking people

Answers to Exercise 3:

(1) 495.1321

(2) 494.541321

(3) 468.6421

(4) 432.471

(5) 428.349171

Exercise 4:

Classify the following topics with the use of Table 6 through Table 2:

(1) School enrollment in the French-speaking world

(2) Conservation of national resources in the Spanish-speaking world

Answers to Exercise 4:

(1) 371.21917541

(2) 339.4917561

CHAPTER 12

Exercise 1:

Classify the following topics with the use of Table 5:

(1) Folksongs of the Romany people

(2) The Dutch people (a social study)

(3) Jewish art

(4) Religion of the Hittites

(5) Traditional religion of Zulus (an African ethnic group)

(6) Contemporary Australian aboriginal paintings

Answers to Exercise 1:

(1) 782.4216291497

(2) 305.83931

(3) 704.03924

(4) 299.199

(5) 299.683986

(6) 759.9940899915

CHAPTER 12 *(Continued)*

Exercise 2:	Answers to Exercise 2:
Classify the following topics with the use of Table 7:	
(1) Jain artists	(1) 704.2944
(2) Ethics of social scientists	(2) 174.93
(3) Church work with Catholic college students	(3) 259.2408822
(4) Reader advisory services for scientists in libraries	(4) 025.540885
(5) Statistical mathematics for librarians	(5) 519.5024092
(6) Introduction to law for police officials	(6) 340.0243632

Exercise 3:	Answers to Exercise 3:
Classify the following topics with the use of Table 7 through Table 2:	
(1) Islamic decorative arts	(1) 745.0917671
(2) Economic conditions in Islamic countries	(2) 330.917671
(3) Adult education in Islamic countries	(3) 374.917671

CHAPTER 13

Exercise 1:

Classify the following topics in science and social sciences involving multiple synthesis:

(1) Social reform movement for heroin addicts in the United States

(2) African-American college students

(3) Behavior of chipmunks

(4) Administration of medical libraries in New York State

(5) Paratroop training in France

(6) Annual administrative reports on proposed budgets of New York State

(7) Viral diseases in maize

Exercise 2:

Classify the following topics in the humanities involving multiple synthesis:

(1) Jewish art in the Victoria and Albert Museum (South Kensington, London)

(2) A critical study of women in British comedy

(3) A study of late nineteenth-century German novels about Berlin

(4) A list of journals on German literature for children

(5) Discography of bluegrass songs

(6) German opera in the eighteenth century

Answers to Exercise 1:

(1) 362.2935240973

(2) 378.1982996073

(3) 599.36415

(4) 025.1966109747

(5) 356.16650944

(6) 352.497470105

(7) 633.1598

Answers to Exercise 2:

(1) 704.03924007442134

(2) 822.052309352042

(3) 833.8093243155

(4) 016.83080928205

(5) 016.7824216420266

(6) 782.1094309033

GLOSSARY

GLOSSARY

For the convenience of users, the glossary includes the terms and definitions found in the glossary in volume 1 of the DDC, Edition 21. The glossary also contains additional terms used in this book.

Add note: A note instructing the classifier to append digits found elsewhere in the Classification to a given base number. *See also* **Base number.**

Add table: *See* **Table (2).**

Application: *See* **Rule of application.**

Approximate the whole: When the topic of a work is nearly coextensive with the topic of a DDC heading, the work is said to "approximate the whole." The term is also used to characterize works that cover more than half the content of the heading, and works that cover representative examples from three or more subdivisions of a class. When a work approximates the whole of a subject, standard subdivisions may be added. Topics that do not approximate the whole are said to be in "standing room" in the number. *See also* **Class-here note; Standard-subdivisions-are-added note; Standing room; Unitary term.**

Area Table: An auxiliary table, the second, that gives geographic areas primarily, but also lists historical periods and several numbers for persons associated with a subject. Areas of the world are listed systematically, not alphabetically. The area table can never be used alone; its provisions are for use only in conjunction with a class number from the schedules.

Arrange-alphabetically note: A note suggesting the option of alphabetical subarrangement where identification by specific name or other identifying characteristic is desired. *See also* **Option.**

Arrange-chronologically note: A note suggesting the option of chronological subarrangement where identification by date is desired. *See also* **Option.**

Artificial digit: A letter or other symbol used optionally as a substitute for digits 0–9 to provide a more prominent location or shorter notation for a jurisdiction; language; literature; religion; racial, ethnic, national group; or other characteristic. *See also* **Option.**

Aspect: An approach to a subject, or a characteristic (facet) of a subject. *See also* **Discipline; Facet; Subject.**

Attraction: *See* **Classification by attraction.**

Author number: *See* **Book number.**

Base number: A number to which other numbers are appended. *See also* **Add note.**

Bibliographic classification: A fully developed classification system that specifies categories down to the finest gradations; it provides the means to relate the categories and to specify in the notation all of the aspects or facets of a work. *See also* **Aspect; Facet.**

Bibliothecal classification: *See* **Library classification.**

Blurb: Information found on the jackets of hardbound books or the back cover of paperbacks that reveals something of the content of the book and the author's background.

Book number: The part of a call number that distinguishes a specific item from other items within the same class number. A library using the Cutter-Sanborn system can have D548d indicate David Copperfield by Dickens (where D stands for the D of Dickens, 548 for "ickens," and d for David Copperfield). *See also* **Call number; Cutter number; Work mark.**

Broad classification: The classification of works in broad categories by logical abridgment, even when more specific numbers are available, e.g., classing a cookbook of Mexican recipes in 641.5 Cooking (instead of in 641.5972 Mexican cooking).

Built number: A number constructed according to add instructions stated or implied in the schedules and tables. *See also* **Number building.**

Call number: A set of letters, numerals, or other symbols (in combination or alone) used by a library to identify a specific copy of a work. A call number may consist of the class number; book number; and other data such as date, volume number, copy number, and location symbol. *See also* **Book number; Class number.**

Centered entry: An entry representing a subject covered by a span of numbers, e.g., 372 - 374 Specific levels of education. The entry is called "centered" because the span of numbers is printed in the center of the page rather than in the number column on the left side of the page. Centered entries are identified by the symbol > in the number column.

Characteristic of division: *See* **Facet.**

Citation order: The order in which two or more characteristics (facets) of a class are to be combined in number building. When number building is not permitted or possible, instructions on preference order with respect to the choice of facets are provided. *See also* **Facet**; **Number Building**; **Preference order.**

Class: (Noun) (1) A group of objects exhibiting one or more common characteristics, identified by a specific notation. (2) One of the ten major groups of the DDC numbered 0–9. *See also* **Main class**. (3) A subdivision of the DDC of any degree of specificity. (Verb) To assign a class number to an individual work. *See also* **Classify.**

Class-elsewhere note: A note instructing the classifier on the location of interrelated topics. The note may show preference order, lead to the interdisciplinary or comprehensive number, override the first-of-two rule, or lead to broader or narrower numbers in the same hierarchical array that might otherwise be overlooked. *See also* **Comprehensive number**; **Interdisciplinary number**; **Preference order.**

Class-here note: An instruction identifying topics that are to be classed in the given number and in its subdivisions. Topics identified in class-here notes, even if broader or narrower than the heading, are said to "approximate the whole" of the number; therefore, standard subdivisions may be added for topics in class-here notes. Class-here notes also may identify the comprehensive or interdisciplinary number for a subject. *See also* **Approximate the whole; Comprehensive number; Interdisciplinary number.**

Class number: Notation that designates the class to which a given item belongs. *See also* **Call number.**

Classification: A logical system for the arrangement of knowledge.

Classification by attraction: The classification of a specific aspect of a subject in an inappropriate discipline, usually because the subject is named in the inappropriate discipline but not mentioned explicitly in the appropriate discipline.

Classification schedule: A printed or otherwise recorded (as in electronic form) list of subjects and their subdivisions arranged in a systematic order with notation given for each subject and its subdivisions. It is a ready source for assigning class numbers to works on the basis of their subject content. *See also* **Schedules.**

Classified catalog: A catalog arranged according to the notational order of a classification system.

Classify: (1) To arrange a collection of items according to a classification system. (2) To assign a class number to an individual work.

Close classification: The classification of works to the fullest extent permitted by the notation.

Coextensive: Describes a topic equal in scope to the concept represented by the number.

Cognate number: A number related to another number by virtue of having been built with the same notation to represent a common aspect. For example, 616.241075 Diagnosis of pneumonia and 616.3623075 Diagnosis of hepatitis are cognate numbers of 616.075 because they are built by addition of notation 075 from 616.075, the general number in medicine for diagnosis of diseases.

Comparative table: A table for a complete or extensive revision that lists in alphabetical order selected topics accompanied by their previous number and their number in the current edition. *See also* **Equivalence table; Revision.**

Complete revision: *See* **Revision** *(Complete revision).*

Complex subject: A complex subject is a subject that has more than one characteristic. For example, "unemployed bibliographers" is a complex subject because it has more than one characteristic (employment status and occupation). *See also* **Preference order.**

Comprehensive number: A number (often identified by a "Class here comprehensive works" note) that covers all the components of the subject treated within that discipline. The components may be in a span of consecutive numbers or distributed in the Classification. *See also* **Interdisciplinary number.**

Coordinate: Describes a number or topic at a level equal to another number or topic in the same hierarchy.

Cross classification: Placing works on the same subject in two different class numbers. This tends to occur when works deal with two or more characteristics of a subject in the same class. Notes on preference order should prevent cross classification. *See also* **Preference order.**

Cross reference: *See* **Class-elsewhere note; See-also reference; See reference.**

Cutter number: The notation in a book number derived from the Cutter-Sanborn tables. *See also* **Book number.**

DDC: Dewey Decimal Classification.

Decimal point: The dot that follows the third digit in a DDC number. In strict usage the word "decimal" is not accurate; however, common usage is followed in this edition's explanatory material.

Definition note: A note indicating the meaning of a term in the heading.

Digit: The smallest individual unit in a notational system. For example, the notation 954 has three digits: 9, 5, and 4.

Discipline: An organized field of study or branch of knowledge, e.g., 200 Religion, 530 Physics, 364 Criminology. In the DDC, subjects are arranged by disciplines. *See also* **Subject.**

Discontinued number: A number from the previous edition that is no longer used because the concept represented by the number has been moved to a more general number in the same hierarchy, or has been dropped entirely. Numbers are discontinued because they identify a concept with negligible current literature or represent a distinction no longer valid in the literature or common perception of the field. Discontinued numbers appear in square brackets. *See also* **Schedule reduction.**

Displaced standard subdivision: A standard subdivision concept given special notation in the schedule in place of its regular notation from Table 1. A do-not-use note is always provided at the regular location of the standard subdivision concept. *See also* **Do-not-use note; Standard subdivisions.**

Division: The second level of subdivision in the Classification, represented by the first two digits in the notation, e.g., 62 in 620 Engineering and allied operations. *See also* **Main class; Section.**

Do-not-use note: A note instructing the classifier not to use all or part of a regular standard subdivision notation or an add table provision in favor of a special provision, or standard subdivisions at a broader number. *See also* **Displaced standard subdivision.**

Document: A generic term for all media capable of conveying, coding, and preserving knowledge. The book is the conventional kind of document. Other documents are journals, reports, sound recordings, motion pictures, and so on.

Dual heading: A heading with two separate terms, the first of which is the main topic and the second of which is a major subordinate topic, e.g., 570 Life sciences Biology. A dual heading is used when the subject as a whole and the subordinate topic as a whole share the same number. Standard subdivisions may be added for either or both topics in a dual heading.

Dual provision: The inadvertent provision of more than one place for the same aspect of a subject in the Classification.

Entry: (1) In the schedules and tables, a self-contained unit consisting of a number or span of numbers, a heading, and often one or more notes. (2) In the Relative Index, a term or phrase usually followed by a DDC number.

Enumerative scheme: A classification or subject headings system in which numbers or headings for complex subjects are precombined and listed.

Equivalence table: A table for a complete or extensive revision that lists in numerical order the classes of the current edition with their equivalent numbers in the previous edition (and vice versa). *See also* **Comparative table**; **Revision.**

Expansion: The development of a class in the schedules or tables to provide further subdivisions. *See also* **Revision.**

Extensive revision: *See* **Revision** *(Extensive revision)*.

Facet: Any of the various categories into which a given class may be divided, e.g., division of the class "people" by the categories race, age, education, and language spoken. Each category contains terms based on a single characteristic of division, e.g., children, adolescents, and adults are characteristics of division of the "ages" category. *See also* **Citation order.**

Facet indicator: A digit used to introduce notation representing a characteristic of the subject. For example, "0" is often used as a facet indicator to introduce standard subdivision concepts.

First-of-two rule: The rule instructing that works dealing equally with two subjects not used to introduce or explain one another are classed in the number coming first in the schedules or tables.

Former-heading note: A note listing the heading associated with the class number in the previous edition. The note is used when the heading has changed so much that it bears little or no resemblance to the previous heading, even though the meaning of the number has remained substantially the same.

Heading: The word or phrase used as the caption of a given class.

Hierarchical force: The principle that the attributes of a class as defined in the heading and in certain basic notes apply to all the subdivisions of the class, and to all other classes to which reference is made.

Hierarchy: The arrangement of a classification system from general to specific. In the Dewey Decimal Classification, the degree of specificity of a class is usually indicated by the length of the notation and the corresponding depth of indention of the heading. Hierarchy may also be indicated by special headings, notes, and centered entries.

Hook number: A number in the Classification without meaning in itself, but used as a "hook" to introduce examples of the topic. Headings for hook numbers may include the words "other," "specific," "special," or "miscellaneous." Standard subdivisions are always bracketed under hook numbers.

Including note: A note enumerating topics that are logically part of the class but are less extensive in scope than the concept represented by the class number. These topics do not have enough literature to warrant their own number. Standard subdivisions may not be added to the numbers for these topics. *See also* **Literary warrant; Standing room.**

Indention: Typographical setting of subheadings below and to the right of the main entry term.

Interdisciplinary number: A number (often identified by a "Class here interdisciplinary works" note) to be used for works covering a subject from the perspective of more than one discipline, including the discipline where the interdisciplinary number is located, e.g., the interdisciplinary number for marriage is 306.81 in Sociology. *See also* **Comprehensive number.**

Library classification: A classification designed to arrange the physical items of a library collection. Also called bibliothecal classification.

Literary form: A mode of literary expression such as poetry, drama, fiction, etc. Each form can be subdivided into kinds of forms, e.g., lyric poetry, comedy, science fiction, etc.

Literary warrant: Justification for the development of a class or naming of a topic in the schedules, tables, or Relative Index, based on the existence of a body of published literature on the topic.

Main class: One of the ten major subdivisions of the Dewey Decimal Classification, represented by the first digit in the notation, e.g., the 3 in 300. *See also* **Division; Section**.

Manual: A guide to the use of the DDC that is made up primarily of extended discussions of problem areas in the application of the Classification. In the schedules and tables, see-Manual references indicate where relevant discussions are located in the Manual.

Notation: Numerals, letters, and/or other symbols used to represent the main and subordinate divisions of a classification scheme. In the DDC, Arabic numerals are used to represent the classes, e.g., notation 07 from Table 1 and 511.3 from the schedules.

Notational synthesis: *See* **Number building**.

Number building. The process of constructing a number by adding notation from the tables or other parts of the schedules to a base number. *See also* **Base number; Citation order.**

Number-building note: *See* **Add note**.

Number column: The column of numbers printed in the left margin of the schedules and tables, and to the right of the alphabetical entries in the Relative Index.

Option: An alternative to standard notation provided in the schedules and tables to give emphasis to an aspect in a library's collection not given preferred treatment in the standard notation. In some cases, an option may provide shorter notation for the aspect. *See also* **Optional number.**

Optional number: (1) A number listed in parentheses in the schedules or tables that is an alternative to the standard notation. (2) A number constructed by following an option. *See also* **Option.**

Order of preference: *See* **Preference order.**

Period table: A table giving chronological time periods with their notation. For many literatures, period tables are given in the schedules. For works not limited to a particular language, the period notation is taken from Table 1 Standard subdivisions.

Phoenix schedule: *See* **Revision** *(Complete revision)*.

Preference order: The order indicating which one of two or more numbers is to be chosen when different characteristics of a subject cannot be shown in full by number building. A note (sometimes containing a table of preference) indicates which characteristic is to be selected for works covering more than one characteristic. When the notation can be synthesized to show two or more characteristics, it is a matter of citation order. *See also* **Citation order.**

Preference table: *See* **Preference order.**

Reduction of schedules: *See* **Schedule reduction.**

Regularization: The replacement of special developments for standard subdivision concepts by use of the regular standard subdivisions found in Table 1.

Relative Index: The index to the DDC, called "Relative" because it relates subjects to disciplines. In the schedules, subjects are arranged by disciplines. In the Relative Index, subjects are listed alphabetically; indented under each subject is an alphabetical list of the disciplines in which the subject is found.

Relocation: The shifting of a topic in a new edition of the DDC from one number to another number which differs from the old number in respects other than length.

Retroactive citation ordder: In number building, starting with a number coming later in the schedule as the base number then adding a instructed from numbers earlier in the sequence.

Reused number: A number with a total change in meaning from one edition to another. Usually numbers are reused only in complete revisions or when the reused number has been vacant for two consecutive editions.

Revision: The result of editorial work that alters the text of any class of the DDC. There are three degrees of revision: *Routine revision* is limited to updating terminology, clarifying notes, and providing modest expansions. *Extensive revision* involves a major reworking of subdivisions but leaves the main outline of the schedule intact. *Complete revision* (formerly called a phoenix) is a new development; the base number remains as in the previous edition, but virtually all subdivisions are changed. Changes for complete and extensive revisions are shown through comparative and equivalence tables rather than through relocation notes in the schedule or table affected. *See also* **Comparative table; Equivalence table.**

Routine revision: *See* **Revision** *(Routine revision).*

Rule of application: The rule instructing that works about the application of one subject to a second subject are classified with the second subject.

Rule of three: The rule instructing that works that give equal treatment to three or more subjects that are all subdivisions of a broader subject are classified in the first higher number that includes all of them.

Rule of zero: The rule instructing that subdivisions beginning with zero should be avoided if there is a choice between 0 and subdivisions beginning with 1–9 in the same position in the notation. Similarly, subdivisions beginning with 00 should be avoided when there is a choice between 00 and 0.

Scatter note: A class-elsewhere, see-reference, or relocation note that leads to multiple locations in the Classification.

Schedule reduction: The elimination of certain provisions of a previous edition, often resulting in discontinued numbers. *See also* **Discontinued number.**

Schedules: The series of DDC numbers 000–999, their headings, and notes.

Scope note: A note indicating that the use of a class number is broader or narrower than is apparent from the heading.

Section: The third level of subdivision in the Classification, represented by the first three digits in the notation, e.g., 625 in 625 Engineering of railroads and roads. *See also* **Division**; **Main class**.

See-also reference: (1) In the schedules and tables, a note leading to classes that are tangentially related to the topic and therefore might be confused with it. (2) In the Relative Index, a note leading to a synonym, broader term, or related term.

See-Manual reference: A note leading to additional information about the number in the Manual.

See reference: A note (introduced by the word "for") that leads from the stated or implied comprehensive or interdisciplinary number for a concept to component parts of the subject located elsewhere. *See also* **Class-elsewhere note.**

Segmentation: The indication of logical breaks in a number by a typographical device, e.g., slash marks or prime marks. Segmentation marks indicate the end of an abridged number or the beginning of a standard subdivision.

Separates: Extensive segments of the DDC that are published between editions.

Shelf mark: *See* **Call number.**

Standard subdivisions: Subdivisions found in Table 1 that represent frequently recurring physical forms (dictionaries, periodicals) or approaches (history, research) applicable to any subject or discipline. They may be used with any number in the schedules and tables for concepts that approximate the whole of the number unless there are instructions to the contrary.

Standard-subdivisions-are-added note: A note indicating which topics in a multiterm heading may have standard subdivisions applied to them. The designated topics are considered to approximate the whole of the number. *See also* **Approximate the whole.**

Standing room: A term characterizing a topic without sufficient literature to have its own number, and considerably narrower in scope than the class number in which it is included. Standard subdivisions cannot be added to a topic in standing room, nor are other number-building techniques allowed. Topics listed in including notes have standing room in the class number, as do minor unnamed topics that logically fall in the same place in the Classification. To have standing room is the opposite of approximating the whole. *See also* **Approximate the whole.**

Subdivisions-are-added note: A note used where subdivisions are provided by add instructions indicating which topics in a multiterm heading may have subdivisions applied to them. The designated topics are considered to approximate the whole of the number. *See also* **Approximate the whole.**

Subject: An object of study. Also called topic. It may be a person or a group of persons, thing, place, process, activity, abstraction, or any combination of these. In the DDC, subjects are arranged by disciplines. A subject is often studied in more than one discipline, e.g., marriage is studied in several disciplines such as ethics, religion, sociology, and law. *See also* **Discipline.**

Subject catalog: An index to the contents of a library's collection. If access is provided alphabetically by words, it is called an alphabetical subject catalog. If access is provided by the notation of a library classification system, it is called a classified catalog. *See also* **Classified catalog.**

Subordinate: Describes a number or topic at a lower (narrower) level than another number or topic in the same hierarchy. *See also* **Superordinate.**

Subtitle: An explanatory title that follows the title proper. It often elucidates the subject of the book.

Summary: A listing of the chief subdivisions of a class that provides an overview of its structure. Summaries are also provided for the main classes, divisions, and sections of the Classification as a whole.

Superordinate: Describes a number or topic at a higher (broader) level than another number or topic in the same hierarchy. *See also* **Subordinate.**

Synthesis of notation: *See* **Number building.**

Table: In the DDC, a table of numbers that may be added to other numbers to make a class number appropriately specific to the work being classified. The numbers found in a table are never used alone. There are two kinds: (1) The seven numbered tables (Tables 1–7) representing standard subdivisions, geographic areas, languages, ethnic groups, etc. (2) Lists of special notation found in add notes under specific numbers throughout the schedules and occasionally in Tables 1–7. These lists are called add tables.

Table of preference: *See* **Preference order**.

Topic: See **Subject.**

Unitary term: A heading or term in a note containing two or more words joined by "and" that have such overlapping meanings that the literature on them is unlikely to be clearly separated. In the DDC, unitary terms are treated as single subjects. Unitary terms that appear in headings or class-here notes may have standard subdivisions added for the whole term or for either of its parts; that is, each part of a unitary term is regarded as approximating the whole. Unitary terms in headings are accompanied by standard-subdivisions-are-added or subdivisions-are-added notes.
The following are examples of unitary terms:

    Religious congregations and orders

    Economic development and growth

    Colleges and universities

    Disputes and conflicts between states

    Educational tests and measurements

The following are not considered unitary terms:

    Culture and institutions

    Marriage and family

    Interest and discount

    See also **Approximate the whole.**

Variant-name note: A note listing synonyms or near synonyms for a topic when they might not be immediately recognized.

Word-by-word alphabetization: Filing entries word by word, not letter by letter, e.g., New York files before Newark in word-by-word alphabetization. Letter-by-letter alphabetization would call for Newark to precede New York.

Work mark: The part of a book number that consists of a letter appended to the author (or biographee) designation to show the first letter of the title (or first letter of the surname of the biographer). *See also* **Book number.**

SELECTED BIBLIOGRAPHY

SELECTED BIBLIOGRAPHY

Aluri, R., and others. "Dewey Decimal and Library of Congress Classifications and Online Catalogs." In *Subject Analysis in Online Catalogs*, 157–209. Englewood, CO: Libraries Unlimited, 1991.

Anglo-American Cataloguing Rules. 2nd ed., 1988 revision. Prepared under the direction of the Joint Steering Committee for Revision of AACR, a committee of: the American Library Association, the Australian Committee on Cataloguing, the British Library, the Canadian Committee on Cataloguing, the Library Association, the Library of Congress. Edited by Michael Gorman and Paul W. Winkler. Chicago: American Library Association, 1988.

Beall, Julianne. "Dewey for Windows." In *Knowledge Organization and Change: Proceedings of the 4th International ISKO Conference, Washington, D.C., 1996.* Edited by Rebecca Green. Frankfurt/Main: INDEKS Verlag, forthcoming.

_____. "Editing the Dewey Decimal Classification Online: The Evolution of the DDC Database." In *Classification Research for Knowledge Representation and Organization: Proceedings of the 5th International Study Conference on Classification Research, Toronto, Canada, 1991.* Edited by Nancy J. Williamson and Michèle Hudon, 29-37. Amsterdam and New York: Elsevier, 1992.

Boll, John J. "DDC Classification Rules: An Outline History and Comparison of Two Sets of Rules." *Cataloging & Classification Quarterly* 8(2):49-70 (1987).

Chan, Lois Mai. *Cataloging and Classification.* 2nd ed. New York: McGraw-Hill, 1994.

_____. "Classification, Present and Future." *Cataloging & Classification Quarterly* 21(2):5-17 (1995).

Cochrane, Pauline A., and Eric Johnson. "Visual Dewey: DDC in a Hypertextual Browser for the Library User." In *Knowledge Organization and Change.*

Comaromi, John P. *Book Numbers: A Historical Study and Practical Guide to Their Use.* Littleton, CO: Libraries Unlimited, 1981.

_____. "Conception and Development of the Dewey Decimal Classification." *International Classification* 3(1):11-15 (1976).

_____. "Dewey, Melvil, 1851-1931." In *ALA World Encyclopedia of Library and Information Services*, 2nd ed., 248-50. Chicago: American Library Association, 1986.

_____. *The Eighteen Editions of the Dewey Decimal Classification*. Albany, N.Y.: Forest Press, 1976.

Comaromi, John P., and Peter J. Paulson. "The Dewey Decimal Classification Approaches the 21st Century." In *Information Communications, and Technology Transfer*. Edited by E. V. Smith and S. Keenan, 469-75. New York and Amsterdam: Elsevier, 1987.

Comaromi, John P., and Mohinder P. Satija. *Dewey Decimal Classification: History and Current Status*. New Delhi: Sterling, 1989.

_____. "History of the Indianization of the Dewey Decimal Classification." *Libri* 35(1):1-20 (1985).

Dewey, Melvil. "Decimal Classification Beginnings." *Library Journal* 45:151-54 (February 15, 1920) (Reprinted in *Library Journal*, 115:87-90, June 15, 1990).

Dewey, Melvil. *Dewey Decimal Classification and Relative Index*. Ed. 21. Edited by Joan S. Mitchell, Julianne Beall, Winton E. Matthews, Jr., and Gregory R. New. 4 vols. Albany, NY: OCLC Forest Press, 1996.

Dewey for Windows. Dublin, OH: OCLC Forest Press, 1996.

Drabenstott, Karen Markey, and others. "Analysis of a Bibliographic Database Enhanced with a Library Classification." *Library Resources & Technical Services* 34(2):179-98 (April 1990).

Foskett, A. C. *The Subject Approach to Information*. 4th ed. London: Clive Bingley; Hamden, CT: Linnet Books, 1982.

Holley, Robert P., ed. *Dewey: An International Perspective: Papers from a Workshop on the Dewey Decimal Classification and DDC 20 Presented at the General Conference of the International Federation of Library Associations and Institutions (IFLA), Paris, France, 1989*. Munich: K.G. Saur, 1991.

Hyman, Richard. *Shelf Access in Libraries*. Chicago: American Library Association, 1982.

Lehnus, Donald. *Book Numbers: History Principles, and Applications*. Chicago: American Library Association, 1980.

Liu, Songqiao. "The Automatic Decomposition of DDC Synthesized Numbers" Ph.D. diss., University of California, Los Angeles, 1993.

Liu, Songqiao, and Elaine Svenonius. "DORS: DDC Online Retrieval System (Model Online Catalog Interface)." *Library Resources & Technical Services* 35:359-75 (October 1991).

Markey, Karen, and Anh N. Demeyer. *Dewey Decimal Classification Online Project: Evaluation of a Library Schedule and Index Integrated into the Subject Searching Capabilities of an Online Catalog: Final Report to the Council on Library Resources*. Dublin, OH: OCLC, 1986. Report No. OCLC/OPR/PR-86/1.

Merrill, W. S. *Code for Classifiers: Principles Governing the Consistent Placing of Books in a System of Classification*. Chicago: American Library Association, 1969.

Mitchell, Joan S. "DDC 21 and Beyond: The Dewey Decimal Classification Prepares for the Future." *Cataloging & Classification Quarterly* 21(2):37-47 (1995).

_____. "The Dewey Decimal Classification at 120: Edition 21 and Beyond." In *Knowledge Organization and Change*.

_____. "Options in the Dewey Decimal Classification System: The Current Perspective." *Cataloging & Classification Quarterly* 19(3/4):89-103 (1995).

Mitchell, Joan S., and Mark A. Crook. "A Study of Libraries Using the Dewey Decimal Classification in the OCLC Online Union Catalog: Preliminary Findings." In *Annual Review of OCLC Research 1994*, 47-50. Dublin, OH: OCLC, 1995.

New, Gregory R. "Revising Life Sciences in Dewey Edition 21." In *Knowledge Organization and Change*.

Paulson, Peter J. "Dewey into the 90s." Paper presented at an ALA Workshop on DDC 20 at the 1989 ALA Conference. *The Bookmark* (Albany, N.Y.) 47:176-78 (Spring 1989).

Svenonius, Elaine, Songqiao Liu, and Bhagirathi Subrahmanyam. "Automation of Chain Indexing." In *Classification Research for Knowledge Representation and Organization*, 351-64.

Vizine-Goetz, Diane. "Cataloging Productivity Tools." In *Annual Review of OCLC Research 1994*, 15-20. Dublin, OH: OCLC, 1995.

_____. "The Dewey Decimal Classification as an Online Classification Tool." In *Classification Research for Knowledge Representation and Organization*, 373-80.

_____. "Online Classification: Implications for Classifying and Document [-like Object] Retrieval." In *Knowledge Organization and Change*.

Winkel, Lois, ed. *Subject Headings for Children: A List of Subject Headings Used by the Library of Congress with Dewey Numbers Added*. 2 vols. Albany, NY: OCLC Forest Press, 1994.

Wursten, Richard B., comp. *In Celebration of Revised 780: Music in Dewey Decimal Classification Edition 20*. MLA Technical Report No. 19. Canton, MA: Music Library Association, 1990.

Wynar, Bohdan S. and Arlene G. Taylor. "Decimal Classification." In *Introduction to Cataloging and Classification*, 8th ed., 328-46. Englewood, CO: Libraries Unlimited, 1992.

INDEX

INDEX

In this index, each reference provides a page number followed by a section number in boldface, e.g., Bilingual dictionaries, 162–63, **11.5**

Language (Main Class 400),
[151]–65, **11.0–11.8**
see also Literature
divisions of Class 400, 153, **11.2**
generalities of language, 153, **11.2**
numbers that cannot be extended,
156, **11.3.2**
Table 4, [151]–52, **11.1**;
153–56, **11.3–11.3.2**
Table 6, 156–64, **11.4–11.6**

Language as literary facet, 129,
10.1.1.1

Last-number, preference for, 58,
4.3.2.4.3.2

Last-resort, table of, 59–60,
4.3.2.4.4.2

Law, citation order for, 118, **9.8**

Lehnus, Donald J., 132, **10.3**

Library classification, [40],
4.0; [95] **8.0**

Library of Congress Decimal
Classification Division, 6, **1.3.1**

Life sciences, complex subjects in,
185–86, **13.2.1**

Linguistics, 153, **11.2**

Literary authors, 130–35, **10.2–10.3.1**
see also Literary collections ... ,
Literature, Table 3
Cutter numbers for, 131–32, **10.3**
number building for, 130–35,
10.2–10.3.1

Literary collections and criticism,
130–48, **10.2–10.8**
see also Literature ... , especially
subheading "facets ... "
in more than one language,
136–40, **10.5–10.5.2.3**
in one language, 140–46,
10.6–10.6.3

in two languages, 136(fn4), **10.5**
of a single author, 131–35,
10.3–10.3.1
of more than one author,
135–36, **10.4–10.4.1**
Tables 3A, 3B, and 3C, 130–47,
10.2–10.7

Literary warrant:
for subjects in the Classification,
6, **1.3.1**
for terms in the Relative Index,
72, **6.3**

Literature, 48, **4.2**; [127]–50,
10.0–10.9; 188–89, **13.3.3**
classification of, [127]–30,
10.0–10.1.1.4
collections *see* Literary collections ...
complex subjects in, 188–89, **13.3.3**
facets of literature, 128–46,
10.1.1–10.6.3
citation order, 128, **10.1.1**; 131,
10.3; 136–46 passim,
10.5–10.6.3
feature/theme/persons, 130,
10.1.1.4; 136–46 passim,
10.5–10.6.3
form, 129–30, **10.1.1.2**; 136–46
passim, **10.5–10.6.3**
language, 129, **10.1.1.1**
period, 130, **10.1.1.3**;
136–46 passim,
10.5–10.6.2.3
precedence over other DDC
realms, 48, **4.2**
preference order for literary forms,
129–30, **10.1.1.2**
scope of Class 800, [127]–28,
10.0–10.1
tables: 3A, 3B, and 3C, 130–47,
10.2–10.7
works about individual works,
133–35, 10.3
works by or about more than one
author, 136, **10.4.1**
works by or about individual
authors, 131–33, **10.3**

Main classes, 9–10, **1.5**; 14, 15, **2.2.1**

number-building notes, 36–38,
  3.5–3.5.2.2
preference notes, 57–58,
  4.3.2.4.3–4.3.2.4.3.2
relocation notes, 34, **3.3.3**
revision notes, 33, **3.3.1**
scope notes, 26–27, **3.1.1.2**
see-also references in schedules,
  32, **3.2.2**
see-Manual notes, 35–36, **3.4**
see references in schedules,
  31–32, **3.2.1.3**
standard-subdivisions-are-added
  notes, 37, **3.5.1**
standing-room notes, 28–29, **3.1.5**
variant-name notes, 27, **3.1.3**

Scope notes, 26–27, **3.1.1.2**

Science and technology, complex
  subjects in, 184–86, **13.2–13.2.1**

Second summary of the DDC, 14, 15,
  2.2.1

Sections, 14, 15, **2.2.1**

See-also references in schedules,
  32, **3.2.2**

See-Manual references in schedules,
  35–36, **3.4**; 68, **5.6**

See references in schedules,
  31–32, **3.2.1.3**

Segmentation in DDC numbers,
  21, **2.5.2**

Several-numbers notes in Manual,
  64–65, **5.2**

Shelf location, 2–3, **1.2**; 45, **4.1.5**

Social sciences, complex subjects in,
  181–84, **13.1–13.1.1**

Spaces in DDC numbers, 21, **2.5.2**

Spans of numbers, 91–92, **7.6**

Special topics (ss—04), 103, **8.6**

Square brackets, numbers in,
  21–22, **2.6–2.6.1**

Standard subdivisions in general
  (Table 1), 52–53, **4.2.2**; 66,
  5.3.1; [95]–109, **8.0–8.11**
add instructions, 102–3, **8.5**
adding to main class or division,
  99–102, **8.4**
characteristics of, 97–98, **8.2**
definition of, [96], **8.1**
displaced, 104, **8.7**
extension by add instruction,
  102–3, **8.5**
how to use, 99, **8.3**
information in Manual, 66, **5.3.1**
introduced, 52–53, **4.2.2**; [95], **8.0**
never stand alone, 98, **8.2**
nonstandard, 103, **8.6**
redundancy risk, 105–6, **8.9.1**
regularization of, 104, **8.7**
special topics —04, 103, **8.6**
summary of scope, [96], **8.1**
table of preference, 104–5, **8.8**
two or more, 104–5, **8.8**
variations in meaning in some
  classes, 103, **8.6**
when not used, 105–6, **8.9–8.9.2**
zeros as facet indicators, 98, **8.2**;
  99–102, **8.4**

Standard subdivisions, special uses:
after an area number, 122, **9.12**
area number after an ss number,
  121, **9.11**
for literary collections, 136–37, **10.5**
ss —024, 173–74, **12.7**
ss —04, 103, **8.6**
ss —088, 173–74, **12.7**;
  175–76, **12.9.1**
ss —089, [166]–67, **12.1**; 172, **12.5**
ss —09, 117–18, **9.7**
use with Table 5, 172, **12.5**
use with Table 7, 175–76, **12.9.1**

Standard-subdivisions-are-added
  note, 37, **3.5.1**

Dewey Decimal Classification: A Practical Guide was designed and composed in Joulliard and Arial typefaces by Lisa Hanifan of Albany, New York. The book was printed and bound by Hamilton Printing Company of Rensselaer, New York.